A Social Systems Approach to Global Problems

Institute for 21st Century Agoras Monograph Series

Kenneth C. Bausch, Ph.D., editor

Volume One

Strategic articulation of actions to cope with the huge challenges of our world today:
A Platform for Reflection

Reynaldo Treviño Cisneros

and

Bethania Arango Hisijara

Strategic Articulation of Actions to Cope with the Huge Challenges of Our
World Today

ISBN-13: 9781482641882
ISBN-10: 1482641887

2011: Reynaldo Treviño Cisneros y Bethania Arango Hisijara

Copyright de la versión en inglés, derivada de la versión original en español.
Número de Registro: 03-2011-041111243800-01

© 2013 Institute for 21st Century Agoras.
Volume One of the monograph series:=A Social Systems Approach to Global Problems

Table of Contents

Preface to the Monograph Series

A Social Systems Approach to Global Problems

This monograph series will present case studies of approaches to complex problems which exist in human systems throughout the globe. The first issue of the monograph illustrates an approach for creating a shared understanding of the challenge of global sustainability itself.

Many concerned citizens view our global and national problems as incapable of solution – even when approached by our best scientists and most dedicated politicians. Complex problems are reduced to partial explanations, and our best efforts for resolving complexity become battlegrounds over specific parts of the problem rather than the shape of the larger problem itself.

Scientists have discovered that large piles of statistics present evidence of the unreasonableness of existing policies and yet fail to change prevailing public opinion and governing policies. Recently, one author of the ground-shaking *Limits to Growth* (Meadows et al, 1972) announced that he had given up hope for a successful democratic resolution of our global predicament (comments during the 40th anniversary celebration of *Limits* at the Native American Museum in Washington DC).

A principal failing of research on large-scale, complex social/technological problems is the excessive reliance upon easily measured technical observations and the accompanying minimal regard for hard-to-measure humanist aspirations, intentions, and hopes (Flanagan and Bausch, 2011). By focusing on the easily harvested quantitative data of technological science, complex systems research too easily excludes people's life experiences, their need for practical relevance, their desires, and their traditions... In doing this, they have alienated popular culture from the research and lay the grounds for ignoring its findings.

A new science is emerging that takes account of people's life concerns in the context of critical human problems. This science accepts the observations of all stakeholders, helps observers as they combine these observations, and results in a composite, rich definition of the problem. This comprehensive definition melds many contexts in which stakeholders view the problem. By using this contextualized definition, scientists and populace working together can reach consensus on the nature of the problem and what they are to do about it. This new science was formulated by Gerard DeZeeuw as Third Phase science (1997).

If we are to reach a common ground for collective action, we need to talk not only with each other but also to reason together. Such a process requires dialogue. And not just any dialogue, but a highly structured one. This dialogue must remain focused and disciplined to avoid the vagaries of ordinary conversation. A good design dialogue would follow seven guidelines:

1) *Requisite Variety:* The diversity of perspectives and stakeholders is essential in managing complex situations.
2) *Requisite Parsimony:* Structured dialogue is needed to avoid the cognitive overload of stakeholder/ designers.
3) *Requisite Saliency:* The relative saliency of observations can only be understood through comparisons within an organized set of observations.
4) *Requisite Meaning:* Meaning and wisdom are produced in a dialogue only when observers search for relationships of similarity, priority, influence, etc, within a set of observations.
5) *Requisite Autonomy and Authenticity:* In distinction-making during the dialogue it is necessary to protect the autonomy and authenticity of each observer in drawing distinctions.

6) *Requisite Evolution of Observations:* Learning occurs in a dialogue as the observers search for influence relationships among members of a set of observations.

7) *Requisite Action:* Any action that plans to reform complex social systems designed without the authentic and true engagement of those whose futures will be influenced by the change are bound to fail.

Christakis 2013

An approach witch embodies these laws was empirically validated during 30 years of action research using Structured Dialogic Design (SDD, Christakis and Bausch 2006; Flanagan and Christakis 2010). SDD emerged and became codified as both a research tool and as a management tool in the 1980s and 90s through the efforts of John Warfield, Aleco Christakis, and their associates. The SDD methodology and its associated continually evolving science, Dialogic Design Science (DDS; Christakis 2013), provide opportunities for implementing Third Phase science in the arena of practice – that is, in complex human systems.

Third Phase science and dialogue science are the touchstones of this monograph series: A Social Systems Approach to Global Problems.

In volume one, Reynaldo Treviño Cisneros and Bethania Arango Hisijara present an analysis that joins the 15 global challenges found by the Millennium Society (Glenn, J., Gordon, T., and Florescu, E., 2010) with the 49 Continuous Critical Problems (CCPs) identified by Hasan Ozbekhan (1970). The method they used is expert-analysis using Interpretive Structural Modeling (ISM). This is not an SDD application because it does not directly involve stakeholders. Instead it relies upon its two source documents to provide the required diversity of observations. It also reflects the considered judgment of only two people. It nevertheless illustrates the complexity that is inherent in a deep consideration of the challenge of global sustainability.

In preparation, the authors immersed themselves in the world as viewed in the 15 challenges and the 49 critical problems. Then they used Interpretive Structural Modeling (Warfield, 1974, 1976; Christakis and Bausch, 2006) to rank the 15 challenges on the basis of the influence they have on each other. In doing this, they generated a map that indicates the most influential challenges. This map points out that these challenges possess leverage and therefore deserve priority of effort for improving the global situation. Second, they clustered the individual CCPs with the corresponding Challenges. Third, they generated actions that work to solve the individual Challenges. Finally, they generated a second map that indicates how the actions can confront the Challenges.

This sequence illustrates similar steps that a serious, diverse, and representative group can take to meaningfully address our global challenges. Should they do this, they will go beyond their previous (perhaps antagonistic) conceptions. They will reach a real consensus of hearts and minds and be ready to share their newfound purpose and enthusiasm. They are then committed to working together.

In the Epilogue, Aleco Christakis places this effort of Reynaldo and Bethania into the context of Achanesian geometry, which is the proper geometry for discourse in social spaces.

Commentaries at the end of this monograph illustrate and evaluate it. They also point the way forward. Patricia Kambitsch's graphic essay captures the essence of a problematique. Thomas Flanagan considers this work in the light of Warfield's Domain of Science model. Heiner Benking discusses how Treviño and Arango have crossed a critical threshold in discussions of our huge global problems. Kevin Dye reviews the development of Social Mediation theory, and recommends integrating it with the theory behind Dialogic Design Science (DDS).

The science behind this monograph series

Several major scientific innovations shape the thoughts to be presented in this monograph series:

- Third Phase science
- Archanesian geometry
- Abductive (Retroductive) reasoning
- Interpretative Structural Modeling (ISM)
- Dialogic Design Science (DDS)
- Structured Dialogic Design (SDD)

The limitations of traditional science in dealing with complex socio/technological challenges have become obvious in the last few years. Gerard de Zeeuw made this point most strongly in his 1997 article: Three Phases of Science (DeZeeuw, 1997). **Third Phase science** considers us as observers immersed, and sometimes entangled, in the processes we are studying. We do not have a privileged objective viewpoint. In dealing with complex social situations where efforts at change are required, this immersion is particularly troublesome. Every effort to define important concepts with precision provokes argument. As a result, Third Phase concepts are defined not in abstract point accuracy, but in a rich context that encompasses the views of multiple researchers.

Good examples of such contextual definitions are the 15 challenges identified by the Millennium project. Challenge #1, for instance, presents 8 markers for identifying the challenge of climate change.

Such contextual definitions do not fit well with abstract Euclidean geometry that deals with abstract points and lines. The real objects in Third Phase science are contextualized and the relations between them are determined by consensus. Alexander Christakis in the epilogue presents a geometry of nodes and paths that is up to the challenge of dealing with contextual definitions and consensual paths. He calls it **Archanesian geometry**.

The definitions and paths derived in Third Phase Science and Dialogic Design Science (DDS) utilize reasoning beyond induction and deduction. They use **abductive** (or retroductive) **reasoning** (Peirce, 1998; Stanford, 2010; Shank. 1996; Flanagan and Bausch, 2012; Romm, 2010) as developed by the great American philosopher Charles Sanders Peirce. When we are entangled in situations, we need to have a feel for what we are dealing with. Just tacking a label on the situation will not cut it. When we use abduction, we play our hunches, trusting our intuitions and past experiences to make decisions that feel right – and leave them to be tested through cognitive reasoning and future experience. This is the kind of body wisdom that is utilized in third phase science.

After contextual definitions are agreed upon and feelings of relative importance among factors are recorded, we can start to determine the influences that these factors have upon each other. The preferred method for doing this is **Interpretive Structural Modeling** (Warfield, 1974, 1976; Christakis, 2013). ISM systematically examines each factor in relation to every other factor in a pair wise process, which asks "if we make progress in overcoming factor **A**, will that significantly help us make progress in overcoming factor **B**? With the help of special software, the abductive answers to this series of questions generate a graphic portrayal of the influence relations between all the factors and indicate the leverage points where interventions can be most effectively applied.

As an example, assume that **A influences B (A→B)** and **(B→C}**, this sequence can be written as **A→B→C**. Now suppose that **C→D**, but also **D→C**; this influence relationship can be written as **C←→D**. If **C/D→E**, the entire sequence can be written as: **A→B→ C/D→E.** This is the very structure behind the two systemic maps in the text. In this example, A,B,C/D, and E are the nodes on the map and the arrows portray the paths of influence among them.

In this first monograph, Treviño and Arango stay on an expert level employing only these first four systemic tools. They work, however, in the spirit of Dialogic Design Science and Structure Dialogic Design. DDS and SDD will figure prominently in the future monographs of this series.

References

Christakis, A.N. (2006). A Retrospective Structural Inquiry of the Predicament of Mankind Prospectus of the Club of Rome. In J. McIntyre, editor, *Critical and Systemic Implications for Democracy* New York: Springer.

Christakis, A.N. (2013). Seven Dialogue Laws (Development Years 1995 - 2006).
http://dialogicdesignscience.wikispaces.com/Laws+%287%29

Christakis, A.N. & Bausch, K.B. (2006). *How People Harness their Collective Wisdom and Power to Construct the Future.* Greenwich: Information Age Publishing.

DeZeeuw, G. (1997). Three Phases of Science: A Methodological Exploration. Research memorandum of the Nijmegen Business School in volume *Organizational Cybernetics.*

Flanagan, T. & Christakis A. (2010). *The Talking Point: Creating an Environment for Exploring Complex Meaning.* Charlotte: Information Age Publishing.

Flanagan, T. & Bausch, K. (2011). *A Democratic Approach to Sustainable Futures: A Workbook for Addressing the Global Problematique.* Riverdale, GA: Ongoing Emergence Press.

Glenn, J., Gordon, T., and Florescu, E. (2010). by Glenn, J., Gordon, T. and Florescu, E. (2010). *2010 State of the Future.*

Meadows D. H., Meadows D., and Randers J. (1972). *The Limits to Growth.* New York: Universe Books.

Ozbekhan, H. (1969). Toward a General Theory of Planning. In E. Jantsch (ed.), *Perspectives of Planning.* Paris: OECD Publications.

Ozbekhan, H. (1970). The Predicament of Mankind: A Quest for Structured Responses to Growing World-Wide Complexities and Uncertainties. www.redesignresearch.com/docs/ThePredicamentofMankind.pdf.

Peirce, C.S. (1998). *The Essential Peirce*, 2 vols. Edited by Nathan Houser, Christian Kloesel, and the Peirce Edition Project. Indiana University Press, Bloomington, Indiana,

Romm, N. (2010). *The New Racism: Revisiting Researcher Accountabilities.* Springer, New York

Shank, G. Modes of Peircean Abduction. (1996). cs.indiana.edu.
http://www.cs.indiana.edu/event/maics96/Proceedings/shank.html

Stanford Encyclopedia of Philosophy (2010) Charles Sanders Peirce/ Deduction, Induction, and Abduction

Warfield, J.N. (1974). *Structural Complex Systems.* Batelle Monograph #4

Warfield, J.N. (1976). *Societal Systems: Planning, Policy, and Complexity.* New York, Wiley.

Kenneth Bausch
Executive Director
Institute for 21st Century Agoras

Prologue to Volume One

Strategic Articulation of Actions to Cope with the Huge Challenges of Our World Today

Brother Reynaldo and Sister Bethania,

I feel that the message telegraphed most transparently through your diligent reflection is that thinking through the problem is going to require a personal investment from all readers.

The problematique is formidable. Descriptions of the problematique are formidable. Each time that we lay siege to the problematique, we must come away with a triumphant favor of digestible knowledge. I am not suggesting that we should take a reductive approach, but rather that we need to sustain the crusade to consume the understanding in a holographic fashion. Each time we take a bite of the problematique, we need to taste all of the flavors. In this sense, the way that we consume and internalize the problematique is more important than the total understand that we express with our cognitive skills.

We need to "feel" the problematique as much as "know" the problematique. Answers have a way of extinguishing the yearning for answers, and in doing this they can extinguish the passion for participating with the question. To engage new and younger audiences, I think that your answer must be offered as an example and must wrap itself in an invitation to explore the problematique for ourselves.

There is authentic value in the message that I feel rising from your work. I can only sense this value. I cannot yet fully wrap my head around it because I lack the mental capacity to hold large segments of your understanding in my mind when I also must challenge myself to question and understand those same understandings. I have to iteratively grab the complexity, juggle it in my mind, and then scoop up more of the mystery while I try to pull it all together into a coherent cognitive structure. I am overwhelmed. Capturing pieces of the story does not help ... The greater promised value exists only in its cohesion.

The story that will move me the most (and maybe others too) is the story of how you constructed this deep and expansive understanding. The creative process is always much more engaging than the artful product alone, and I believe that an invitation to be part of the creative process is a compelling invitation in a time of great confusion. I think that we all agree that the case has already been made that your inclusive approach is an unavoidable necessity of planning today. Inviting others to walk the path that you have worked is more meaningful at the human level than offering the short cut of describing the views from path.

So, you have a story about views along a path of inquiry. This is an authentic story. The views that you captured in the form of relationships had a sense of presence for you as you captured them. The moment when connections were made was alive for you. Telling the story of the path is valuable ... like promoting a tour in a travel agency. The story of the path is essential, but not sufficient. We need to invite others to walk the path. When they understand that this is a voyage that we can take together, it will matter less if they capture slightly different relationships as they walk the path. What will matter is that we have agreed that walking along the shared path is essential for our collective well being. Our differences then will be invitations to dialogue.

Your work invites people of good faith to a banquet. The banquet, however, must be the work that they do together. I do feel that your invitation should be celebrated through its publication.

With most sincere love,

Tom Flanagan

Acknowledgments

The authors would like to make especial mention of the work of a fine man, who is one of the most important systems thinkers and philosophers of the present century, Kenneth C. Bausch, who did for us the Spanish original version translation into the English language. He is our personal friend and counselor. He has been during many years an inspiration for our research achievements and has always done whatever we asked him for with full dedication and love. We cannot ever thank him in the required measure, but we intimately know that he shares with us the same ideals of service for the humankind, and possibly this has helped to make his contributions easier in a spiritual sense.

We also want to thank Thomas Flanagan for the words written in the Prologue. He has always had stimulating sentences for the work of many people who enjoy his friendship as we also do. His brilliant mind is empathetically disposed to anyone and anything having to do with the welfare of our close communities and the whole world. His contributions around Structural Dialogic Design are a demonstration of our statement here.

Another inspiration of the present research achievement and results is Alexander Christakis in the first place. Aleco, as we friendly call him, has taught us all we know about the practice of Structural Dialogic Design, but most of all, he has given us the opportunity of working directly with him in several occasions in very important workshops and settings, where we could appreciate the great skills he possesses for conducting dialog in interdisciplinary groups and achieve difficult and relevant goals. Heiner Benking, Peter Jones, Kevin Dye, Norma Romm, Rafael Alberto Pérez and Gayle Underwood have been contributing all along to make this monograph a better thought and written document. We appreciate their spontaneous collaboration very much. Our gratitude to Patricia Kambitsch; she applied her wonderful skills portraying the essential steps of the process that we ran over.

We want to express our gratitude to many brilliant thinkers who preceded us. John Warfield, Hasan Ozbekhan, Eric Jantsch, George Klir, Erwin Laszlo, Ludwig von Bertalanffy, Michael C. Jackson, Jerome Glenn, Theodore Gordon, Elizabeth Florescu, Rafael Alberto Pérez, Barry B. Hughes, Antonio Alonso Concheiro, and our well remembered Thomas Berry, whose minds and hearts remain connected no matter the distances and times between us all.

Dedication

To: Hasan Ozbekhan, John Warfield and Alexander Christakis,
who have exerted a deep influence in our thinking.

"Human social systems are, within definable and relatively narrow limits, capable of adjusting to changes internal and external (environmental) to the system. However, they also possess the characteristic of creativity by which we mean that they can both adapt to their environment and interfere with it, thereby changing it so that they might be able to adapt to its altered form. Human and social systems are reproductive, and insofar as reproduction can be viewed as a purposeful activity, the continued –hence future- existence of the system becomes a rational consideration (or decision) in such systems". (Ozbekhan, H., 1968, p. 3)

"...if we extend, as is increasingly being done nowadays, the definition of ecology to comprise the dimensions of occurrence in our world-wide environments it becomes possible to say that we are confronted with a problematique which is eco-systemic in character. The normative statement that describes the value-content of any ecosystem is "ecological balance". Consequently it is the idea of ecological balance that can, and will, be taken as the underlying value-base of the study; for in the terms dictated by our situation the "good" is self-evidently and most generally capable of being defined as the re-establishment of that many-dimensional dynamic balance that seems to have been lost in the modern world". (Ozbekhan., 1970, p. 23)

"One of the primary motivations – for presenting a thorough discussion of the management of complexity through system design – comes from recognizing that society today involves large socio-technical systems whose performance is far from ideal. It is clear that many of these large systems have taken their present forms primarily through evolutionary change that did not involve any systematic overview design, but may have involved some systematic design of parts. Other systems are said to have been designed, but still fail in ways that produce disasters" (Warfield, J. 1990, p. XXV)

"Dialogue is a vehicle for understanding cultures and subcultures in organizations. And organizational learning depends upon such cultural understanding. It facilitates the development of a common language and collective mental models. Thus, the ability to engage in dialogue becomes one of the most fundamental and most needed human capabilities. Dialogue becomes a central component of any model of evolutionary transformation". (Banathy (2000), quoted by Christakis, A., and Bausch, K., 2006, p.15)

The Path We Took
by Bethania Arango Hisijara

We began our work by trying to conceptually integrate 3 theoretical-methodological issues:

1. Alexander Christakis´ methodology "Structured Dialogic Design" (SDD), based on John Warfield´s methodology of Interactive Management, especially his Interpretive Structural Modelling (ISM) methodology.

2. The 49 Continuous Critical Problems identified in 1970 by Hasan Ozbekhan for The Club of Rome (1970).

3. The Challenges of the Millennium, identified by the Project of the Millennium research team (2010).

These issues were selected because they all strive to integrate a systemic vision of our complex world reality. Also, from these 3 issues we can distinguish problematic multi-dimensional relationships without losing systematization. This is the essence of chapter 4 (Methodology) in our article.

The methodology as it´s described in our article, was developed in a 4 phase process, and guided by the SDD methodology.

- **First phase: Getting the structural pattern.**

We found this structure by using ISM to chart the interrelationships among the 15 world challenges.

- **Second phase: "Problematique" definition.**

We aligned the 15 world challenges and the 50 Continuous Critical Problems (49 Hasan Ozbekhan´s and 1 Ken Bausch´s). They meshed together very well despite the different periods in which they were written. (Have a look at the first matrix).

- **Third Phase: Strategic actions definition.**

In this phase, we identified actions that can eliminate or lessen the impact of individual Continuous Critical Problems and thereby enable us to meet their associated global challenges. (See matrix 2).

- **Fourth phase: Strategic routes definition and global strategy integration.**

In this phase, we again use ISM to indicate a strategic route of actions that can lead to global systemic change. This route can be understood as a solution that needs to be applied in its totality. The individual actions are not to be understood as "solutions" that can be applied separate ways. Nor is this "route" to be seen as a lineal sequence of solution, because the actions are highly interdependent.

At the end of this research, a global strategy is integrated. We can even visualize a concept model that allows us to see "the weave" of movements among our actions. We firmly believe that with the application of "Collective

Intelligence" (SDD), and the specialized dedication of multidisciplinary action groups, we can intervene to achieve changes in the actual state of the world.

Addendum

The following graphic illustrates the process we followed.

It would be naive to think that one proposal includes all the different perspectives needed to comprehend the reality of our world. Multidisciplinary understanding and action by an organized group will always be needed to get the desired change. But by applying the collective intelligence through SDD, we get more than just a self-theory strategy, because SDD also allows us, collectively and individually, to create cognitive models about the world's complexity (WEB). See model below.

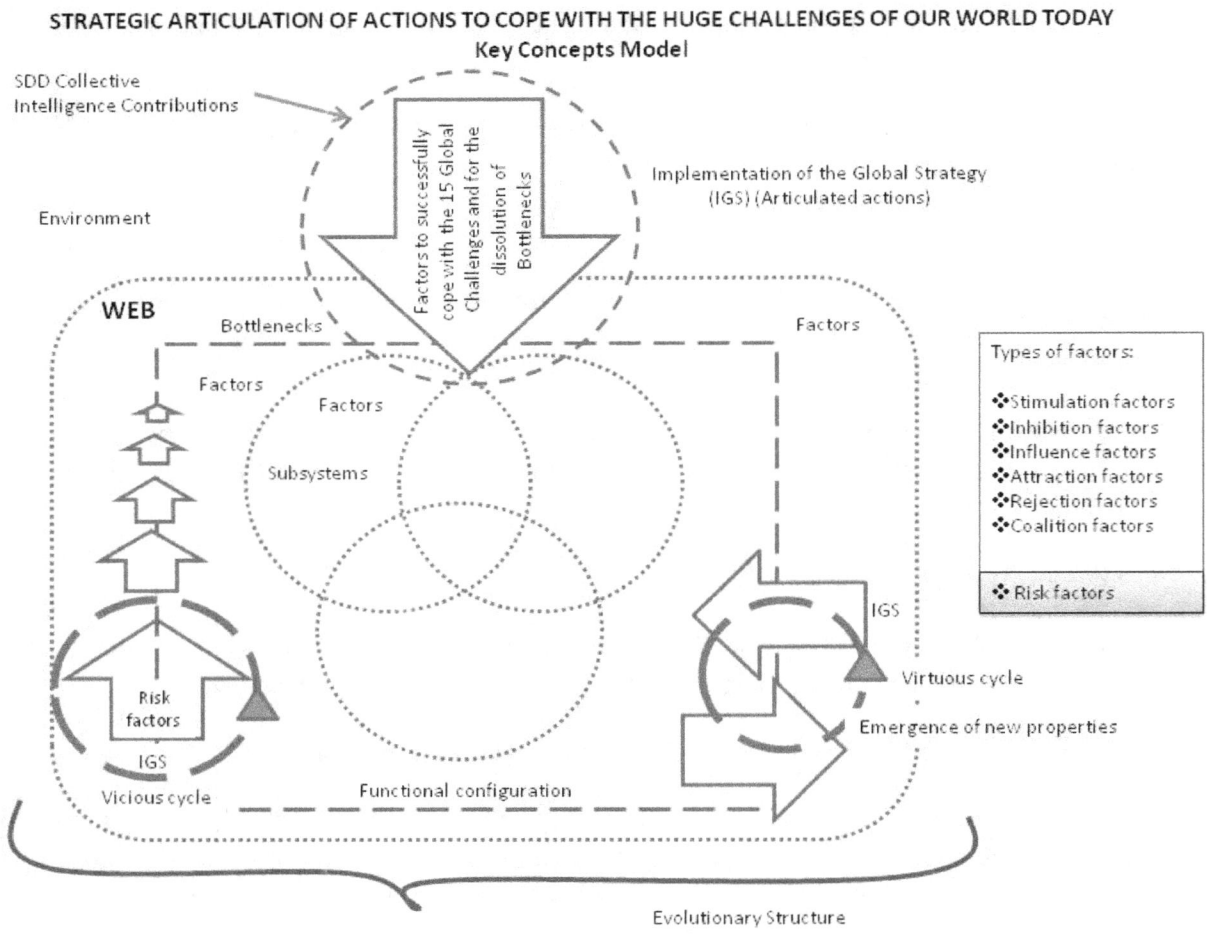

STRATEGIC ARTICULATION OF ACTIONS TO COPE WITH THE HUGE CHALLENGES OF OUR WORLD TODAY
Key Concepts Model

Graphic comments:

The 3-circle Venn diagram represents the WEB interactions within the whole system. At the beginning of the process, the risk factors have distorted the WEB, so it resembles a chaotic tangle. The collective intelligence contributions during the SDD processes can design strategic actions introducing factors that may diminish the effects or impacts of the risk factors, or make them disappear. At the end, those strategic actions might eliminate the vicious cycles of the present situation and facilitate the emergence of the virtuous cycles of the future.

The outputs of the SDD application in our work integrate system ideas from Ozbekhan and the Millennium Project. They allowed us to develop a strategy that, should it be totally applied (simultaneously or at different rhythms), would dissolve the bottlenecks. It would lead us through those conditions that hinder our progress. Its actions would harmonize the system´s components (subsystems) to make them perform virtuous cycles.

The strategy's actions introduce factors into the WEB to install virtuous cycles, but it's well known that their implementation might involve risks. The strategy could go off track. It might be attacked in many ways. Using SDD, we can anticipate these complications and devise ways to minimize their impact. It is convenient to mention, according to our perspective, that no factor by itself could be strong enough to produce the expected strategy's effects. To get the evolutionary progress that we are seeking will require a homeostasis among many factors at the time of their combination and complementation.

Bethania Arango Hisijara
Doctorate in Pedagogy
Member of the Communication Strategies
Ibero-American Forum (FISEC)

1. INTRODUCTION

The report *2010 State of the Future* (Glenn, Gordon, and Florescu) identifies 15 major Global Challenges and justifies them with qualitative and quantitative argument. Their analysis discloses a web of interdependent situations, which bode ill for anybody on the planet.

Upon reading this report, we considered the challenge of making practical sense of that web of 15 Global Challenges. This present document examines the 15 Global Challenges, utilizes tools of systemic analysis, and prescribes steps we can take to create a more desirable future. It calls upon governments, organizations, and individuals to design public policies and actions by common citizens, which can cope with the wicked problem posed by those challenges.

Each challenge is multidimensional and multisided. This book describes dimensions and sides for each challenge and establishes clear differences between them. It enables readers and people, who look at the corresponding videos accessible online (http://www.youtube.com/view_play_list?p=2C7D2B78000F1C2D), to accurately identify the issues requiring the greatest attention. It indicates the organized multidisciplinary actions, their proper moments and sequences needed to accomplish the required changes in the world.

As authors and common citizens, we asked ourselves if we could do something to change the complex and pernicious situation described by the 15 Global Challenges. Could we increase our survival chances and create the possibility of a better life for all of us? Could we invest now in sustainable development and give the next generations a more livable place? The costs of postponing action will increase exponentially if we ignore what we now recognize as negative and serious dangers.

These dangers are not only our concern. They are the concern of every living being on the planet. They disturb the order implied by our planet's physical and chemical systems, which support life and the transcendental development of humanity as well.

Many people cooperated in identifying, selecting, and refining these most relevant 15 global challenges. They worked under the aegis and inspiration of the Millennium Project beginning in 1996. As we have advanced in diagnosing and prescribing actions for the world, we have discovered unsuspected interdependencies between local, national and international situations. These interdependencies can turn internal or worldwide policies upside down. This turbulence has progressed to such an extent that optimism for the future has radically diminished, and apathy has increased. This, in spite of the wealth of knowledge, skills, institutional strengths and natural resources possessed by any country.

From the dawn of the Club of Rome in 1970, when an extended platform for reflection between people of different nationalities and concerns was inaugurated, we have searched for structured responses to the growing complexities and uncertainties of our age. The global scope of the problems prompts pertinent questions for widening our perspectives on the problems identified then and actually happening today. Some contributions made then, such as the ones Hasan Ozbekhan made in 1970 in the document *The Predicament of Mankind,* were not quite understood during his presentation and were dismissed as mere academic conceptual articulations made by a small group of scientists.

The footprint of Hasan Ozbekhan fructified some years later through the achievements of close friends like John Warfield and Alexander Christakis, who searched and developed proper methodologies to cope with complex challenges. They dealt with the challenges faced by corporations and governmental agencies as well as the challenges confronting organized groups interested in finding feasible and viable solutions to undesirable states of affairs.

A Science of Generic Design and its consolidation in Structured Dialogic Design processes bring adequate tools for addressing open systems of high degrees of complexity (Warfield, J., 1995; Christakis, A. and Bausch K., 2006). Many persons contributed since 1970 to the crystallization of these advances with new ideas, new structuring concepts and ad hoc improvements. Their efforts have produced an unending win-win game, giving everyone better ways of approaching the future and grounding successful decision-making processes.

The 15 Global Challenges *"provide a framework to assess the global and local prospects for humanity. The Challenges are interdependent: an improvement in one makes it easier to address others; deterioration in one makes it harder to address others. Arguing whether one is more important than another is like arguing that the human nervous system is more important than the respiratory system"* (Glenn et al, 2010, p.10). The structure of the 15 Global Challenges might be considered as the problematique that all of us are now confronted with. We can look upon this structure as a network of subsystems intertwining behaviors, mutually influencing their dimensions, and adding boundaries with multiple sides. These more or less fluid interactions give a unique identity and unexpected performances to the whole. The systemic axiom that "the whole is more than the sum of its parts" finds in this network of the world and in the network of the universe its best prototypes.

Figure 1. The 15 Global Challenges

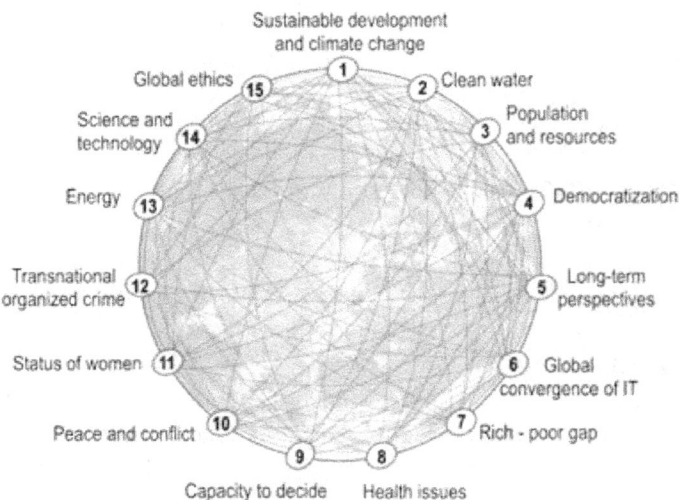

Quoted from: "2010, State of the Future" by Glenn, J., Gordon, T. and Florescu, E., 2010.

The illustration above is remarkable. It shows the 15 global challenges as little circles on the circumference of a sphere that are connected (therefore influenced), by lines on the sphere's surface from all of them to all of them, and go in every direction possible. There has not been until now, however, an explicit treatment that articulates in a more penetrating way the most significant influences between the 15 global challenges. This was the first objective concerning us. We built upon the inspiration offered by Rafael Alberto Pérez and Sandra Massoni (2009), in their book *Toward a General Theory of Strategy*. We quote:

- *"Saying goodbye to the fragmentation and reductionism of the previous models in science. That implies saying goodbye to the directive/economic paradigm(p.319)*
- *Thinking about reality as a web of fluid, complex, and sometimes chaotic processes. Complex is defined etymologically as "what is weaved together". Thus, we are talking about a dynamic web that becomes both configured through energetic and physical interconnections and through symbolic and cultural links (conversational threads), which sometimes are more explicit while being more profound in other occasions (p.319).*
- *Nevertheless, saying goodbye to disjunctive thinking (that separates) to welcome complex thinking (that fits consistently) does not mean denying the first one, since that alone could be done by denying also the second one. Precisely, because thinking is complex, two kinds of perspective may be included: one referred to continuity and another one referred to discontinuities. And we should link both. Again, the new paradigm involves the previous one (p.320).*
- *All that makes us face a new scenario that leads to different approaches. Understanding what we name reality (without breaking it, cutting it or stopping it) will also imply another way of thinking about human relationships and their strategies"* (p.320).

These observations by Pérez illuminate the trajectory to try first: to articulate relationships that the 15 Global Challenges have among themselves, in order to focus on their relationships. This approach might bring superior and distinct benefits distinct from just taking into account the ones that could derive from a detailed characterization of each one of the challenges individually, that is, from a mere analytical examination inside each challenge. In other words, we see the trees but we also want to see the forest; we see the forest, but we also want to see the rest of the geography: the mountains, the rivers, the lakes; and later the atmosphere, the starry firmament and the limits of the horizon. And further beyond, our imagination might help us to have a glimmering sight of the sea, the glaciers, the incandescent tropics, the continental coastlines, the lighting on big extensions of the world during the night, and the almost spherical form and blue color of the Earth from a standpoint outside in space. By looking at relationships we find new ways of looking at challenges as they combine themselves to give us ever more and more information and to increase our possibilities of knowledge and wonder.

As soon as we finished reading the book by Pérez and Massoni, the seed of this peculiar research was sown. We began by asking ourselves: Can we articulate the 15 Global Challenges in a map that discloses how successfully addressing some specific challenges can help us to successfully cope with other specific challenges? We confidently immersed ourselves in this task thanks to the previous work of John Warfield and Alexander Christakis who showed the way to do it. They in turn, inherited many of their stimulating ideas from Hasan Ozbekhan.

2. KEY CONCEPTS

For the purposes of the actual research, we highlight definitions of key concepts. This will help us to understand the whole document. It will also allow us to unfold the mentality implied in our systemic approach.

2.1. Web:

The Web is a set of components (subsystems), processes, stimulation factors, inhibition factors, dissuasion factors, influencing factors, attraction factors, rejection factors, coalition factors and risk factors that are involved in continued and discontinued interactions. These interactions are at work inside both space and time frameworks. They constitute the world, its structure and evolution, its characteristics, its virtuous and vicious cycles, and its emergent properties. They operate in realms where chaos dominates, this being understood as different levels of disorganization of the components related to some grand criteria forged by human groups. Interactions were present at the world's beginnings and will be there at its ultimate end. They are operational in evolution's advances, backings, deviations and inflection points. They are also integral to the world's manifested trends in relation to its survival and probable transcendence, to the velocity and acceleration of its changes, to its inertias and left behind opportunities, to its level of harmonization with the longings of humanity as a whole, and to everything that constitutes a part of its becoming. Some synonyms might appear later like System, Tangle, Bond, Framework, Puzzle or Set of Subsystems.

2.2. Bottlenecks:

Bottlenecks are sets of conditions notably preventing, obstructing, or restraining the impacts of a given strategy that if implemented could achieve a new configuration that would be more functional for the whole of the Web for:

A) Stimulating and influencing factor flow;
B) Disentangling and re-localizing rejection factors;
C) Appropriating and operating attraction factors in a timely manner;
D) Fully intervening and inhibiting dissuasion factors;
E) Installing a dynamic order promoting interactions that might remain latent;
F) Accelerating transportation of defenses needed in case of perceived risks or chaining of risks;
G) Eliminating unnecessary conflicts;
H) Fostering the emergence of properties that could be multipliers of opportunities;
I) Achieving the ultimate objectives of the strategy, and
J) Achieving global ecological balance.

On the Map of the Global Challenges, the bottlenecks will be the steps that due to their chaining and intrinsic complexity pre-condition against fast installation of solutions to adequately cope with their problematiques.

2.3. Subsystems:

Systems components that deploy specialized functions which are necessary for the sustainability of the system, while they become strengthened and strive for interactions with the rest of the subsystems. In doing this they produce virtuous cycles, whose permanence and functioning might be able to produce at different paces emergent properties of potential advantage for the whole system to which they pertain. The subsystems are interdependent and have permeable boundaries that allow interactions that can be profitable for the system. A list of the subsystems here implied could be the following: ecologic, political, socio-demographic, economic, physical-chemical, biological, psychic, ethical, or juridical-legal. They can be influential in areas of justice management, religion, communication, techno-science, and culture. Subsystems are permanently interdependent and interacting through flows of matter, energy, information, knowledge, emotions, behaviors and values.

2.4. Strategy:

Strategies are sets of actions to be deployed in order to get a desired effect in the System; an effect such as global ecological balance. Those actions can be simultaneous or can be deployed at different paces, but all of them must be implemented if someone wishes to achieve the intended effect in the system. These actions introduce factors into the Web that stimulate the subsystems in order to install virtuous cycles, i.e. auto-maintained order situations. They also incorporate factors that directly influence the behavior of the subsystems and system by changing their configuration from time to time. The intended effect of the strategy becomes a permanent attraction factor, which would be for our ecological subsystem example, the survival of the whole Web. Some actions also generate factors that reject every factor that prevents the achievement of the intended effect. During deployment of the strategy, risk factors of different kinds and intensities may appear that will provoke complementary or corrective actions.

The set of stimulating, influencing and attracting factors is generally fortified after the installation of a virtuous cycle. Such a cycle might produce a property called an emergent property, whose existence was not foreseen in the strategy design and this new property might potentiate the strategic capacity to achieve the desired result. Every strategy will as much as possible avoid or reduce to a minimum the formation of vicious cycles that prevent, restrain or inhibit the achievement of the desired effect in the system.

These considerations work within the paradigm of flow. As pronounced by Rafael Alberto Pérez, paraphrasing the words of Heinz von Foerster, the paradigm of flow rejects *"seeing the world as a collection of static objects that we can take, manipulate, classify and turn back to their physical space'.* [Instead it turns] *to understanding it as a set of processes and dynamic systems permanently flowing.* [This leads us to] *become aware that we are handling objects which are in fact processes"* (2009, p. 146).

2.5. Factor:

A factor is every condition existing, whose endurance can be extended until it becomes significant as change agent; that is, it influences the emergence or modification of interactions and properties, reinforces trends, makes them disappear or changes their course. There are stimulation factors, inhibition factors, dissuasion factors, influencing factors, attraction factors, rejection factors, coalition factors and risk factors, which are defined in accord with their intended effects in the system.

The first ones, i.e. the stimulation factors, induce the rise of new events or interactions and the modification of trends that could remain without change if they did not exist. Certain interactions between interdependent subsystems that were in a latent period could begin to function thanks to them. The stimulation factors generally remain unaltered through the processes that they influence. They resemble chemical catalysts. Their final effect is potentiating the system performance as such.

Inhibition factors permanently suspend or partially postpone the ability of some subsystem(s) to face risks. They can also prevent the emergence of inadequate conditions that would hinder the intended effect in the system. In the political, juridical-legal, socio-demographic, economic, and judicial subsystems dissuasion factors promote the waiving of some purposes maintained in the system by certain agents of change. In the strategy, many of the inhibition and dissuasion factors exist because of reactions to undesired behaviors of the subsystems, of the system environment, or of its agents of change. Some of these reactions already exist or are foreseen.

Influencing factors are immersed or incorporated in the existent interactions between interdependent subsystems. They produce or maintain changes that can be favorable to the achievement of the intended effect in the system. They generally change the course of trends and produce events considered as inflection points. They might increase the probability of virtuous cycle and configuration formations that are successively more functional for attaining the intended effect in the system. They tend to disappear if they are not part of the strategy, but if they do form part of it, then they generally become incorporated by pro-active actions.

The attraction factors are intimately bonded with the intended effect in the system. They might be real or virtual sources of light (distant lanterns in space or time that lead the subsystems safe and sound to the right port, i.e. to the desired effect for the system). These lanterns may already exist or only be imagined as part of the future of the system (utopias).

The rejection factors are installed by the strategy to offset some events, properties, or trends that are foreseen and are anticipated to interfere with efforts to create an intended effect in the system.

The coalition factors appear when high imminent and intense risk factors sprout. They are installed through negotiation between subsystems in order to achieve the intended effect in the system, without taking into account that they might slant certain proper functions of the subsystems. Thus they are antagonistic conditions in a normal context. Nevertheless, they enter in negotiation if there is a superior value to be achieved. They possess the same quality of contingency as the risk factors, and they can only be contemplated when a big menace is perceived. They cannot be discarded during the implantation of the strategy, though it would be preferable to evade them from the beginning. The problem with these factors is that their permanence and arrangement is unknown after the intended effect of the system is attained.

The risk factors are generally introduced by contingent interactions arising in the subsystems or by actions of the system environment. They produce unexpected effects, undesirable properties or prolonged deviations from the track designed to achieve the intended effect in the system. It is desirable to account for them from the beginning of the design and during the deployment of the strategy. To do that, we need to anticipate them based upon a well developed imagination and upon a precise detection system for alterations that they might produce in the subsystems or in the system. We also need to provide for the immediate ceasing of their activities if possible just after they have been detected.

The vast majority of risk factors are multisided, i.e., they can influence various subsystems by simultaneously attacking their functionalities and unchaining interactions capable of transforming themselves in vicious cycles (chaining of undesirable effects). To constrain these risks, we can establish early warning systems that let us know about the emergence of likely risk factors. Once they emerge, we need to understand how they will function and of their probable effects. To do this we need a diagnosis going beyond the perception of symptoms. Once they have been diagnosed, strategy must take charge of them in multiple ways and from diverse flanks.

Knowing the existence of continuous critical problems, which are the result of different combinations of risk factors, allows us to do an a-posteriori design of strategies with attraction factors, stimulation factors, influence factors, inhibition and dissuasion factors, rejection and coalition factors that will stand up to the risk factors in continuous or intermittent processes. This always requires follow-up tasks, monitoring, evaluation and circumspection of the effects achieved in the subsystem and system levels. This induces a dialectic in addressing the risk factors that goes from subsystems to the system and vice versa. The stages of design and deployment of the strategy should become clearly differentiated and we should periodically evaluate the results considering the intended effect for the system, and also to introduce substantive or secondary changes that may be required during its implementation.

A characteristic of a good strategy lies in its imagining a good combination of factors that can multiply the possibilities and increase the probabilities for attaining the intended effect in the system in the minimum time with the least cost.

2.6. Factors applicable for the dissolution of bottlenecks:
These are all those factors that individually or conjunctly can reduce the number of already complex steps that make possible the installation of virtuous cycles inside each of the subsystems or in the whole system. They generally represent large savings of effort, time and resources during the deployment of the strategy or a good investment that would bring forth substantial benefits in the future. They help to produce the desired state of the system. All the factors listed in section 2.5, with the exception of the risk factors, might become factors applicable for the dissolution of bottlenecks whenever they function in a bonded or individual way to establish new relationships between the subsystems giving rise to a new dynamic inside of the Web. As Pérez and Massoni (2009) point out, to produce changes *"what is required is to change the nature of the relationship"* (p.149).

2.7. Virtuous cycle:
This is a chaining of factors allowing a fluidity of interaction thanks to an auto-maintained persistent order and savings of energy, resources, time, and effort. After a variable lapse of performance in a virtuous cycle, the emergence of new properties becomes real. Then the emergent properties are reinforced and potentiate performance toward higher levels of the system's evolution.

2.8. Vicious cycle:
This is a chaining of risk factors that prevents, hinders, or restrains the fluidity of interactions between the subsystems or between the system and its environment. This gives rise to a progressive degradation that might destroy one or various subsystems. In the extreme case, vicious cycles can destroy a system and cause it to disappear.

2.9. Evolutionary structures:
These are configurations of the system that generate modifications in the subsystems and their interactions. They are derived from the deployment of strategies or from the intervention of risk factors. The way we perceive the configurations of a system varies with time in accordance with changes during the implementation of strategies and our periodic evaluations. Each evolutionary structure implies different orders, new interdependencies, different processes and interactions than the previous ones, and consequently different perceptions of the relative importance of its components. Times for jumping from one configuration to another are variable, but the leaps are generally too large in the case of the Web (our world).

2.10. Random combination of factors:
Factors that are introduced into the Web by a strategy might become affected by a system environment that can incorporate random risk factors into one or more of its subsystems and changing the whole configuration of the system, thus also changing its performance in time. This same effect might be produced by the massive harnessing of emergent properties during the evolutionary trajectory. For example, man's ability to control fire, the invention of the wheel, the sedentary condition based in agriculture, and the invention of writing altered our Web or World so drastically it could never be the same as it was in the Pleistocene of the quaternary period of the Cenozoic era. Now humanity lives in the Holocene, after the Ice Age, and the Web continues its evolution (http://es.wikipedia.org/wiki/Era_Cenozoica).

Besides, all the subsystems through their own interactions at different paces might incorporate some factors into the Web, whose random combination could produce determinate effects in certain stages of its evolution. No factor alone might be the cause of a global challenge, i.e., none might become a necessary and sufficient cause to produce complex effects of the nature and intensity of the global challenges. The random combination of sets of factors is responsible for raising continuous critical problems to the rank of global challenges. Sometimes, the continuous critical problems are bonded together and produce bottlenecks and vicious cycles that are constituents of the global challenges. There is the need to strategize diverse combinations of factors that might dissolve bottlenecks and to investigate factors capable of eliminating vicious cycles in the subsystems and in the Web.

The analogy of the Web as an intricate Tangle of threads of different diameters and longitudinal sizes preventing the use of its components as a highly functional and fluid configuration leads us to think that we need to dismantle or loosen certain knots, to untie the threads, classify them, order them, and arrange them in order to make possible a weaving of them into a new configuration usable by the whole of the Web in its evolutionary process. The demand for harmonizing subsystems and relations between the Web and its environment becomes predominant. Its main effect should be the global ecological balance and, consequently, the survival of the Web.

3. AIMS OF THIS RESEARCH

Our original aim was to show readers and organizations in charge of the design of global public policies a non-linear strategy that could be widely shared to adequately cope with the global challenges of the Millennium Project. These challenges were identified, described and summarized in the work *"2010, State of the Future"*, based on the participation of more than 2,700 persons around the world. These people collaborated, from 1996 until now, with the directors of the above mentioned Project (Glenn, J., Gordon, T., and Florescu, E., 2010).

After developing the actual research, the authors humbly realize that this framing of the strategy is only an approximation of the set of actions that need to be implemented, developed, evaluated, pondered, modified or corrected if we are to later achieve a superior discerned strategy with real impact and effectiveness over the Web and its evolutionary behavior. This later strategy could promise the survival of the Earth against any risk factors of our own creation. We consider that the environment lies far from human beings control and capacity for transformation at least until now.

A second aim arose during the research work. It consisted in demonstrating the existence of a methodology based on collective intelligence for the treatment and confrontation of very complex affairs, a methodology capable of producing sound and widely shared results. In our case, the methodology arose from two relevant collaborations. The first collaboration developed the 15 global challenges previously mentioned. The second collaboration was led by Hasan Ozbekhan and his conceptualization of the 49 Continuous Critical Problems in the global problematique (Ozbekhan, H., 1970), plus a set of additional collaborations, remarkably the methodological ones for the treatment of complexity from John Warfield (1990) and Alexander Christakis (2006). There is also a need to mention a further set of diverse collaborations. All of them are pertinent. They are directed to specific issues that emerged during the research work and ground some actions pertaining to the strategy. We should also mention, that a problem # 50 was added to the list of the 49 continuous critical problems espoused by Ozbekhan. This last one was offered by Kenneth Bausch after his research on Body Wisdom (2010).

Other particular research objectives took form after many intuitions which were developed during the research as working hypotheses. As soon as some results derived from them were put in practice, they allowed for their ulterior presentation and concretion. Those particular objectives will be presented in section 6: Interpretation of Results.

It should be clear to our readers that we are not pretending to solve every acute problem that the intelligence of individuals or groups has discovered. These problems might involve security, survival, or better living situations. Also, the Web might in its evolution draw on its own resources now unknown to human beings. These might contribute more definitive and adequate answers to the challenges it now possesses.

These clarifications around the scope of the research made, we propose now to go the methodological route required to understand the aims presented and the real coverage of this research.

4. METHODOLOGICAL ROUTE

The methodology employed will be shown stage by stage as follows:

4.1. 15 global challenges
The first approach to the Web was through the 15 global challenges, which defined the framework for developing this strategic proposal. These 15 challenges were developed by a holistic integration of an international diagnosis. From 1996 on, a number of organizations, universities and individuals working in collaboration with the Millennium Project authorities have built, studied and perfected the diagnosis just mentioned.

List of the 15 Millennium Project global challenges:

1. How can sustainable development be achieved for all while addressing global climate change?
2. How can everyone have sufficient clean water without conflict?
3. How can population growth and resources be brought into balance?
4. How can genuine democracy emerge from authoritarian regimes?
5. How can policymaking be made more sensitive to global long-term perspectives?
6. How can global convergence of information and communications technologies work for everyone?
7. How can ethical market economies be encouraged to help reduce the gap between rich and poor?
8. How can the threat of new and reemerging diseases and immune microorganisms be reduced?
9. How can the capacity to decide be improved as the nature of work and institutions change?
10. How can shared values and new security strategies reduce ethnic conflicts, terrorism, and the use of weapons of mass destruction?
11. How can the changing status of women help improve the human condition?
12. How can transnational organized crime networks be stopped from becoming more powerful and sophisticated global enterprises?
13. How can growing energy demands be met safely and efficiently?
14. How can scientific and technological breakthroughs be accelerated to improve the human condition?
15. How can ethical considerations become more routinely incorporated into global decisions?

Using the CogniScope II (Christakis, 1996) software and the generic question: *"Assuming we made progress coping with challenge "X", would that significantly increase the probability of successfully coping with challenge "Y"?,* we obtained the first structural pattern. This constitutes the base for the study of the interrelationships and influences existing between the 15 global challenges. (See figure 2: 'Systemic Map of the Millennium Project Global Challenges" in section 5 of this document). Here are the first four clusters of the framework:

1. The first cluster focuses on challenges 4, 15, 5, and 11 (on the Map they appear in levels X to VII), and refers to a stage of extremely important requirements for the development of democracy, consciousness (awareness) and values (political will and acceptation of ethical principles).
2. The second cluster takes into account the previous groundings, and applies intelligence and cleverness to the next two levels in the Map (second cluster, levels VI and V, challenges 3, 7, 9, 14, 2, and 6). This cluster deals with advantages from technology and the use of an economy for the benefit of humanity as a whole and not for only few.
3. The third cluster, corresponding to challenges 12, 10, and 8 (levels IV, III, and II) proposes the possibility of foreseeing and reducing the self-destructive actions of humans that derive from not giving adequate attention to the two previous clusters.

4. And, finally, obviously linked to the three previous clusters, the fourth one (last section of the Map) allows us to design strategies (estrategar, new word in Spanish) for our reasonably benefiting from natural resources in our planet as well as for incorporating preventive actions to achieve health and sustainability (challenges 13, 8 and 1; levels III, II and I).

The result of this first analysis produced the following learning:

- The 15 global challenges are, from a theoretical conceptual perspective, risk factors resulting from interactions of subsystems with bad side effects. These dysfunctional subsystems have been operating without remedial attention for years. They have now been recognized by the Millennium Project Organization.
- The Systemic Map is only a holistic view of how the 15 challenges influence themselves. If this map is incorporated into a new comprehension of the Web, the probability for successfully addressing these challenges from different flanks is increased.

4.2. 49 continuous critical problems from Hasan Ozbekhan (1970)

As we considered the 15 global challenges as risk factors inside of the system, we saw the need for a wider and deeper scrutiny of the actual problematique implied by each one of them. Under this perspective, we decided to integrate the Hasan Ozbekhan's 49 continuous critical problems into the methodological work. His proposal was made to the Club of Rome through the document *"The Predicament of Mankind" (1970).*

Therefore, we elaborated a first Research Matrix to intuitively incorporate each problem from Hasan's list into one or more global challenges, (see Research Matrix Number 1: *"Categorization of the Continuous Critical Problems identified by Hasan Ozbekhan (1970) according to the Millennium Project Global Challenges (2009)",* in section 5 of the present document). Later, we added Ken Bausch's proposal (2010) of continuous critical problem number 50, since the original "problematique" espoused by Hasan Ozbekhan did not involve it. Next we show the list of the

50 continuous critical problems:

1. Explosive population growth with consequent escalation of social, economic and other problems.
2. Widespread poverty throughout the world.
3. Increase in the production, destructive capacity and accessibility of all weapons of war.
4. Uncontrolled urban spread.
5. Generalized and growing malnutrition.
6. Persistence of widespread illiteracy.
7. Expanding mechanization and bureaucratization of almost all human activity.
8. Growing inequalities in the distribution of wealth throughout the world.
9. Insufficient and irrationally organized medical care.
10. Hardening discrimination against minorities.
11. Hardening prejudices against differing cultures.
12. Affluence and its unknown consequences.
13. Anachronistic and irrelevant education.
14. Generalized environmental deterioration.
15. Generalized lack of agreed on alternatives to present trends.
16. Widespread failure to stimulate man's creative capacity to confront the future.
17. Continuing deterioration of inner-cities or slums.
18. Growing irrelevance of traditional values and continuing failure to evolve new value systems.

19. Inadequate shelter and transportation.
20. Obsolete and discriminatory income distribution systems.
21. Accelerating wastage and exhaustion of natural resources.
22. Growing environmental pollution.
23. Generalized alienation of youth.
24. Major disturbances of the world's physical ecology.
25. Generally inadequate and obsolete institutional arrangements.
26. Limited understanding of what is feasible in the way of corrective measures.
27. Unbalanced population distribution.
28. Ideological fragmentation and semantic barriers to communication between individuals, groups and nations.
29. Increasing a-social and anti-social behavior and consequent rise in criminality.
30. Inadequate and obsolete law enforcement and correctional practice.
31. Widespread unemployment and generalized under-employment.
32. Spreading "discontent" throughout most classes of society.
33. Polarization of military power and psychological impacts of the policy of deterrence.
34. Fast obsolescing political structures and processes.
35. Irrational agricultural practices.
36. Irrational use of pesticides, chemical additives, insufficiently tested drugs, fertilizers, etc.
37. Growing use of distorted information to influence and manipulate people.
38. Fragmented international monetary system.
39. Growing technological gaps and lags between developed and developing areas.
40. New modes of localized warfare.
41. Inadequate participation of people at large in public decisions.
42. Unimaginative conceptions of world-order and the rule of law.
43. Irrational distribution of industry supported by policies that will strengthen the current patterns.
44. Growing tendency to be satisfied with technological solutions for every kind of problem.
45. Obsolete system of world trade.
46. Ill conceived use of international agencies for national or sectoral ends.
47. Insufficient authority of international agencies.
48. Irrational practices in resource investment.
49. Insufficient understanding of Continuous Critical Problems, of their nature, their interactions and of the future consequences both they and current solutions to them are generating.
50. An absence of individuals with appropriate and sufficient psychological formation (Bausch, K. C., 2010).

A deeper diagnostic examination of each of the 15 global challenges was searched for in a similar manner. We selected some relevant indicators inside the analysis made by Glenn, Gordon, and Florescu to compare with the "International Futures Model" developed in the University of Denver. The diagnostic perspective generated during the selection of indicators was another key element that stimulated the need to design actions and integrate them in a Global Strategy.

From this first categorization – which we named the "bridge" – an approach to the risk factors corresponding to each global challenge was produced and we profited from the following lessons:

- The categorization of the 50 continuous critical problems in Research Matrix Number 1 provided us with a base to design Actions as a first approach to the Global Strategy that we wanted to define for the System.

- The problematic areas presented a chaining of interdependent and interactive factors that transcended the boundaries of each challenge, since the same problems might be directly immersed in more than one challenge.
- It was very likely that the components of each cluster in the problematique that were categorized under each one of the 15 challenges would not finally be all the factors integrating them. Nevertheless, they certainly would correspond to some of the most critical and sensible components in the Research Matrix Number 1.
- The problematic version of the 15 global challenges already allowed us to visualize and design Actions needed to achieve a first approach toward a Global Strategy of the System.

During the handling of the information gathered, the authors permanently installed a dialectical procedure of analysis and synthesis. This helped us produce refinements and successive incorporations into the Matrix as soon as information accumulated and the new results were contemplated.

4.3. Strategic actions to cope with the 15 global challenges.
The following sections show the design process of this research:

4.3.1. From the 50 continuous critical problems to the 60 strategic actions to cope with the 15 global challenges.
In this stage the Continuous Critical Problems assigned to each global challenge were "transformed" into Actions that could undermine, eliminate or reduce the impacts of the problems. These transformations are described in Research Matrix Number 1; i.e., to each one of the Continuous Critical Problems, we associated from one to nine Actions to cope with or mitigate the risk factors implied by it. We did this for each critical problem as it relates to each of the global challenges (Research Matrix Number 2: *"Design of Actions based on the definition of continuous critical problems (Hasan Ozbekhan, 1970) to successfully cope with the Millennium Project Global Challenges (Jerome C. Glenn, Theodore J. Gordon and Elizabeth Florescu, 2010)"* in section 5 of this document).

Sixty Actions to successfully cope with the Global Challenges were placed in this Matrix:

1. Achieving personal responsibility and commitment over reproduction processes among humans according to local circumstances, including job, health, and educational capabilities.
2. Creating combined financing and education programs that enhance productivity, long term self sufficiency, and amelioration of living conditions of poor communities. These programs are to be specifically chosen for each community taking into account due respect for their cultural traditions and always looking for easiness of replication in other communities.
3. Destroying under each country governmental responsibility, every arsenal of massive destruction weapons.
4. Hardening sanctions against arms traffickers.
5. Increasing intelligence against that crime (arms trafficking) with the highest technology at hand.
6. Creating new cities under a fair-regulated development plan.
7. Creating economic and political incentives for diminishing the concentration of population in few megacities.
8. Interconnecting cities with physical and logistic infrastructure that produce economic surpluses.
9. Lowering population illiteracy using every media possible.
10. Reducing transactions (official procedures) all over the world, conveniently using the new Information and Communication Technologies with secure services that preserve the confidentiality of information.

11. Humanizing labor with the creativity necessary to efficiently solve every problem linked to human rights.
12. Gradually increasing organized medical care until it becomes a universally accessible service.
13. Putting to work local Commissions of Human Rights all over the world.
14. Advancing legislative agendas that protect minorities against any type of discrimination.
15. Educating with a philosophy of happiness linked to the appreciation of human dignity and also linked to human rewards deeper than private property and accumulation.
16. Educating and training people on the seven necessary types of knowledge for addressing the future (Morin, E., 1999). This implies a necessary reorientation of all the present educational systems.
17. Improving everywhere the environment, through local progressive restoration of the atmosphere, water, and soil necessary conditions for preserving life.
18. Inserting the general practice of rigorously tested methodologies for attaining focused and structured dialog among people who need to take decisions which affect other people (Flanagan, T. and Christakis, A., 2010).
19. Creating and spreading a new theory of strategy which takes into account the relational nature of the human being, its new value system and the main trends observed in its environment (Pérez, R., and Massoni, S., 2009)
20. Gradually installing of restoration programs to recuperate the dignity of inhabitable spaces within the cities.
21. Establishing a value system that incorporates as guiding principles: world sustainable development, equity, peace, the well-being of children all over the world, love, gender equality, harmony, and mutual respect for cultural differences.
22. Building ecological housing in rural and urban areas with complete water and energy systems, including water recycling facilities and all types of energy saving technologies.
23. Producing, distributing and operating ecology friendly transportation at accessible costs for the average inhabitant in every community.
24. Gradually increasing the capacity to work at home or near home.
25. Inaugurating a fair global financial and salary system, that will transform finance into a Global Commons and tighten the salary system in order to provide for all the basic necessities in accordance with a global recognition of human rights (Henderson, H. in Gutiérrez, L., 2010).
26. Progressively diminishing wastage and the actual levels of natural resources exploitation.
27. Increasing the recycling of organic and inorganic chemicals that can be income-producing.
28. Gradually reducing environmental pollution.
29. Gradually reversing global climate change.
30. Establishing a general system of law that favors the conscious evolution of institutions and the continuous improvement of their practices.
31. Building a consensual linguistic domain through the participation of individuals from different groups and nations in processes of Structured Dialogic Design (Christakis, A., and Bausch, K., 2006).
32. Addressing the hopes of young people internationally for better living conditions and human development opportunities.
33. Strengthening the law enforcement system with highly professional people who become, through their actions, the most respected people in their communities.
34. Facilitating participants in non-structured economy legitimate activities the incorporation into a regulated structured economy, by offering them a fairer fiscal system and the minimum of restraints.
35. Inserting a respectable world managerial system that privileges the whole new value system of humanity over any interest that favors only a part of the world's population.
36. Strengthening the participation of the common citizens in the design of better political structures and also in the impartial evaluation of political processes.

37. Improving agricultural techniques to avoid the contamination of soils and underground water, as well as fertile soil erosion and progressive desertification.
38. Producing organic food and prime materials.
39. Educating people to discern between types of information through the careful examination of the methods of production and presentation, and the original intentions of its producers.
40. Agreeing on an international globally accepted monetary system (Wikipedia, 2010).
41. Establishing a new "intellectual property system" that fairly prizes original inventors and innovators whenever they honestly offer their knowledge on products and processes to anyone in the world through public media like internet.
42. Using higher forms of security intelligence to disarticulate any possible form of localized warfare.
43. Gradually establishing a balanced division of labor which accounts for the advantages offered by different countries, recognizes the real strengths of the people involved, and also searches for the equitable participation of every single country.
44. Applying holistic systemic solutions for complex problems in world, regional, national, and local situations, keeping sustainability in mind, and properly following up and periodically evaluating strategies.
45. Gradually establishing a new world trade system that privileges the benefit of final consumers over the particular interests of investors.
46. Establishing an effective global Rule of Law.
47. Installing tested mechanisms for attaining democracy within international agencies and from the top to the bottom of every hierarchical system.
48. Investing in well-balanced resource projects.
49. Enriching all possible foods with proteins and vitamins which help stop malnutrition all over the world.
50. Including in the international law system norms for protecting the world's physical ecological balance.
51. Educating in the appropriate balance between the feminine and masculine polarities existing in every human being no matter its gender, with especial attention during infancy and adolescence (Gutiérrez, L., 2010).
52. Effectively increasing the use of alternative sources of clean energy.
53. Gradually dismantling the local, national and international networks engaged in persons and drugs trafficking, using the most sophisticated intelligence and technology for detection of criminal activities.
54. Globally legalizing the personal consumption of the least human damaging drugs, and building in parallel an effective personalized control system for their sale.
55. Incorporating practices that lead to the gradual dismantling of the corruption existing in institutions all over the world.
56. Designing and applying systems of water capture, recycling, and transport from areas of abundance to scarcity, in such a way that all of them can be eco-friendly, use upgraded technology to reduce its final cost and secure its reconditioning or sanitation.
57. Designing and launching successful community scale projects of water management including equity factors in accordance with the different economic situations of the beneficiaries, and allowing each specific community to become sensible to the real value of this resource and the need to protect it.
58. Dramatically increasing investments in research for developing effective, integral, preventive medicine that can be accessed in any country of the world.
59. Hardening sanctions against criminals who attempt to injure any person through physical violence, sexual abuse, rape, kidnapping, torture, persons trafficking or any behavior based on discrimination, or just accentuated because of a state of defenselessness of the victim.

60. Installing international online co-laboratories among trans-disciplinarian groups of experts, that are opened to general public access and its selective collaboration, in order to make science and technology progress, evaluate each one of the breakthroughs and try to harmonize them with a vision of the universe, supported by the new value system and the new philosophy of happiness.

Transforming the Continuous Critical Problems into Actions was a creative stage during this research. Thanks to the contributions of different disciplines, proposals, different trends, perspectives, empirical knowledge, and "body wisdom" (Bausch, K., 2010), the procedure attained integration. It did this in a single Matrix, which allows us to see the confluence of all this diversity. Again, the use of "collective intelligence" emerged as a *"sine qua non"* step for the conscious evolution of humanity.

4.3.2. Map of Superposition of Actions on the Systemic Map of the 15 Global Challenges.

The Research Matrix Number 2 titled *"Design of Actions based on the definition of Continuous Critical Problems (Hasan Ozbekhan, 1970) to successfully cope with the Millennium Project Global Challenges (Jerome C. Glenn, Theodore J. Gordon, and Elizabeth Florescu, 2010)* presented in analytic form, was a response to the Global Challenges of the Millennium Project. However, it is fragmented and does not correspond to the desired and searched for vision of an integral strategy with a real holistic approach. For that reason, a new structural pattern was elaborated using CogniScope II™. This second map was titled *"Map of Actions to successfully cope with the Global Challenges of the Millennium Project"* (See figure 3 in section 5 of this document). For every pair of Action-Challenge the next generic question was used:

If we implemented action "X", would this increase the probability
of successfully coping with challenge "Y"?

Using the criterion of *transitivity* for the relationships displayed on the map of superposition allowed us to apply the generic question to quite a minor number of pairs of Action-Challenge. Had we not employed transitivity and the software program's inherent properties, the number of feasible pairs to evaluate would have been 900 in total.

Through the examination of this result we learned:

- The proposed Actions to cope with the Global Challenges cannot be considered as separate solutions. They should be applied as components of a Global Strategy in order to reach sustainable development for all while addressing global climate change (Global Challenge 1) by settling down Earth's foundations. It is hoped that the Web, as we now understand it, will achieve during its evolution successive configurations, each one more functional than the previous one thanks to the implementation of the diverse Actions already designed to cope with the whole of the 15 Global Challenges. As Ozbekhan (1970) pointed out: *"When we consider the truly critical issues of our time such as environmental deterioration, poverty, endemic ill-health, urban blight, criminality, etc., we find it virtually impossible to view them as problems that exist in isolation – or, as problems capable of being solved in their own terms".*

- The proposed Actions cannot be considered as linear sequential solutions to the Global Challenges, because their interdependence requires contributions from the rest of the Actions, which have a very different nature. Working together the Actions incorporate the holistic approach into the foreground of the Global Strategy and, in the middle distance, provide the Global Strategy with a clear and defined course toward the achievement of its final objective: overcoming the Global Challenge 1 just mentioned above, and represented at the right end of the Map.

- Consequently, Actions are not precisely causes but diverse factors which function through appropriate combinations. Such combinations of factors would collaborate to disentangle the dysfunctional knots residing in the Web (bottlenecks, vicious cycles).

- As was previously suggested, *"We work with processes instead of objects."* Map 2 is neither a static representation nor a definitive representation. It is, analogically speaking, only a photograph, captured with the lens of the researchers, of the moment the Web is going through. (The duration of this "moment" is unknown; however, we should not make it equivalent to the accustomed temporary dimensions that we as individuals go through in our everyday activities. We may simply observe that the 49 Continuous Critical Problems identified by Ozbekhan in 1970 prevail more than forty years later.)

- The Global Strategy proposed is, in conclusion, a holistic statement that might be continuously improved by implementing trans-disciplinary "Co-Laboratories of Democracy" in the whole world (see the web page of the Institute for the 21st Century Agoras: http://www.globalagoras.com). To the extent that other "collective intelligence" results emerge some previous results might become endorsed, tuned, or modified in accordance with the accumulation of perceptions, analytical-synthetic studies, and broader technological capacities for detecting new risk factors.

5. RESULTS

The results of this research are shown next. There were six months of effort, reflection, and expectation before we knew what the methodology would deliver and which discoveries would gradually evolve until we became satisfied.

The results are two maps and two matrices with ample but sufficiently compact information. Other researchers might draw from them unexpected conclusions or use them as points of departure for a another set of reflections outside the ones here stated.

Figure 2: Systemic Map of the Millennium Project Global Challenges

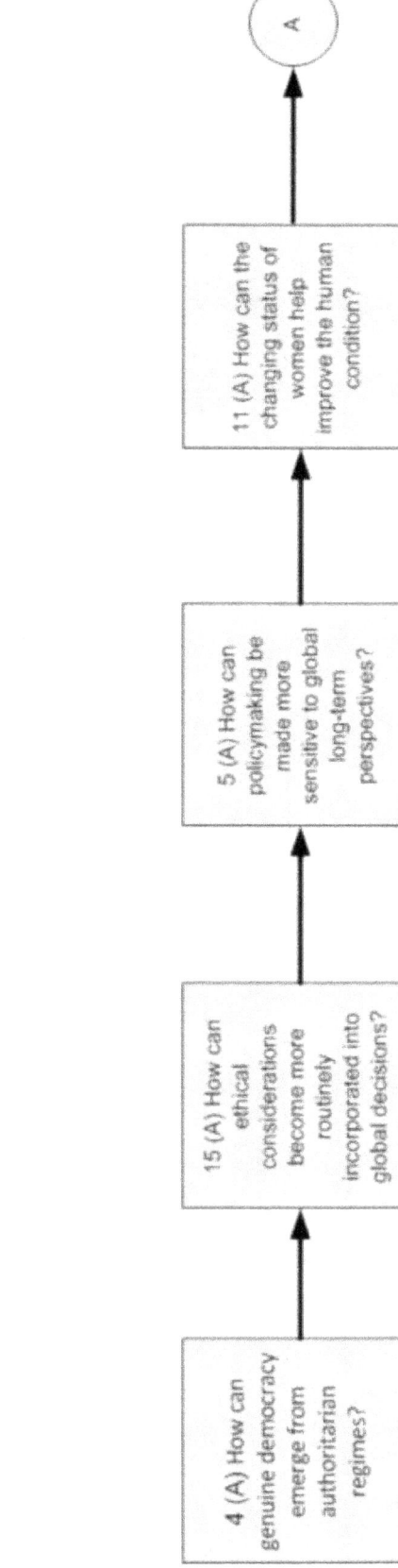

VII

11 (A) How can the changing status of women help improve the human condition?

VIII

5 (A) How can policymaking be made more sensitive to global long-term perspectives?

IX

15 (A) How can ethical considerations become more routinely incorporated into global decisions?

X

4 (A) How can genuine democracy emerge from authoritarian regimes?

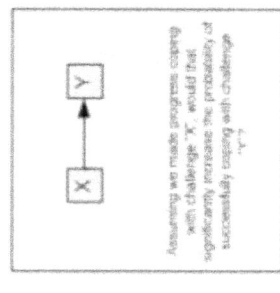

Assuming we made progress coping with challenge "X", would that significantly increase the probability of successfully coping with challenge "Y"?

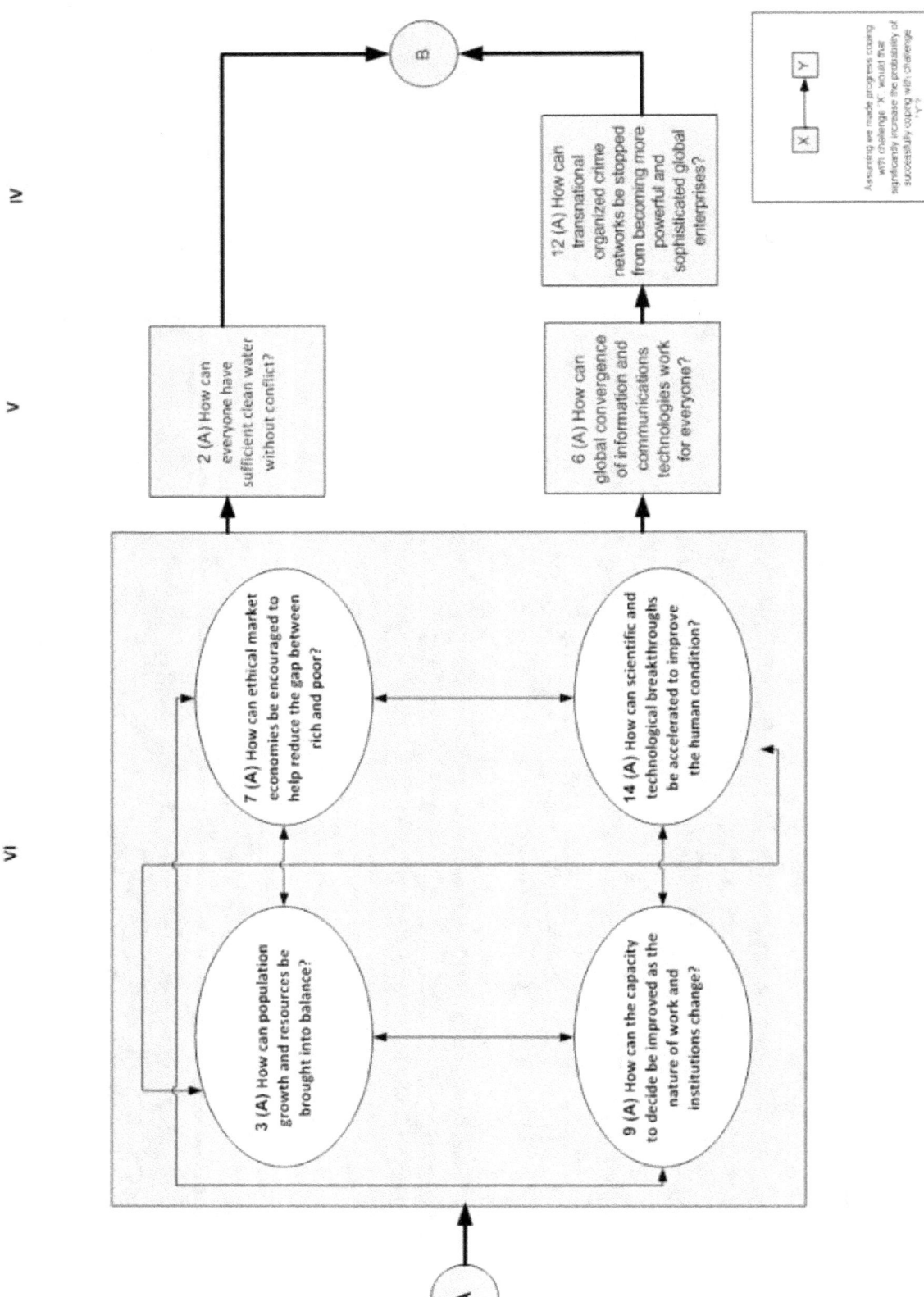

IV

V

VI

B

2 (A) How can everyone have sufficient clean water without conflict?

12 (A) How can transnational organized crime networks be stopped from becoming more powerful and sophisticated global enterprises?

6 (A) How can global convergence of information and communications technologies work for everyone?

7 (A) How can ethical market economies be encouraged to help reduce the gap between rich and poor?

14 (A) How can scientific and technological breakthroughs be accelerated to improve the human condition?

3 (A) How can population growth and resources be brought into balance?

9 (A) How can the capacity to decide be improved as the nature of work and institutions change?

A

X → Y

Assuming we made progress coping with challenge "X", would that significantly increase the probability of successfully coping with challenge "Y"?

44

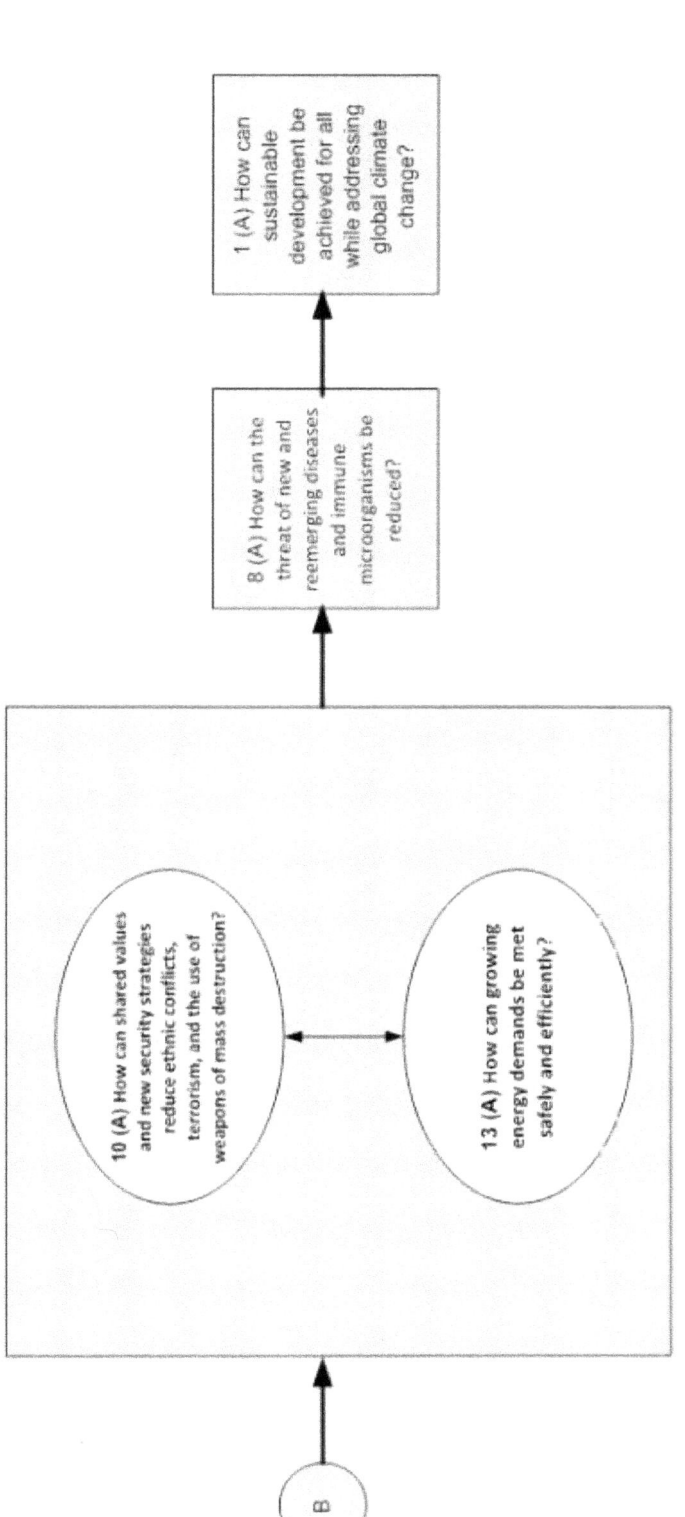

I   1 (A) How can sustainable development be achieved for all while addressing global climate change?

II   8 (A) How can the threat of new and reemerging diseases and immune microorganisms be reduced?

III   10 (A) How can shared values and new security strategies reduce ethnic conflicts, terrorism, and the use of weapons of mass destruction?

13 (A) How can growing energy demands be met safely and efficiently?

B

X → Y

Assuming we made progress coping with challenge "X", would that significantly increase the probability of successfully coping with challenge "Y"?

45

Research Matrix Number 1:

"Categorization of the Continuous Critical Problems

identified by Hasan Ozbekhan (1970)

according to the Millennium Project Global Challenges (2010)"

GLOBAL CHALLENGES[1]	CONTINUOUS CRITICAL PROBLEMS[2]
1. How can sustainable development be achieved for all while addressing global climate change? "Challenge 1 will be addressed seriously when green GDP increases while poverty and global greenhouse gas emissions decrease for five years in a row". (Glenn, J., Gordon, T., & Florescu, E., 2010, p.13) 1.1 "Climate change threatens the well-being of all humans, especially the poor, who have contributed the least to global warming". (Glenn, J., Gordon, T., & Florescu, E., 2010, p.12) 1.2 "By 2015 climate change is expected to reduce wheat yields by 30% and rice yields by 15% and to increase their prices by 194% and 121% respectively". (Glenn, J., Gordon, T., & Florescu, E., 2010, p.12) 1.3 "By 2050 another 2.3 billion people could be added to the planet and income per capita could more than double, dramatically increasing greenhouse gases". (Glenn, J., Gordon, T., & Florescu, E., 2010, p.12) 1.4 "There is a growing fear that the target itself is inadequate –that the world needs to lower CO_2 to 350 ppm or else the momentum of climate change could grow beyond human ability to reverse it". (Glenn, J., Gordon, T., & Florescu, E., 2010, p.12) 1.5 "Glaciers are melting, polar ice caps are thinning, and coral reefs are dying. Some	CCP-14 Generalized environmental deterioration. CCP-21 Accelerating wastage and exhaustion of natural resources. CCP-22 Growing environmental pollution. CCP-24 Major disturbances of the world´s physical ecology. CCP-35 Irrational agricultural practices. CCP-36 Irrational use of pesticides, chemical additives, insufficiently tested drugs, fertilizers, etc. CCP-48 Irrational practices in resource investment.

[1] It refers to the 15 Global Challenges published in "2010 State of the Future" of the Millennium Project, by Glenn, J., Gordon, T., & Florescu, E., (2010).

[2] The first 49 continuous critical problems (CCP) come from an illustrative list that grounds the *ptoblematique* created by Hasan Ozbekhan (1970). Only CCP 50 refers to a different proposal made by Ken Bausch (2010).

GLOBAL CHALLENGES[1]	CONTINUOUS CRITICAL PROBLEMS[2]
30% of fish stocks have already collapsed, and 21% of mammal species and 70% of plants are under threat. Oceans absorb 30 million tons of CO_2 each day, increasing their acidity". (Glenn, J., Gordon, T., & Florescu, E., 2010, p.12) 1.6 "The number of dead zones –areas with too little oxygen to support life- has doubled every decade since the 1960s. Mangrove forests, salt marshes, and sea grass beds cover less than 1% of the world's seabed but sequester over half the carbon buried in the ocean floor". (Glenn, J., Gordon, T., & Florescu, E., 2010, p.12) 1.7 "Human consumption of natural resources is 30% larger than nature's capacity to regenerate". (Glenn, J., Gordon, T., & Florescu, E., 2010, p.12) 1.8 "Large reinsurance companies estimate the annual economic loss due to climate change could reach $300 billion per year within a decade". (Glenn, J., Gordon, T., & Florescu, E., 2010, p.13)	
2. How can everyone have sufficient clean water without conflict? "Challenge 2 will be addressed seriously when the number of people without clean water and those suffering from water-borne diseases diminishes by half from their peaks and when the percentage of water used in agriculture drops for five years in a row". (Glenn, J., Gordon, T., & Florescu, E., 2010, p.14) 2.1 "An additional 1.3 billion people gained access to improved drinking water and 500 million got better sanitation since 1990, yet 900 million still lack clean water and 2.6 billion lack adequate sanitation". (Glenn, J., Gordon, T., & Florescu, E., 2010, p.14) 2.2 "By 2025 about 3 billion people could	CCP-21 Accelerating wastage and exhaustion of natural resources. CCP-20 Obsolete and discriminatory income distribution system(s). CCP-22 Growing environmental pollution. CCP-24 Major disturbances of the world´s physical ecology. CCP-35 Irrational agricultural practices. CCP-36 Irrational use of pesticides, chemical additives, insufficiently tested drugs, fertilizers, etc.

GLOBAL CHALLENGES[1]	CONTINUOUS CRITICAL PROBLEMS[2]
face water scarcity (defined as fewer than 1,000 cubic meters per person per year) due to climate change, population growth, and increasing demand for water per capita". (Glenn, J., Gordon, T., & Florescu, E., 2010, p.14) 2.3 "Some 2.2 million children under five die due to unsafe water, inadequate sanitation, and the lack of hygiene every year". (Glenn, J., Gordon, T., & Florescu, E., 2010, p.14) 2.4 "Diarrheal disease in children under 15 has a greater impact than HIV, malaria, and tuberculosis combined". (Glenn, J., Gordon, T., & Florescu, E., 2010, p.14) 2.5 "Some 90% of developing countries' wastewater is discharged untreated directly into rivers, lakes, or oceans, contributing to the rapid expansion of de-oxygenated dead zones". (Glenn, J., Gordon, T., & Florescu, E., 2010, p.14) 2.6 "About 2 million tons of sewage and industrial and agricultural waste is annually discharged into the world's waterways". (Glenn, J., Gordon, T., & Florescu, E., 2010, p.14) 2.7 "Unless major political and technological changes occur, global water demand could be 40% more than current supply by 2030". (Glenn, J., Gordon, T., & Florescu, E., 2010, p.14) 2.8 "Agriculture already accounts for 70% of human usage of fresh water, but it needs even more to feed growing populations with increasing incomes. Some 30% of global cereal production could be lost in current production regions due to water scarcity, yet new areas in Russia and Canada could open due to climate change". (Glenn, J., Gordon, T., & Florescu, E., 2010, p.14) 2.9 "Access to clean water and basic sanitation should become human rights. About 80% of diseases in the developing world are water-related; most are due to poor management of human excreta".	

GLOBAL CHALLENGES[1]	CONTINUOUS CRITICAL PROBLEMS[2]
(Glenn, J., Gordon, T., & Florescu, E., 2010, p.14) 2.10 "The world is on track to meet the MDG goal on drinking water but not the one on sanitation". (Glenn, J., Gordon, T., & Florescu, E., 2010, p.14)	
3. How can population growth and resources be brought into balance? "Challenge 3 will be addressed seriously when the annual growth in world population drops to fewer than 30 million, the number of hungry people decreases by half, the infant mortality rate decreases by two-thirds between 2000 and 2015, and new approaches to aging become economically viable". (Glenn, J., Gordon, T., & Florescu, E., 2010, p.16) 3.1 "Today's 6.9 billion population is expected to grow to 9.1 billion by 2050 and could reach 11 billion if fertility rates do not continue to fall". (Glenn, J., Gordon, T., & Florescu, E., 2010, p.16) 3.2 "If the (fertility) rates do continue to fall, then world population could actually shrink by 2100, creating an elderly world difficult to support". (Glenn, J., Gordon, T., & Florescu, E., 2010, p.16) 3.3 "Nearly all the population increases will be in urban areas in developing countries". (Glenn, J., Gordon, T., & Florescu, E., 2010, p.16) 3.4 "Scientific and medical breakthroughs over the next 50 years will give people longer and more productive lives than most would believe possible today". (Glenn, J., Gordon, T., & Florescu, E., 2010, p.16) 3.5 "The global population profile is changing from high mortality and high fertility to low mortality and low fertility". (Glenn, J., Gordon, T., & Florescu, E., 2010, p.16)	CCP-1 Explosive population growth with consequent escalation of social, economic and other problems. CCP-4 Uncontrolled urban spread. CCP-5 Generalized and growing malnutrition. CCP-8 Growing inequalities in the distribution of wealth throughout the world. CCP-19 Inadequate shelter and transportation. CCP-20 Obsolete and discriminatory income distribution system(s). CCP-21 Accelerating wastage and exhaustion of natural resources. CCP-24 Major disturbances of the world´s physical ecology. CCP-27 Unbalanced population distribution. CCP-48 Irrational practices in resource investment.

GLOBAL CHALLENGES[1]	CONTINUOUS CRITICAL PROBLEMS[2]
3.6 "About 20% of the world will be over 60 by 2050, and 20% of the older population will be aged 80 or more. Some 20% of Europeans are 60 or older compared with 10% in Asia and Latin America and 5% in Africa". (Glenn, J., Gordon, T., & Florescu, E., 2010, p.16) 3.7 "The economic slowdown and unemployment, combined with elevated food and fuel prices, pushed some 100 million people into chronic hunger". (Glenn, J., Gordon, T., & Florescu, E., 2010, p.16) 3.8 "Over 1 billion people were undernourished in 2009". (Glenn, J., Gordon, T., & Florescu, E., 2010, p.16) 3.9 "In 2010, WFP plans to bring food assistance to more than 90 million people in 73 countries, yet in some of these countries, agricultural lands are being bought by foreign investors". (Glenn, J., Gordon, T., & Florescu, E., 2010, p.16) 3.10 "Meanwhile, 25% of all fish stocks are overharvested; the entire value of fish caught is $85 billion, but $27 billion spent on government subsidies, mostly in rich countries, lead to overexploitation". (Glenn, J., Gordon, T., & Florescu, E., 2010, p.16) 3.11 "To keep up with population and economic growth, food production should increase by 70% and meat production by over 200 million metric tons to reach 470 million metric tons by 2050, which increases demands on water and land, further increasing prices and competition between rural and urban requirements. An additional $83 billion per year will be needed to keep up with these new demands". (Glenn, J., Gordon, T., & Florescu, E., 2010, p.16) 3.12 "Cutting the number of hungry people in half by 2015 would generate global annual incremental benefits of $120 billion by 2015". (Glenn, J., Gordon, T., & Florescu, E., 2010, p.16)	

GLOBAL CHALLENGES[1]	CONTINUOUS CRITICAL PROBLEMS[2]
3.13 "Some 30-40% of food production from farm to mouth is lost in many countries". (Glenn, J., Gordon, T., & Florescu, E., 2010, p.16) 3.14 "Developing countries could experience a decline of 9-21% in overall potential agricultural productivity by 2050 as a result of global warming". (Glenn, J., Gordon, T., & Florescu, E., 2010, p.16) 3.15 "Urban population is expected to jump from 3.4 billion in 2009 to 6.3 billion in 2050". (Glenn, J., Gordon, T., & Florescu, E., 2010, p.16) 3.16 "During the same period, the 1 billion people living in slums today could double". (Glenn, J., Gordon, T., & Florescu, E., 2010, p.16) 3.17 "Without sufficient nutrition, shelter, water, and sanitation produced by more intelligent human-nature symbioses, increased migrations, conflicts, and disease seem inevitable". (Glenn, J., Gordon, T., & Florescu, E., 2010, p.16)	
4. How can genuine democracy emerge from authoritarian regimes? "Challenge 4 will be addressed seriously when strategies to address threats to democracy are in place, when less than 10% of the world lives in nondemocratic countries, when Internet and media freedom protection is internationally enforced, and when voter participation exceeds 60% in most democratic elections". (Glenn, J., Gordon, T., & Florescu, E., 2010, p.18) 4.1 "According to Freedom House's 2010 report, world democracy and freedom declined for the fourth consecutive year, and press freedom for the eight consecutive years". (Glenn, J., Gordon, T., & Florescu, E., 2010, p.18) 4.2 "Freedom declined in 40 countries, while	CCP-6 Persistence of widespread illiteracy. CCP-13 Anachronistic and irrelevant education. CCP- 18 Growing irrelevance of traditional values and continuing failure to evolve new value systems. CCP-20 Obsolete and discriminatory income distribution system(s). CCP-33 Polarization of military power and psychological impacts of the policy of deterrence. CCP-37 Growing use of distorted information to influence and manipulate people. CCP-40 New modes of localized warfare.

GLOBAL CHALLENGES[1]	CONTINUOUS CRITICAL PROBLEMS[2]
it improved in only 16 countries and the number of electoral democracies decreased by three, to 116 countries". (Glenn, J., Gordon, T., & Florescu, E., 2010, p.18)	CCP-47 Insufficient authority of international agencies.
4.3 "While 46% of the world lives in 89 "free" countries, and 20% lives in 58 "partly free" countries, 34% (over 2.3 billion people) lives in 47 countries with "not free" status". (Glenn, J., Gordon, T., & Florescu, E., 2010, p.18)	
4.4 "Freedom of the press also declined almost worldwide, with worse signs in sub-Saharan Africa, Latin America, and the Middle East and North Africa. (Glenn, J., Gordon, T., & Florescu, E., 2010, p.18)	
4.5 "Only 16% of the world lives in the 69 countries with "free" press, 44% in 64 countries with "partly free" press, and 40% lives in 63 countries without freedom of the press". (Glenn, J., Gordon, T., & Florescu, E., 2010, p.18)	
4.6 "Injustices in different parts of the world become the concern of thousands or millions of people who then pressure local, regional, or international governing systems to address the issue". (Glenn, J., Gordon, T., & Florescu, E., 2010, p.18)	
4.7 "The increasing role of digital media also responds to increasing concerns over monopolization and control of the news media". (Glenn, J., Gordon, T., & Florescu, E., 2010, p.18)	
4.8 "Authoritarian regimes increasingly apply censorship, crackdown on bloggers and Internet journalism, and even use forms of cyber warfare to undermine democratic functions". (Glenn, J., Gordon, T., & Florescu, E., 2010, p.18)	
5 How can policymaking be made more sensitive to global long-term perspectives?	
"Challenge 5 will be addressed seriously when foresight functions are a routine part of	CCP-15 Generalized lack of agreed on alternatives to present trends.

GLOBAL CHALLENGES[1]	CONTINUOUS CRITICAL PROBLEMS[2]
most organizations and governments, when national SOFIs are used in at least 50 countries, when the consequences of high-risk projects are routinely considered before they are initiated, and when standing Committees for the Future exist in at least 50 national legislatures". (Glenn, J., Gordon, T., & Florescu, E., 2010, p.21)	CCP-16 Widespread failure to stimulate man´s creative capacity to confront the future.
	CCP-18 Growing irrelevance of traditional values and continuing failure to evolve new value systems.
5.1 "The BP oil spill and the cancellation of flights across Europe due to the volcano in Iceland expose the need for global, national, and local systems for resilience –the capacity to anticipate, respond, and recover from disasters while identifying future technological and social innovations and opportunities. Implementing resilience systems is one way to make policymaking more sensitive to global long-term perspectives". (Glenn, J., Gordon, T., & Florescu, E., 2010, p.20)	CCP-25 Generally inadequate and obsolete institutional arrangements.
	CCP-26 Limited understanding of what is feasible in the way of corrective measures.
	CCP-30 Inadequate and obsolete law enforcement and correctional practice.
	CCP-34 Fast obsolescing political structures and processes.
	CCP-41 Inadequate participation of people at large in public decisions.
5.2 "Government future strategies units (see the CD Chapter 4.1) are being informally connected by Singapore's Future Strategy Unit to share best practices, compare research, and verify assumptions, just as the UN Strategic Planning Group connects 12 UN agency strategy units". (Glenn, J., Gordon, T., & Florescu, E., 2010, p.20)	
5.3 "Foresight for development.org –in Africa- makes research documents, projects, scenarios, people, and blogs available to support African futures research". (Glenn, J., Gordon, T., & Florescu, E., 2010, p.21)	
5.4 "Japan includes private-sector companies in its long-term strategic planning unit". (Glenn, J., Gordon, T., & Florescu, E., 2010, p.21)	
5.5 "Forecasts of migrations from Asia and Africa are forcing Europe to reassess its future, as are the EU2020 strategy, Lisbon Strategy, emergence of China, and forecasts of public finances for social and health services for an aging population".	

GLOBAL CHALLENGES[1]	CONTINUOUS CRITICAL PROBLEMS[2]
(Glenn, J., Gordon, T., & Florescu, E., 2010, p.21)	

5.6 "The rotating six-month EU presidency may have been necessary to enhance pan-European identification, but it makes long-term policy management difficult". (Glenn, J., Gordon, T., & Florescu, E., 2010, p.21)

5.7 "The 7th Framework Programme of the EU expands foresight support; the Institute for Prospective Technological Studies provides future studies for EU decision-making; the European Foresight Monitoring Network connects futurists; an annual European Futurists Conference is held in Switzerland; and the European Regional Foresight College improves future methods". (Glenn, J., Gordon, T., & Florescu, E., 2010, p.21)

5.8 "Yet futures approaches are ignored by the academic and mass media, which focus on urgent and confrontational issues over ideologies, unmet basic needs, growing inequality, and large economic groups that monopolize services". (Glenn, J., Gordon, T., & Florescu, E., 2010, p.21)

5.9 "The Global Millennium Prize was initiated in Mexico for students worldwide who have the best ideas for addressing global long-range challenges. Since the average age in Latin America is only 23, it is fundamental to incorporate the visions of the next generation". (Glenn, J., Gordon, T., & Florescu, E., 2010, p.21)

5.10 "There are increasing efforts to link academic research and future-oriented policymaking by special initiatives in universities, think tanks, NGOs, and government departments". (Glenn, J., Gordon, T., & Florescu, E., 2010, p.21)

5.11 "Global perspectives in decision-making are emerging due to perpetual collaboration among different institutions and nations that has become the norm to

GLOBAL CHALLENGES[1]	CONTINUOUS CRITICAL PROBLEMS[2]
address the increasing complexity and speed of global change". (Glenn, J., Gordon, T., & Florescu, E., 2010, p.21) 5.12 "Global long-term perspectives continue to be evident in the climate change policies of many local governments". (Glenn, J., Gordon, T., & Florescu, E., 2010, p.21)	
6 How can the global convergence of information and communications technologies work for everyone? "Challenge 6 will have been addressed seriously when Internet access and basic tele-education are free and available universally and when basic tele-medicine is commonplace everywhere". (Glenn, J., Gordon, T., & Florescu, E., 2010, p.23) 6.1 "Nearly 30% of humanity is connected to Internet, which has evolved from a passive information repository (Web 1.0) to a user-generated and participatory system (Web 2.0) and is morphing into Web 3.0, a more intelligent partner that has knowledge about the meaning of the information it stores and the ability to reason with that knowledge. (Glenn, J., Gordon, T., & Florescu, E., 2010, p.22) 6.2 "Today, mobile devices have become personal electronic companions, combining computer, GPS, telephone, camera, projector, music player, TV, and a library that is "aware" of its surroundings". (Glenn, J., Gordon, T., & Florescu, E., 2010, p.22) 6.3 "Self-organizing social networks are augmenting hierarchical management of natural disasters, scientific research, and environmental monitoring. These new forms of transnational democracy are giving birth to unprecedented international conscience and action". (Glenn, J., Gordon, T., & Florescu, E.,	CCP- 18 Growing irrelevance of traditional values and continuing failure to evolve new value systems. CCP-28 Ideological fragmentation and semantic barriers to communication between individuals, groups and nations. CCP-37 Growing use of distorted information to influence and manipulate people. CCP-39 Growing technological gaps and lags between developed and developing areas. CCP-44 Growing tendency to be satisfied with technological solutions for every kind of problem.

GLOBAL CHALLENGES[1]	CONTINUOUS CRITICAL PROBLEMS[2]
2010, p.22)	
6.4 "Open source software's non ownership model may become a significant element in the next economic system". (Glenn, J., Gordon, T., & Florescu, E., 2010, p.22)	
6.5 "Real-time stream communications shorten the time it takes from situational awareness to decisions". (Glenn, J., Gordon, T., & Florescu, E., 2010, p.22)	
6.6 "...growth of live streaming video puts stress on the Internet's capacities, requiring new approaches to keep up with bandwidth demand". (Glenn, J., Gordon, T., & Florescu, E., 2010, p.22)	
6.7 "Businesses are building offices and holding meetings in Second Life and other cyber worlds that compete with conventional reality". (Glenn, J., Gordon, T., & Florescu, E., 2010, p.22)	
6.8 "Wikipedia has become the world's encyclopedia, albeit with information reliability problems and struggles to counter disinformation campaigns..." (Glenn, J., Gordon, T., & Florescu, E., 2010, p.22)	
6.9 "The Net has also created a new "virtual world" of a different type, blending into a single intercommunicating entertainment/image entity the domains of television, film, photography, music, and the visual Web (e.g. YouTube), so that images and performances flow freely among the various modalities. (There are also 14,000 Net "radio stations")". (Glenn, J., Gordon, T., & Florescu, E., 2010, p.22)	
6.10 "It has also created an analogous intellectual world of information, linking newspapers, magazines, Web blogs and searches, TV news and information, and books and libraries". (Glenn, J., Gordon, T., & Florescu, E., 2010, p.22)	
6.11 "Issues of intellectual property are unresolved, however, and governments are wrestling with how to control harmful content". (Glenn, J., Gordon, T., &	

GLOBAL CHALLENGES[1]	CONTINUOUS CRITICAL PROBLEMS[2]
Florescu, E., 2010, p.22) 6.12 "Humanity, the built environment, and ubiquitous computing are becoming a continuum of consciousness and technology reflecting the full range of human behavior, from individual philanthropy to organized crime". (Glenn, J., Gordon, T., & Florescu, E., 2010, p.22) 6.13 "Low-cost computers are replacing high-cost weapons as an instrument of power in asymmetrical warfare". (Glenn, J., Gordon, T., & Florescu, E., 2010, p.22) 6.14 "Cyberspace is also becoming a battle zone among competing commercial interests and ideological adversaries as well as a key tool for extremists and a battleground between cybercriminals and law enforcement". (Glenn, J., Gordon, T., & Florescu, E., 2010, p.22) 6.15 "Meanwhile, Internet bases with wireless transmission are being constructed in remote villages; cell phones with Internet access are being designed for educational and business access by the lowest-income groups; and innovative programs are being created to connect the poorest 2 billion people to the evolving nervous system of civilization". (Glenn, J., Gordon, T., & Florescu, E., 2010, p.22) 6.16 "Social networking spurs the growth of political consciousness and popular power, and e-government systems allow citizens to receive valuable information from their leaders, provide feedback to them, and carry out needed transactions without time-consuming and possibly corrupt human intermediaries". (Glenn, J., Gordon, T., & Florescu, E., 2010, p.22) 6.17 "...the UN has conducted comparative assessments of e-government status of its 191 member states since 2003". (Glenn, J., Gordon, T., & Florescu, E., 2010, p.22)	

GLOBAL CHALLENGES[1]	CONTINUOUS CRITICAL PROBLEMS[2]
7 How can ethical market economies be encouraged to help reduce the gap between rich and poor? "Challenge 7 will be addressed seriously when market economy abuses and corruption by companies and governments are intensively prosecuted and when the inequality gap –by all definitions- declines in 8 out of 10 years". (Glenn, J., Gordon, T., & Florescu, E., 2010, p.24) 7.1 "According to the IMF the world economy shrunk by 0.6% during 2009, per capita income fell about 2% to $10,500, and global unemployment reached 9%". (Glenn, J., Gordon, T., & Florescu, E., 2010, p.24) 7.2 "Nevertheless, the world still appears to be on track to halve the 1990 poverty rate (except in sub-Saharan Africa) by 2015". (Glenn, J., Gordon, T., & Florescu, E., 2010, p.24) 7.3 "The IMF estimates a 4.2% growth in 2010. Much of this recovery is led by the developing world, with expected growth of 6.3% in 2010 and 6.6% in 2011-13, compared with growth in advanced economies at 2.3% and 2.4% in those years". (Glenn, J., Gordon, T., & Florescu, E., 2010, p.24) 7.4 "The contribution of BRIC to world GDP in 2009 was over 23.5%, while a growing middle-class in developing countries opens new markets". (Glenn, J., Gordon, T., & Florescu, E., 2010, p.24) 7.5 "By 2015, the IMF expects unemployment to be 6.2% in advanced economies and 5.4% in emerging and developing economies". (Glenn, J., Gordon, T., & Florescu, E., 2010, p.24) 7.6 "The World Bank estimates that the number of people living on less than $1.25 a day might be about 1 billion in	CCP-1 Explosive population growth with consequent escalation of social, economic and other problems. CCP-2 Widespread poverty throughout the world. CCP-5 Generalized and growing malnutrition. CCP-8 Growing inequalities in the distribution of wealth throughout the world. CCP-12 Affluence and its unknown consequences. CCP-17 Continuing deterioration of inner-cities or slums. CCP- 18 Growing irrelevance of traditional values and continuing failure to evolve new value systems. CCP-19 Inadequate shelter and transportation. CCP-20 Obsolete and discriminatory income distribution system(s). CCP-31 Widespread unemployment and generalized under-employment. CCP-38 Fragmented international monetary system. CCP-43 Irrational distribution of industry supported by policies that will strengthen the current patterns. CCP-45 Obsolete system of world trade.

GLOBAL CHALLENGES[1]	CONTINUOUS CRITICAL PROBLEMS[2]
2015 and 826 million in 2020, while those living on less than $2 a day might be 2.06 billion and 1.92 billion respectively". (Glenn, J., Gordon, T., & Florescu, E., 2010, p.24) 7.7 "The 2009 net ODA from DAC countries was $120 billion and is expected to grow to $126 billion in 2010". (Glenn, J., Gordon, T., & Florescu, E., 2010, p.24) 7.8 "Remittances account for 20% of GDP in some countries. These fell by an estimated 6% in 2009, to about $317 billion, and are expected to grow by 2% in 2010". (Glenn, J., Gordon, T., & Florescu, E., 2010, p.24) 7.9 "UNCTAD forecasts FDI inflows to recover and grow from $1 trillion in 2009 to $1.8 trillion in 2011". (Glenn, J., Gordon, T., & Florescu, E., 2010, p.24) 7.10 "While FDI flows to developed countries continue to decline (falling 41% in 2009), FDI between developing countries (South-South) is growing rapidly". (Glenn, J., Gordon, T., & Florescu, E., 2010, p.24) 7.11 "The WTO forecasts world trade to grow 9.5% in 2010, after a 12.2% drop in 2009". (Glenn, J., Gordon, T., & Florescu, E., 2010, p.24) 7.12 "In 2011, the trade balance of emerging and developing economies might reach $663.5 billion, while that of advanced economies could further deteriorate to -$423.9 billion". (Glenn, J., Gordon, T., & Florescu, E., 2010, p.24) 7.13 "By 2015, the account balance of emerging and developing economies is expected to grow to $769 billion". (Glenn, J., Gordon, T., & Florescu, E., 2010, p.24) 7.14 "The high tech-low wage conditions of China and India make it very difficult for other developing countries to compete; hence, developing countries should rethink their export-led growth strategies". (Glenn, J., Gordon, T., &	

GLOBAL CHALLENGES[1]	CONTINUOUS CRITICAL PROBLEMS[2]
Florescu, E., 2010, p.24) 7.15 "Although agriculture employs 37.5% of the labor force, its contribution to GDP is barely 6%". (Glenn, J., Gordon, T., & Florescu, E., 2010, p.24) 7.16 "Since 1976, microfinance institutions provided loans to over 113 million clients worldwide". (Glenn, J., Gordon, T., & Florescu, E., 2010, p.24) 7.17 "Financing to the private sector by the MDBs increased from less than $4 billion 20 years ago to $40 billion in 2009, while the IFC mobilized $14.5 billion in the new investments in private companies in developing countries". (Glenn, J., Gordon, T., & Florescu, E., 2010, p.24)	
8 How can the threat of new and reemerging diseases and immune microorganisms be reduced? "At the moment, the best ways to address infectious diseases remain early detection, accurate reporting, prompt isolation, transparency of information, increased investment in clean drinking water, sanitation, and hand washing. Also are WHO's eHealth systems, International Health Regulations to address SARS-like threats, immunization programs, and the Global Outbreak Alert and Response Network as global responses to this challenge. (Glenn, J., Gordon, T., & Florescu, E., 2010, pp. 26 and 27) 8.1 "Even though population is increasing, 30% fewer children under five died in 2008 than in 1990 and total mortality from infectious disease fell from 25% in 1998 to 16% in 2008". (Glenn, J., Gordon, T., & Florescu, E., 2010, p. 26) 8.2 "Vaccines supplied by UNICEF reach 55% of the world's children". (Glenn, J., Gordon, T., & Florescu, E., 2010, p. 26)	CCP-5 Generalized and growing malnutrition. CCP-9 Insufficient and irrationally organized medical care. CCP-17 Continuing deterioration of inner-cities or slums. CCP-24 Major disturbances of the world's physical ecology. CCP-27 Unbalanced population distribution. CCP-36 Irrational use of pesticides, chemical additives, insufficiently tested drugs, fertilizers, etc. CCP-46 Ill conceived use of international agencies for national or sectoral ends.

GLOBAL CHALLENGES[1]	CONTINUOUS CRITICAL PROBLEMS[2]
8.3 "Partnerships between the Global Alliance for Vaccines and Immunization and the Gates Foundation, WHO, UNICEF, and the World Bank have greatly improved global health cooperation over the past 10 years". (Glenn, J., Gordon, T., & Florescu, E., 2010, p. 26) 8.4 "Because the world is aging and increasingly sedentary, cardiovascular disease is now the leading cause of death in the developing as well as the industrial world; however infectious diseases are the second largest killer and cause about 67% of all preventable deaths of children under five (pneumonia, diarrhea, malaria and measles)". (Glenn, J., Gordon, T., & Florescu, E., 2010, p. 26) 8.5 "Urbanization, travel, trade, increased encroachment on animal territory, and concentrated livestock production move infectious organisms to more people in less time than ever before and could trigger new pandemics". (Glenn, J., Gordon, T., & Florescu, E., 2010, p. 26) 8.6 "The H1N1 virus (swine flu) infected millions of humans in all 214 countries and territories within a year, killing 18,000, and will be active another year. Although spreading very fast, the mortality was relatively low, causing WHO to review its decision to declare it a pandemic". (Glenn, J., Gordon, T., & Florescu, E., 2010, p. 26) 8.7 "H5N1 (avian flu) killed half of the people infected, spread very slowly, has mutated three times in the last 15 years, and could mutate again, increasing its impact". (Glenn, J., Gordon, T., & Florescu, E., 2010, p. 26) 8.8 "Over the past 40 years, 39 new infectious diseases have been discovered, 20 diseases are now drug-resistant, and old diseases have reappeared, such as cholera, yellow fever, plague, dengue fever, meningitis, hemorrhagic fever, and diphtheria. In the last five years, more	

GLOBAL CHALLENGES[1]	CONTINUOUS CRITICAL PROBLEMS[2]
than 1,100 epidemics have been verified. About 75% of emerging pathogens are zoonotic (they jump species)". (Glenn, J., Gordon, T., & Florescu, E., 2010, p. 26)	

than 1,100 epidemics have been verified. About 75% of emerging pathogens are zoonotic (they jump species)". (Glenn, J., Gordon, T., & Florescu, E., 2010, p. 26)

8.9 "Some 33 million people are living with HIV/AIDS; 2.7 million were newly infected and 2 million died during 2009. The virus is unstable and mutates enough that $800 million of research has not produced a successful vaccine. So far, it cannot be cured, only stabilized, and it has become resistant to multiple drugs. While it appears that new cases peaked in the late 1990s and mortality peaked in 2004, predictions of 2.3 million new cases per year are likely to be true into the 2030s unless prevention is more successful. Sharing needles is thought to be three times more likely than sexual intercourse to transmit HIV; male circumcision may reduce infection by 50%; and since HIV crosses the placenta and breast milk to children, preventive treatments are important". (Glenn, J., Gordon, T., & Florescu, E., 2010, p. 26)

8.10   "While small numbers of people with Ebola and West Nile viruses have received (sic) media attention, the bigger health impacts are from schistosomiasis (200 million cases), dengue fever (50 million new cases a year), measles (30 million cases a year), onchocerciasis (18 million cases in Africa), typhoid and leishmaniasis (approximately 12 million each globally), rotavirus (600,000 child deaths per year), and shigella childhood diarrhea (600,000 deaths per year)". (Glenn, J., Gordon, T., & Florescu, E., 2010, p. 26)

8.11   "About half of the world's population is at risk of several endemic diseases". (Glenn, J., Gordon, T., & Florescu, E., 2010, p. 26)

8.12   "Climate change is altering insect and disease patterns. Vector reproduction, parasite development cycle, and byte

GLOBAL CHALLENGES[1]	CONTINUOUS CRITICAL PROBLEMS[2]
frequency generally rise with temperature; therefore, malaria, tick-borne encephalitis, and dengue fever are expected to become increasingly widespread". (Glenn, J., Gordon, T., & Florescu, E., 2010, p. 26) 8.13 "Hepatitis B infects up to 2 billion people. There is more TB in the world now than ever before (2 million deaths, 9 million new infections in 2009), yet in the last 15 years 43 million TB cases have been treated and 36 million have been cured". (Glenn, J., Gordon, T., & Florescu, E., 2010, p. 26) 8.14 "There were 863,000 malaria deaths in 2009 (80% occurred in children younger than 5 in sub-Saharan Africa), yet 38 countries (9 in Africa) documented reductions of more than 50% in the number of malaria cases between 2000 and 2008". (Glenn, J., Gordon, T., & Florescu, E., 2010, p. 26)	
9 How can the capacity to decide be improved as the nature of work and institutions change? "Challenge 9 will be addressed seriously when the State of the Future Index or similar systems are used regularly in decision-making, when national corporate law is modified to recognize transinstitutional organizations, and when at least 50 countries require elected officials to be trained in decision-making". (Glenn, J., Gordon, T., & Florescu, E., 2010, p. 29) 9.1 "The number and complexity of choices seem to be growing beyond our abilities to analyze and make decisions". (Glenn, J., Gordon, T., & Florescu, E., 2010, p. 28) 9.2 "The acceleration of change reduces the time from recognition of the need to make a decision to completion of all the steps to make the right decision". (Glenn, J., Gordon, T., & Florescu, E., 2010, p. 28)	CCP-7 Expanding mechanization and bureaucratization of almost all human activity. CCP-15 Generalized lack of agreed on alternatives to present trends. CCP-16 Widespread failure to stimulate man´s creative capacity to confront the future. CCP-20 Obsolete and discriminatory income distribution system(s). CCP-25 Generally inadequate and obsolete institutional arrangements. CCP-26 Limited understanding of what is feasible in the way of corrective measures. CCP-31 Widespread unemployment and generalized

GLOBAL CHALLENGES[1]	CONTINUOUS CRITICAL PROBLEMS[2]
9.3 "The global challenges…show that the world is increasingly interdependent and intricate, requiring improved abilities for collaborative decision-making across institutional, political and cultural boundaries". (Glenn, J., Gordon, T., & Florescu, E., 2010, p. 28) 9.4 "Many of the world's decision-making processes are inefficient, slow, and ill informed". (Glenn, J., Gordon, T., & Florescu, E., 2010, p. 28) 9.5 "Previous economic models continue to mistakenly assume that human beings are well informed, rational decision makers in spite of research to the contrary". (Glenn, J., Gordon, T., & Florescu, E., 2010, p. 28) 9.6 "…relying on computer models for decisions proved unreliable in the financial crisis". (Glenn, J., Gordon, T., & Florescu, E., 2010, p. 28) 9.7 "The region's dependence (North America) on computer-augmented decision-making –from e-government to tele-business- creates new vulnerabilities to manipulation by organized crime, corruption, and cyber-terrorism…" (Glenn, J., Gordon, T., & Florescu, E., 2010, p. 29) 9.8 "More open systems, democratization, and interactive media are involving more people in decision-making, which further increases complexity". (Glenn, J., Gordon, T., & Florescu, E., 2010, p. 28) 9.9 "DSS improves decisions by filtering out bias and providing a more objective assessment of facts and potential options". (Glenn, J., Gordon, T., & Florescu, E., 2010, p. 28) 9.10 "Some software lets groups select criteria and rate options, some averages people's bets on future events, while others show how issues have alternative positions and how each is supported or refuted by research". (Glenn, J., Gordon, T., & Florescu, E., 2010, p. 28)	under-employment. CCP-43 Irrational distribution of industry supported by policies that will strengthen the current patterns. CCP-47 Insufficient authority of international agencies.

GLOBAL CHALLENGES[1]	CONTINUOUS CRITICAL PROBLEMS[2]
9.11 "Self-organization of volunteers around the world via Web sites is increasing transparency and creating new forms of decision-making. Nearly half of the 200 million blogs were created from 2007 to 2009". (Glenn, J., Gordon, T., & Florescu, E., 2010, p. 28) 9.12 "Issues-based information software in e-government allows decision-making to be more transparent and accountable". (Glenn, J., Gordon, T., & Florescu, E., 2010, p. 28) 9.13 "Unfortunately, we are still so flooded with so much trivial news that serious attention to serious issues gets little interest, and too much time is wasted going through useless information". (Glenn, J., Gordon, T., & Florescu, E., 2010, p. 28) 9.14 "Expert advice was most often the view of single individuals or very small groups, but now decision-making benefits from online, open systems that invite broad and transparent participation". (Glenn, J., Gordon, T., & Florescu, E., 2010, p. 28) 9.15 "Ubiquitous computing will increase the number of decisions per day, constantly changing schedules and priorities". (Glenn, J., Gordon, T., & Florescu, E., 2010, p. 28)	
10 How can shared values and new security strategies reduce ethnic conflicts, terrorism, and the use of weapons of mass destruction? "Challenge 10 will be addressed seriously when arms sales and violent crimes decrease by 50% from their peak". (Glenn, J., Gordon, T., & Florescu, E., 2010, p. 31) 10.1 "Although the vast majority of the world is living in peace, half the world continues to be vulnerable to social instability and violence due to the global	CCP-3 Increase in the production, destructive capacity, and accessibility of all weapons of war. CCP-10 Hardening discrimination against minorities. CCP-15 Generalized lack of agreed on alternatives to present trends. CCP- 18 Growing irrelevance of traditional values and

GLOBAL CHALLENGES[1]	CONTINUOUS CRITICAL PROBLEMS[2]
recession, to aging populations and decreasing water, food, and energy supplies per person, to climate change, and to increasing migrations due to political, environmental, and economic conditions". (Glenn, J., Gordon, T., & Florescu, E., 2010, p. 30)	continuing failure to evolve new value systems.
10.2 "There were 14 conflicts with 1,000 or more deaths in 2010. These occurred in Africa (5), Asia (3), the Americas (2), and the Middle East (3), with 1 conflict classified as worldwide anti-extremism". (Glenn, J., Gordon, T., & Florescu, E., 2010, p. 30)	CCP-29 Increasing a-social and anti-social behavior and consequent rise in criminality. CCP-40 New modes of localized warfare. CCP-46 Ill conceived use of international agencies for national or sectoral ends.
10.3 "The U.S. and Russia signed a nuclear arms reduction treaty, and the Cluster Munitions Convention will come into force in the fall of 2010". (Glenn, J., Gordon, T., & Florescu, E., 2010, p. 30)	CCP-47 Insufficient authority of international agencies. CCP-23 Generalized alienation of youth.
10.4 "The Global Peace Index's rating of 144 countries' peacefulness again declined slightly, reflecting intensification of some conflicts and the economic crisis". (Glenn, J., Gordon, T., & Florescu, E., 2010, p. 30)	
10.5 "In 2010, there are 124,000 UN peacekeepers from 115 countries in 16 operations". (Glenn, J., Gordon, T., & Florescu, E., 2010, p. 30)	
10.6 "Total military expenditures are about $1.5 trillion per year. There are an estimated 8,100 active nuclear weapons, down from 20,000 in 2002 and 65,000 in 1985. However, there are approximately 1,700 tons of highly enriched uranium and 500 tons of separated plutonium that could produce nuclear weapons". (Glenn, J., Gordon, T., & Florescu, E., 2010, p. 30)	
10.7 "Unmanned aircraft and robot land vehicles are increasingly being used". (Glenn, J., Gordon, T., & Florescu, E., 2010, p. 30)	
10.8 "The nexus of transnational extremist violence is changing from complex organized plots to attacks by single individuals or small independent groups".	

GLOBAL CHALLENGES[1]	CONTINUOUS CRITICAL PROBLEMS[2]
(Glenn, J., Gordon, T., & Florescu, E., 2010, p. 30) 10.9 "Future desktop molecular and pharmaceutical manufacturing and organized crime's access to nuclear materials give single individuals the ability to make and use weapons of mass destruction –from biological weapons to low-level nuclear ("dirty") bombs". (Glenn, J., Gordon, T., & Florescu, E., 2010, p. 30) 10.10 "IAEA reports that between 1993 and the end of 2009, the Illicit Trafficking Database recorded 1,784 nuclear trafficking incidents (222 during 2009), ranging from illicit disposal efforts to nuclear material of unknown provenance". (Glenn, J., Gordon, T., & Florescu, E., 2010, p. 30) 10.11 "The ICRC has pointed out that the Geneva Convention needs to be modified to cover intra-state conflicts". (Glenn, J., Gordon, T., & Florescu, E., 2010, p. 30)	
11 How can the changing status of women help improve the human condition? "Challenge 11 will be addressed seriously when there is gender parity in school enrollment, literacy, and access to capital, when discriminatory laws are gone, when discrimination and violence against women is prosecuted, and when there are essentially equal numbers of men and women in policymaking positions". (Glenn, J., Gordon, T., & Florescu, E., 2010, p. 32) 11.1 "The ratio of women in national parliaments has increased from 13.8% in 2000 to 18.9% in 2010, while the current ratio of women in ministerial positions is 29% in health, 26% in culture, 25% in education, and 4% in defense, while 5% are heads of government. Some 100 countries have mandatory or voluntary	CCP-18 Growing irrelevance of traditional values and continuing failure to evolve new value systems. CCP-20 Obsolete and discriminatory income distribution system(s). CCP-29 Increasing a-social and anti-social behavior and consequent rise in criminality.

GLOBAL CHALLENGES[1]	CONTINUOUS CRITICAL PROBLEMS[2]
gender quotas for their legislatures". (Glenn, J., Gordon, T., & Florescu, E., 2010, p. 32)	

11.2　"The Gender Equity Index 2009 computed by Social Watch shows that in most countries the gender gap is not closing and progress is largely dependent on the gender discrimination status in the country, and not on the region or economic development. The index decreased from 35% in 2008 to 34.5% in 2009, with setbacks in 51% of the countries that were already in the worse relative situation, while 77% of those in a comparatively better situation made progress". (Glenn, J., Gordon, T., & Florescu, E., 2010, p. 32)

11.3　"Most progress was made in achieving universal primary education. Of the estimated 72 million primary-age children who are not in school, girls only slightly outnumber boys. However, only 53% of countries achieved gender parity in both primary and secondary education, with the gap for secondary schooling widening in some regions". (Glenn, J., Gordon, T., & Florescu, E., 2010, p. 32)

11.4　"Around 126 million children are still involved in hazardous work, and the economic crisis threatens the education status of a whole generation of children". (Glenn, J., Gordon, T., & Florescu, E., 2010, p. 32)

11.5　"Meanwhile, 50% of university students worldwide are women, and in many countries they outnumber men". (Glenn, J., Gordon, T., & Florescu, E., 2010, p. 32)

11.6　"Women account for over 40% of the world's workforce but earn less than 25% of the wages. In developing countries, they represent over 60% of all unpaid family workers, typically with no job security and benefits". (Glenn, J., Gordon, T., & Florescu, E., 2010, p. 32)

11.7　"Environmental disasters, food and

GLOBAL CHALLENGES[1]	CONTINUOUS CRITICAL PROBLEMS[2]
financial crises, armed conflicts, and forced displacement further increase vulnerabilities and generate new forms of disadvantages for women and children". (Glenn, J., Gordon, T., & Florescu, E., 2010, p. 32)	

11.8 "...women control over 70% of global consumer spending and by 2015 might generate 70% of the global household income growth". (Glenn, J., Gordon, T., & Florescu, E., 2010, p. 32)

11.9 "Some religious and patriarchal structures continue to impede women's liberty and access to family planning in many cultures. Unsafe and illegal abortions cause some 5.3 million disabilities and 68,000 deaths each year. Of the more than 500,000 maternal deaths per year, 99% happen in developing countries, with the highest prevalence in Africa and Asia due to high fertility rates and weak health systems". (Glenn, J., Gordon, T., & Florescu, E., 2010, p. 32)

11.10 "At the current rate of improvement, the UN goal to reduce maternal mortality to 120 deaths per 100,000 live births by 2015 will not be achieved". (Glenn, J., Gordon, T., & Florescu, E., 2010, p. 32)

11.11 "About 2.5 million people from 127 different countries are being trafficked around the world, out of which approximately 70% are women and girls and up to 50% are minors, the "largest slave trade in history"". (Glenn, J., Gordon, T., & Florescu, E., 2010, p. 32)

11.12 "The Protocol to Prevent, Suppress and Punish Trafficking in Persons, especially Women and Children, has 137 parties and 117 signatories, but it has yet to be adopted and enforced by some key countries". (Glenn, J., Gordon, T., & Florescu, E., 2010, p. 32)

11.13 "Despite significant progress in setting international mechanisms to eradicate all forms of violence against

GLOBAL CHALLENGES[1]	CONTINUOUS CRITICAL PROBLEMS[2]
women, about half of the countries have no legislation to stop gender-based discrimination, and crimes against women continue to be perpetrated with impunity". (Glenn, J., Gordon, T., & Florescu, E., 2010, p. 32) 11.14 "About one-third of women suffer gender-based violence during their lives, and one in five has been a victim of rape or attempted rape, especially during armed conflicts". (Glenn, J., Gordon, T., & Florescu, E., 2010, p. 32)	
12 How can transnational organized crime networks be stopped from becoming more powerful and sophisticated global enterprises? "Challenge 12 will be seriously addressed when money laundering and crime income sources drop by 75% from their peak". (Glenn, J., Gordon, T., & Florescu, E., 2010, p. 34) 12.1 "Havocscope.com estimates world illicit trade to be just over $1 trillion per year, with counterfeiting and intellectual property piracy accounting for $300 billion to $1 trillion, the global drug trade at $386 billion, trade in environmental goods at $63 billion, human trafficking and prostitution at $141 billion, smuggling at $96 billion, and weapons trade at $12 billion". (Glenn, J., Gordon, T., & Florescu, E., 2010, p. 34) 12.2 "The FBI estimates that online fraud cost U.S. businesses and consumers $560 million in 2009, up from $265 million in 2008. These figures do not include extortion or organized crime's part of the $1 trillion in bribes that the World Bank estimates are paid annually or its part of the estimated $1.5-6.5 trillion in laundered money". (Glenn, J., Gordon, T., & Florescu, E., 2010, p. 34) 12.3 "Hence the total income could be $2-	CCP-1 Explosive population growth with consequent escalation of social, economic and other problems. CCP-3 Increase in the production, destructive capacity, and accessibility of all weapons of war. CCP-29 Increasing a-social and anti-social behavior and consequent rise in criminality. CCP-40 New modes of localized warfare. CCP-46 Ill conceived use of international agencies for national or sectoral ends. CCP-23 Generalized alienation of youth.

GLOBAL CHALLENGES[1]	CONTINUOUS CRITICAL PROBLEMS[2]
3 trillion –about twice as big as all the military budgets in the world". (Glenn, J., Gordon, T., & Florescu, E., 2010, p. 34) 12.4 "The financial crisis and bankrupt financial institutions have opened new filtration routes for TOC crime". (Glenn, J., Gordon, T., & Florescu, E., 2010, p. 34) 12.5 "The world recession has increased human trafficking and smuggling. Human body parts for transplantation are a new element in TOC. There are up to 27 million people being held in slavery today (the vast majority in Asia), more than during the peak of the African slave trade. UNICEF estimates that 1.2 million children are trafficked every year". (Glenn, J., Gordon, T., & Florescu, E., 2010, p. 34) 12.6 "The online market in illegally obtained data and tools for committing data theft and other cybercrimes continues to grow, and criminal organizations are offering online hosting of illegal applications". (Glenn, J., Gordon, T., & Florescu, E., 2010, p. 34) 12.7 "Computer transfers of $2 trillion per day make tempting targets for international cybercriminals". (Glenn, J., Gordon, T., & Florescu, E., 2010, p. 34)	
13 How can growing energy demands be met safely and efficiently? "Challenge 13 will have been addressed seriously when the total energy production from environmentally benign processes surpasses other sources for five years in a row and when atmospheric CO_2 additions drop for at least five years". (Glenn, J., Gordon, T., & Florescu, E., 2010, p. 36) 13.1 "World energy demand is expected to increase by between 40% to 50% over the next 25 years, with the vast majority of the increase being in China and India".	CCP-21 Accelerating wastage and exhaustion of natural resources. CCP-20 Obsolete and discriminatory income distribution system(s). CCP-24 Major disturbances of the world´s physical ecology.

GLOBAL CHALLENGES[1]	CONTINUOUS CRITICAL PROBLEMS[2]
(Glenn, J., Gordon, T., & Florescu, E., 2010, p. 36) 13.2 "Without major policy and technological changes (which could be triggered by the BP oil spill), fossil fuels will dominate energy sources, making large-scale carbon capture, storage, and/or reuse a top priority to reduce climate change". (Glenn, J., Gordon, T., & Florescu, E., 2010, p. 36) 13.3 "The total global renewable energy investment for 2010 is estimated at $200 billion, up nearly 50% from 2009. To meet total energy demand, an annual $1.1 trillion (1.4% of global GDP) is needed, and an additional $10.5-trillion investment by 2030 will be necessary if the world is to meet the goal of keeping atmospheric CO_2 concentration below 450ppm". (Glenn, J., Gordon, T., & Florescu, E., 2010, p. 36) 13.4 "...the world spends more than $310 billion on energy subsidies every year. G20 leaders pledged to phase out fossil fuel subsidies in the medium term. Eliminating subsidies could lead to a 10% reduction of GHG emissions by 2050". (Glenn, J., Gordon, T., & Florescu, E., 2010, p. 36) 13.5 "In 2008, for the first time, the majority of US and EU increases in the production of electricity came from renewable sources instead of fossil or nuclear sources". (Glenn, J., Gordon, T., & Florescu, E., 2010, p. 36) 13.6 "Meanwhile, 1.5 billion people have no access to electricity and 3 billion still rely on traditional biomass for cooking and heating". (Glenn, J., Gordon, T., & Florescu, E., 2010, p. 36) 13.7 "In the IEA reference scenario, the number of people lacking access to electricity drops by only 200 million by 2030 and the number actually increases in Africa". (Glenn, J., Gordon, T., & Florescu, E., 2010, p. 36)	

GLOBAL CHALLENGES[1]	CONTINUOUS CRITICAL PROBLEMS[2]
13.8 "The World Bank estimates that countries with underperforming energy systems may lose up to 1-2% of growth potential every year, while billions of gallons of petroleum are wasted in traffic jams around the world". (Glenn, J., Gordon, T., & Florescu, E., 2010, p. 36)	
14 How can scientific and technological breakthroughs be accelerated to improve the human condition? "Challenge 14 will have been addressed seriously when the funding of R&D for societal needs reaches parity with funding for weapons and when an international science and technology organization is established that routinely connects world S&T knowledge for use in R&D priority setting and legislation". (Glenn, J., Gordon, T., & Florescu, E., 2010, p. 39) 14.1 "The ability to invent life has been demonstrated. The J. Craig Venter Institute synthesized a 1.08-million base pair chromosome to construct the bacterial cell *Mycoplasma mycoides JCVI-syn1.0,* the first self-replicating synthetic cell". (Glenn, J., Gordon, T., & Florescu, E., 2010, p. 38) 14.2 "Synthetic neurobiologists are creating "co-processors" for the brain to cure blindness or make us more intelligent. The lab-created Isx-9 molecule can make nerve stem cells mature into brain cells, leading the way to brain regeneration". (Glenn, J., Gordon, T., & Florescu, E., 2010, p. 38) 14.3 "IBM plans to have the Sequoia 20-petaflops computer ready for DOE by 2012, which is estimated to be the first computer with the processing power of a human brain". (Glenn, J., Gordon, T., & Florescu, E., 2010, p. 38) 14.4 "A transistor has been built from	CCP- 18 Growing irrelevance of traditional values and continuing failure to evolve new value systems. CCP-19 Inadequate shelter and transportation. CCP-20 Obsolete and discriminatory income distribution systems. CCP-26 Limited understanding of what is feasible in the way of corrective measures. CCP-39 Growing technological gaps and lags between developed and developing areas. CCP-44 Growing tendency to be satisfied with technological solutions for every kind of problem.

GLOBAL CHALLENGES[1]	CONTINUOUS CRITICAL PROBLEMS[2]
seven atoms". (Glenn, J., Gordon, T., & Florescu, E., 2010, p. 38) 14.5 "There are already machines that can be controlled by thought alone". (Glenn, J., Gordon, T., & Florescu, E., 2010, p. 38) 14.6 "The acceleration of S&T innovations from improved instrumentation, communications among scientists, and synergies among nanotechnology, biotechnology, information technology, cognitive science, and quantum technology continues to fundamentally change the prospects for civilization". (Glenn, J., Gordon, T., & Florescu, E., 2010, p. 38) 14.7 "Millions of people passively volunteer their computers' excess capacity to run data analysis programs to help speed up research in biomedicine, mathematics, artificial intelligence, and cancer. Over 50 million volunteer citizen scientists gather and analyze data, dramatically expanding the capacity of scientific research around the world". (Glenn, J., Gordon, T., & Florescu, E., 2010, p. 38) 14.8 "Patients with rare diseases share real-time clinical data to assist doctors". (Glenn, J., Gordon, T., & Florescu, E., 2010, p. 38) 14.9 "Free university courses, curricula, and tools in science and technology are increasing on the Web to share extraordinary breakthroughs". (Glenn, J., Gordon, T., & Florescu, E., 2010, p. 38) 14.10 "Scanning electron microscopes can see 0.01 nanometers (the distance between a hydrogen nucleus and its electron), and the Hubble telescope has seen 13.2 billion light-years away". (Glenn, J., Gordon, T., & Florescu, E., 2010, p. 38) 14.11 "The Large Hadron Collider is exploring the nature of dark energy". (Glenn, J., Gordon, T., & Florescu, E., 2010, p. 38)	

GLOBAL CHALLENGES[1]	CONTINUOUS CRITICAL PROBLEMS[2]
14.12 "Photons have been slowed and accelerated, and four photons have been precisely controlled on a silicon chip to learn how to create optical computers". (Glenn, J., Gordon, T., & Florescu, E., 2010, p. 38)	
14.13 "Over 450 planets have been discovered orbiting other stars". (Glenn, J., Gordon, T., & Florescu, E., 2010, p. 38)	
14.14 "A record five photons have been entangled (quantum entanglement is the simultaneous change of entangled objects separated in space) to explore futuristic communications, security, simple teleportation, and the transport of energy". (Glenn, J., Gordon, T., & Florescu, E., 2010, p. 38)	
14.15 "External light can be concentrated inside the body for photodynamic therapy and to power implanted devices". (Glenn, J., Gordon, T., & Florescu, E., 2010, p. 38)	
14.16 "MRI brain imaging shows primitive pictures of real-time thought processes". (Glenn, J., Gordon, T., & Florescu, E., 2010, p. 38)	
14.17 "Magnetic signals from a single electron buried inside a solid sample have been detected". (Glenn, J., Gordon, T., & Florescu, E., 2010, p. 38)	
14.18 "A new sensor can detect over 2,000 viruses and about 900 bacteria within 24 hours". (Glenn, J., Gordon, T., & Florescu, E., 2010, p. 38)	
14.19 "Extinct mammoth's blood now lives using ancient DNA". (Glenn, J., Gordon, T., & Florescu, E., 2010, p. 38)	
14.20 "Nanotechnology-based products have grown by 25% in the last year to over 800 items today for the release of medicine in the body, thin-film photovoltaics, super hard surfaces, and many lightweight strong objects". (Glenn, J., Gordon, T., & Florescu, E., 2010, p. 38)	
14.21 "DNA scans open the possibility of customized medicine and eliminating	

GLOBAL CHALLENGES[1]	CONTINUOUS CRITICAL PROBLEMS[2]
inherited diseases". (Glenn, J., Gordon, T., & Florescu, E., 2010, p. 38) 14.22 "Viruses have been used to help build efficient batteries that are half the size of a human cell". (Glenn, J., Gordon, T., & Florescu, E., 2010, p. 38) 14.23 "Transistors measuring 10-by-1 atoms have been produced out of graphene, a material just 1 atom thick –the thinnest material in the world-. Graphene may ultimately replace silicon in many nano-electronic applications". (Glenn, J., Gordon, T., & Florescu, E., 2010, p. 38) 14.24 "Over 12 million robots do everything from routine surgery to building cars and managing farms, even marrying couples in Japan". (Glenn, J., Gordon, T., & Florescu, E., 2010, p. 38)	
15 How can ethical considerations become more routinely incorporated into global decisions? "Challenge 15 will be addressed seriously when corruption decreases by 50% from the World Bank estimates of 2006, when ethical business standards are internationally practiced and regularly audited, when essentially all students receive education in ethics and responsible citizenship, and when there is a general acknowledgement that global ethics transcends religion and nationality". (Glenn, J., Gordon, T., & Florescu, E., 2010, p. 41) 15.1 "The global financial crisis demonstrated the interdependence of economics and ethics. While quick fixes have pulled the world out of recession, it is not clear that ethics have been addressed sufficiently to prevent future crises". (Glenn, J., Gordon, T., & Florescu, E., 2010, p. 40) 15.2 "International meetings of the G-20 and other forums are trying to reach agreements about how to improve	CCP-10 Hardening discrimination against minorities. CCP-11 Hardening prejudices against differing cultures. CCP- 18 Growing irrelevance of traditional values and continuing failure to evolve new value systems. CCP-20 Obsolete and discriminatory income distribution system(s). CCP-28 Ideological fragmentation and semantic barriers to communication between individuals, groups and nations. CCP- 32 Spreading "discontent" throughout most classes of society. CCP-42 Unimaginative conceptions of world-order and the rule of law. CCP-47 Insufficient authority of international agencies.

GLOBAL CHALLENGES[1]	CONTINUOUS CRITICAL PROBLEMS[2]
systems in order to increase integrity, financial transparency, and accountability". (Glenn, J., Gordon, T., & Florescu, E., 2010, p. 40)	

15.3   "At the same time, 12-27 million people are slaves today, more than at the height of the nineteenth century slave trade". (Glenn, J., Gordon, T., & Florescu, E., 2010, p. 40)

15.4   "The World Bank estimates over $1 trillion is paid each year in bribes". (Glenn, J., Gordon, T., & Florescu, E., 2010, p. 40)

15.5   "...organized crime takes in $2-3 trillion annually". (Glenn, J., Gordon, T., & Florescu, E., 2010, p. 40)

15.6   "Concerns are also growing about ties between organized crime and terrorism threatening the future of democracy". (Glenn, J., Gordon, T., & Florescu, E., 2010, p. 40)

15.7   "Meanwhile, trivial news and entertainment flood people's minds with unneeded products and unethical behavior". (Glenn, J., Gordon, T., & Florescu, E., 2010, p. 40)

15.8   "Some experts speculate that the world is heading for a "singularity"-a time in which technological change is so fast and significant that people today are incapable of conceiving what life might be like beyond 2025. This acceleration of technological change seems beyond the ability of most people and institutions to comprehend, leading to ethical uncertainties". (Glenn, J., Gordon, T., & Florescu, E., 2010, p. 40)

15.9   "Individuals can now experiment with genetics to create new life forms in home labs without the safeguards of government and commercial laboratories". (Glenn, J., Gordon, T., & Florescu, E., 2010, p. 40)

15.10   "Globalization and advanced technology allow fewer people to do more damage and in less time, so that

GLOBAL CHALLENGES[1]	CONTINUOUS CRITICAL PROBLEMS[2]
possibly one day a single individual may be able to make and deploy a weapon of mass destruction". (Glenn, J., Gordon, T., & Florescu, E., 2010, p. 40) 15.11 "New technologies also allow more people to do more good than ever before, such as single individuals organizing worldwide actions around specific ethical issues via the Internet". (Glenn, J., Gordon, T., & Florescu, E., 2010, p. 40) 15.12 "The moral will to act in collaboration across national, institutional, religious, and ideological boundaries that are necessary to address today's global challenges requires global ethics". (Glenn, J., Gordon, T., & Florescu, E., 2010, p. 40) 15.13 "Public morality based on religious metaphysics is challenged daily by growing secularism, leaving many unsure about the moral basis for decision-making". (Glenn, J., Gordon, T., & Florescu, E., 2010, p. 40) 15.14 "Unfortunately, religions and ideologies that claim moral superiority give rise to "we-they" splits". (Glenn, J., Gordon, T., & Florescu, E., 2010, p. 40)	
For the whole set of global challenges. "Ethics in the post-crisis world must be rooted in placing the common good above individual ambition; in ensuring a government's right to regulate the economy and to provide basic services for all; and in promoting infinite benefits, such as spiritual ones, over the consumption of finite, material goods. The ethics of a new project for civilization must incorporate environmental preservation into the concept of sustainable development, value solidarity economy and fair trade networks, and strengthen civil society as a regulator of government action" (Frey Betto, 2010, p. 21, in World Economic Forum *"Faith and the Global Agenda: Values for the Post-Crisis Economy"*)	CCP-49 Insufficient understanding of Continuous Critical Problems, of their nature, their interactions and of the future consequences both they and current solutions to them are generating. CCP-50 An absence of individuals with appropriate and sufficient psychological formation (Bausch, K. C., 2010).

Research Matrix Number 2:

*"Design of Actions based on the definition of continuous critical problems
(Hasan Ozbekhan, 1970)
to successfully cope with the Millennium Project Global Challenges
(Jerome C. Glenn, Theodore J. Gordon and Elizabeth Florescu, 2010)"*

GLOBAL CHALLENGES[3]	CONTINUOUS CRITICAL PROBLEMS[4]/ ACTIONS OVER CHALLENGES[5]
1. How can sustainable development be achieved for all while addressing global climate change?	
"Challenge 1 will be addressed seriously when green GDP increases while poverty and global greenhouse gas emissions decrease for five years in a row". (Glenn, J., Gordon, T., & Florescu, E., 2010, p.13)	CCP-14 Generalized environmental deterioration. AOCH-17 Improving everywhere the environment, through local progressive restoration of the atmosphere, water and soil necessary conditions for preserving life. AOCH-52 Effectively increasing the use of alternative sources of clean energy.
1.1 "Climate change threatens the well-being of all humans, especially the poor, who have contributed the least to global warming". (Glenn, J., Gordon, T., & Florescu, E., 2010, p.12)	CCP-21 Accelerating wastage and exhaustion of natural resources. AOCH-26 Progressively diminishing wastage and the actual levels of natural resources exploitation. AOCH-27 Increasing recycling of organic and inorganic chemicals that can be income-producing.
1.2 "By 2015 climate change is expected to reduce wheat yields by 30% and rice yields by 15% and to increase their prices by 194% and 121% respectively". (Glenn, J., Gordon, T., & Florescu, E., 2010, p.12)	AOCH-52 Effectively increasing the use of alternative sources of clean energy. AOCH-56 Designing and applying systems of water capture, recycling, and transport from areas of abundance to scarcity, in such a way that all of them can be eco-friendly, use upgraded technology to reduce its final costs, and secure its reconditioning or sanitation.
1.3 "By 2050 another 2.3 billion people could be added to the planet and income per capita could more than double, dramatically increasing greenhouse gases". (Glenn, J., Gordon, T., & Florescu, E., 2010, p.12)	AOCH-57 Designing and launching successful community-scale projects of water management including equity factors in accordance with the different economic situations of the beneficiaries, and allowing each specific community to become sensible to the real value of this resource and the need to protect it.
1.4 "There is a growing fear that the target itself is inadequate –that the world needs to lower CO_2 to 350 ppm or else the momentum of climate change could grow beyond human ability to reverse it". (Glenn, J., Gordon, T., & Florescu, E., 2010, p.12)	
1.5 "Glaciers are melting, polar ice caps are thinning, and coral reefs are dying. Some 30% of fish stocks have already collapsed, and 21% of mammal species and 70% of plants are under threat. Oceans absorb 30 million tons of CO_2 each day, increasing their acidity". (Glenn, J., Gordon, T., & Florescu, E., 2010, p.12)	CCP-22 Growing environmental pollution. AOCH-28 Gradually reducing environmental pollution. AOCH-52 Effectively increasing the use of alternative sources of clean energy.
1.6 "The number of dead zones –areas with too little oxygen to support life- has doubled every decade since the	CCP-24 Major disturbances of the world´s physical ecology. AOCH-29 Gradually reversing global climate change. AOCH-50 Including in the international law system

GLOBAL CHALLENGES[3]	CONTINUOUS CRITICAL PROBLEMS[4]/ ACTIONS OVER CHALLENGES[5]
1960s. Mangrove forests, salt marshes, and sea grass beds cover less than 1% of the world's seabed but sequester over half the carbon buried in the ocean floor". (Glenn, J., Gordon, T., & Florescu, E., 2010, p.12) 1.7 "Human consumption of natural resources is 30% larger than nature's capacity to regenerate". (Glenn, J., Gordon, T., & Florescu, E., 2010, p.12) 1.8 "Large reinsurance companies estimate the annual economic loss due to climate change could reach $300 billion per year within a decade". (Glenn, J., Gordon, T., & Florescu, E., 2010, p.13)	norms for protecting the world's physical ecological balance. AOCH-52 Effectively increasing the use of alternative sources of clean energy. CCP-35 Irrational agricultural practices. AOCH-37 Improving agricultural techniques to avoid the contamination of soils and underground water, as well as fertile soil erosion, and progressive desertification. CCP-36 Irrational use of pesticides, chemical additives, insufficiently tested drugs, fertilizers, etc. AOCH-38 Producing organic food and prime materials. CCP-48 Irrational practices in resource investment. AOCH-48 Investing in well-balanced resource projects.
2. How can everyone have sufficient clean water without conflict? "Challenge 2 will be addressed seriously when the number of people without clean water and those suffering from water-borne diseases diminishes by half from their peaks and when the percentage of water used in agriculture drops for five years in a row". (Glenn, J., Gordon, T., & Florescu, E., 2010, p.14) 2.1 "An additional 1.3 billion people gained access to improved drinking water and 500 million got better sanitation since 1990, yet 900 million still lack clean water and 2.6 billion lack adequate sanitation". (Glenn, J., Gordon, T., & Florescu, E., 2010, p.14) 2.2 "By 2025 about 3 billion people could face water scarcity (defined as fewer than 1,000 cubic meters per person per year) due to climate change, population growth, and increasing	CCP-21 Accelerating wastage and exhaustion of natural resources. AOCH-26 Progressively diminishing wastage and the actual levels of natural resources exploitation. AOCH-27 Increasing recycling of organic and inorganic chemicals that can be income-producing. AOCH-52 Effectively increasing the use of alternative sources of clean energy. AOCH-56 Designing and applying systems of water capture, recycling, and transport from areas of abundance to scarcity, in such a way that all of them can be eco-friendly, use upgraded technology to reduce its final costs, and secure its reconditioning or sanitation. AOCH-57 Designing and launching successful community-scale projects of water management including equity factors in accordance with the different economic situations of the beneficiaries, and allowing each specific community to become sensible to the real value of this resource and the

GLOBAL CHALLENGES[3]	CONTINUOUS CRITICAL PROBLEMS[4]/ ACTIONS OVER CHALLENGES[5]
demand for water per capita". (Glenn, J., Gordon, T., & Florescu, E., 2010, p.14) 2.3 "Some 2.2 million children under five die due to unsafe water, inadequate sanitation, and the lack of hygiene every year". (Glenn, J., Gordon, T., & Florescu, E., 2010, p.14) 2.4 "Diarrheal disease in children under 15 has a greater impact than HIV, malaria, and tuberculosis combined". (Glenn, J., Gordon, T., & Florescu, E., 2010, p.14) 2.5 "Some 90% of developing countries' wastewater is discharged untreated directly into rivers, lakes, or oceans, contributing to the rapid expansion of de-oxygenated dead zones". (Glenn, J., Gordon, T., & Florescu, E., 2010, p.14) 2.6 "About 2 million tons of sewage and industrial and agricultural waste is annually discharged into the world's waterways". (Glenn, J., Gordon, T., & Florescu, E., 2010, p.14) 2.7 "Unless major political and technological changes occur, global water demand could be 40% more than current supply by 2030". (Glenn, J., Gordon, T., & Florescu, E., 2010, p.14) 2.8 "Agriculture already accounts for 70% of human usage of fresh water, but it needs even more to feed growing populations with increasing incomes. Some 30% of global cereal production could be lost in current production regions due to water scarcity, yet new areas in Russia and Canada could open due to climate change". (Glenn, J., Gordon, T., & Florescu, E., 2010, p.14) 2.9 "Access to clean water and basic sanitation should become human rights. About 80% of diseases in the developing world are water-related; most are due to poor management of human excreta". (Glenn, J., Gordon, T.,	need to protect it. CCP-20 Obsolete and discriminatory income distribution system(s). AOCH-25 Inaugurating a fair global financial and salary system, transforming finance into a Global Commons and tightening the salary system to the satisfaction of all basic necessities in accordance to a global recognition of human rights. (A fair financial system implies: a) Stabilizing the value of national currencies and establishing a reliable global currency regime; b) Channeling savings into productive and sustainable investments that build real wealth; c) Managing fail-safe, transparent payment and settlement systems; d) Appropriate, dependable, transparent tools for managing financial risks and assuring that issuers, insurers and counterparties are accountable) (Henderson, H. in Gutierrez, L., 2010). CCP-22 Growing environmental pollution. AOCH-28 Gradually reducing environmental pollution. AOCH-52 Effectively increasing the use of alternative sources of clean energy. CCP-24 Major disturbances of the world's physical ecology. AOCH-29 Gradually reversing global climate change. AOCH-50 Including in the international law system norms for protecting the world's physical ecological balance. AOCH-52 Effectively increasing the use of alternative sources of clean energy. CCP-35 Irrational agricultural practices. AOCH-37 Improving agricultural techniques to avoid the contamination of soils and underground water, as well as fertile soil erosion and progressive desertification. CCP-36 Irrational use of pesticides, chemical additives, insufficiently tested drugs, fertilizers, etc.

GLOBAL CHALLENGES[3]	CONTINUOUS CRITICAL PROBLEMS[4]/ ACTIONS OVER CHALLENGES[5]
& Florescu, E., 2010, p.14) 2.10 "The world is on track to meet the MDG goal on drinking water but not the one on sanitation". (Glenn, J., Gordon, T., & Florescu, E., 2010, p.14)	AOCH-38 Producing organic food and prime materials.

3. How can population growth and resources be brought into balance?

"Challenge 3 will be addressed seriously when the annual growth in world population drops to fewer than 30 million, the number of hungry people decreases by half, the infant mortality rate decreases by two-thirds between 2000 and 2015, and new approaches to aging become economically viable". (Glenn, J., Gordon, T., & Florescu, E., 2010, p.16)

3.1 "Today's 6.9 billion population is expected to grow to 9.1 billion by 2050 and could reach 11 billion if fertility rates do not continue to fall". (Glenn, J., Gordon, T., & Florescu, E., 2010, p.16)

3.2 "If the (fertility) rates do continue to fall, then world population could actually shrink by 2100, creating an elderly world difficult to support". (Glenn, J., Gordon, T., & Florescu, E., 2010, p.16)

3.3 "Nearly all the population increases will be in urban areas in developing countries". (Glenn, J., Gordon, T., & Florescu, E., 2010, p.16)

3.4 "Scientific and medical breakthroughs over the next 50 years will give people longer and more productive lives than most would believe possible today". (Glenn, J., Gordon, T., & Florescu, E., 2010, p.16)

3.5 "The global population profile is changing from high mortality and high fertility to low mortality and low fertility". (Glenn, J., Gordon, T., & Florescu, E., 2010, p.16)

3.6 "About 20% of the world will be over 60 by 2050, and 20% of the older population

CCP-1 Explosive population growth with consequent escalation of social, economic and other problems.
AOCH-1 Achieving personal responsibility and commitment over reproduction processes among humans according to local circumstances, including job, health and educational capabilities.

CCP-4 Uncontrolled urban spread.
AOCH-6 Creating new cities under a fair-regulated development plan.
AOCH-7 Creating economic and political incentives for diminishing the concentration of population in few megacities.
AOCH-8 Interconnecting cities with physical and logistic infrastructures that produce economic surpluses.

CCP-5 Generalized and growing malnutrition.
AOCH-49 Enriching all possible foods with proteins and vitamins which help stop malnutrition all over the world.

CCP-8 Growing inequalities in the distribution of wealth throughout the world.
AOCH-25 Inaugurating a global fair financial and salary system, transforming finance into a Global Commons and tightening the salary system to the satisfaction of all basic necessities in accordance to a global recognition of human rights. (A fair financial system implies: a) Stabilizing the value of national currencies and establishing a reliable global currency regime; b) Channeling savings into productive and sustainable investments that build real wealth; c) Managing fail-safe, transparent payment and settlement systems; d) Appropriate, dependable, transparent tools for managing financial risks and

GLOBAL CHALLENGES[3]	CONTINUOUS CRITICAL PROBLEMS[4]/ ACTIONS OVER CHALLENGES[5]
will be aged 80 or more. Some 20% of Europeans are 60 or older compared with 10% in Asia and Latin America and 5% in Africa". (Glenn, J., Gordon, T., & Florescu, E., 2010, p.16) 3.7 "The economic slowdown and unemployment, combined with elevated food and fuel prices, pushed some 100 million people into chronic hunger". (Glenn, J., Gordon, T., & Florescu, E., 2010, p.16) 3.8 "Over 1 billion people were undernourished in 2009". (Glenn, J., Gordon, T., & Florescu, E., 2010, p.16) 3.9 "In 2010, WFP plans to bring food assistance to more than 90 million people in 73 countries, yet in some of these countries, agricultural lands are being bought by foreign investors". (Glenn, J., Gordon, T., & Florescu, E., 2010, p.16) 3.10 "Meanwhile, 25% of all fish stocks are overharvested; the entire value of fish caught is $85 billion, but $27 billion spent on government subsidies, mostly in rich countries, lead to overexploitation". (Glenn, J., Gordon, T., & Florescu, E., 2010, p.16) 3.11 "To keep up with population and economic growth, food production should increase by 70% and meat production by over 200 million metric tons to reach 470 million metric tons by 2050, which increases demands on water and land, further increasing prices and competition between rural and urban requirements. An additional $83 billion per year will be needed to keep up with these new demands". (Glenn, J., Gordon, T., & Florescu, E., 2010, p.16) 3.12 "Cutting the number of hungry people in half by 2015 would generate global annual incremental benefits of $120 billion by 2015". (Glenn, J., Gordon, T., & Florescu, E., 2010, p.16) 3.13 "Some 30-40% of food production from farm to mouth is lost in many	assuring that issuers, insurers and counterparties are accountable] (Henderson, H. in Gutierrez, L., 2010). CCP-19 Inadequate shelter and transportation. AOCH-22 Building ecological housing in rural and urban areas with complete water and energy systems, including water recycling facilities and all types of energy saving technologies. AOCH-23 Producing, distributing and operating ecology-friendly transportation at accessible costs for the average inhabitant in every community. AOCH-24 Gradually increasing the capacity to work at home or near home. CCP-20 Obsolete and discriminatory income distribution system(s). AOCH-25 Inaugurating a global fair financial and salary system, transforming finance into a Global Commons and tightening the salary system to the satisfaction of all basic necessities in accordance to a global recognition of human rights. (A fair financial system implies: a) Stabilizing the value of national currencies and establishing a reliable global currency regime; b) Channeling savings into productive and sustainable investments that build real wealth; c) Managing fail-safe, transparent payment and settlement systems; d) Appropriate, dependable, transparent tools for managing financial risks and assuring that issuers, insurers and counterparties are accountable) (Henderson, H. in Gutierrez, L., 2010). CCP-21 Accelerating wastage and exhaustion of natural resources. AOCH-26 Progressively diminishing wastage and the actual levels of natural resources exploitation. AOCH-27 Increasing recycling of organic and inorganic chemicals that can be income-producing. AOCH-52 Effectively increasing the use of alternative sources of clean energy. CCP-24 Major disturbances of the world's physical ecology. AOCH-29 Gradually reversing global climate change. AOCH-50 Including in the international law system norms for protecting the world's physical ecological balance.

GLOBAL CHALLENGES[3]	CONTINUOUS CRITICAL PROBLEMS[4]/ ACTIONS OVER CHALLENGES[5]
countries". (Glenn, J., Gordon, T., & Florescu, E., 2010, p.16) 3.14 "Developing countries could experience a decline of 9-21% in overall potential agricultural productivity by 2050 as a result of global warming". (Glenn, J., Gordon, T., & Florescu, E., 2010, p.16) 3.15 "Urban population is expected to jump from 3.4 billion in 2009 to 6.3 billion in 2050". (Glenn, J., Gordon, T., & Florescu, E., 2010, p.16) 3.16 "During the same period, the 1 billion people living in slums today could double". (Glenn, J., Gordon, T., & Florescu, E., 2010, p.16) 3.17 "Without sufficient nutrition, shelter, water, and sanitation produced by more intelligent human-nature symbioses, increased migrations, conflicts, and disease seem inevitable". (Glenn, J., Gordon, T., & Florescu, E., 2010, p.16)	AOCH-52 Effectively increasing the use of alternative sources of clean energy. CCP-27 Unbalanced population distribution. AOCH-6 Creating new cities under a fair-regulated development plan. AOCH-7 Creating economic and political incentives for diminishing the concentration of population in few megacities. CCP-48 Irrational practices in resource investment. AOCH-48 Investing in well-balanced resource projects. AOCH-55 Incorporating practices that lead to the gradual dismantling of the corruption existing in institutions all over the world.
4. How can genuine democracy emerge from authoritarian regimes? "Challenge 4 will be addressed seriously when strategies to address threats to democracy are in place, when less than 10% of the world lives in nondemocratic countries, when Internet and media freedom protection is internationally enforced, and when voter participation exceeds 60% in most democratic elections". (Glenn, J., Gordon, T., & Florescu, E., 2010, p.18) 4.1 "According to Freedom House's 2010 report, world democracy and freedom declined for the fourth consecutive year, and press freedom for the eight consecutive years ." (Glenn, J., Gordon, T., & Florescu, E., 2010, p.18) 4.2 "Freedom declined in 40 countries, while it improved in only 16 countries and the number of electoral democracies	CCP-6 Persistence of widespread illiteracy. AOCH-9 Lowering population illiteracy using every media possible. CCP-13 Anachronistic and irrelevant education. AOCH-16 Educating people including the seven necessary types of knowledge for addressing the future (Morin, E., 1999). This implies a necessary reorientation of all the present educational systems. CCP- 18 Growing irrelevance of traditional values and continuing failure to evolve new value systems. AOCH-21 Establishing a value system that incorporates as guiding principles: world sustainable development, equity, peace, the well-being of children all over the world, love, gender equality, harmony and mutual respect for cultural differences. AOCH-55 Incorporating practices that lead to the gradual dismantling of the corruption existing in

GLOBAL CHALLENGES[3]	CONTINUOUS CRITICAL PROBLEMS[4]/ ACTIONS OVER CHALLENGES[5]
decreased by three, to 116 countries". (Glenn, J., Gordon, T., & Florescu, E., 2010, p.18) 4.3 "While 46% of the world lives in 89 "free" countries, and 20% lives in 58 "partly free" countries, 34% (over 2.3 billion people) lives in 47 countries with "not free" status". (Glenn, J., Gordon, T., & Florescu, E., 2010, p.18) 4.4 "Freedom of the press also declined almost worldwide, with worse signs in sub-Saharan Africa, Latin America, and the Middle East and North Africa. (Glenn, J., Gordon, T., & Florescu, E., 2010, p.18) 4.5 "Only 16% of the world lives in the 69 countries with "free" press, 44% in 64 countries with "partly free" press, and 40% lives in 63 countries without freedom of the press". (Glenn, J., Gordon, T., & Florescu, E., 2010, p.18) 4.6 "Injustices in different parts of the world become the concern of thousands or millions of people who then pressure local, regional, or international governing systems to address the issue". (Glenn, J., Gordon, T., & Florescu, E., 2010, p.18) 4.7 "The increasing role of digital media also responds to increasing concerns over monopolization and control of the news media". (Glenn, J., Gordon, T., & Florescu, E., 2010, p.18) 4.8 "Authoritarian regimes increasingly apply censorship, crackdown on bloggers and Internet journalism, and even use forms of cyber warfare to undermine democratic functions". (Glenn, J., Gordon, T., & Florescu, E., 2010, p.18)	institutions all over the world. CCP-20 Obsolete and discriminatory income distribution system(s). AOCH-25 Inaugurating a global fair financial and salary system, transforming finance into a Global Commons and tightening the salary system to the satisfaction of all basic necessities in accordance to a global recognition of human rights. (A fair financial system implies: a) Stabilizing the value of national currencies and establishing a reliable global currency regime; b) Channeling savings into productive and sustainable investments that build real wealth; c) Managing fail-safe, transparent payment and settlement systems; d) Appropriate, dependable, transparent tools for managing financial risks and assuring that issuers, insurers and counterparties are accountable) (Henderson, H. in Gutierrez, L., 2010). CCP-33 Polarization of military power and psychological impacts of the policy of deterrence. AOCH-35 Inserting a respectable world managerial system that privileges the whole new value system of humanity over any interest that favors only a part of the world's population. CCP-37 Growing use of distorted information to influence and manipulate people. AOCH-39 Educating people to discern between types of information through the careful examination of the methods of production and presentation, and the original intentions of its producers. AOCH-55 Incorporating practices that lead to the gradual dismantling of the corruption existing in institutions al over the world. CCP-40 New modes of localized warfare. AOCH-42 Using higher forms of security intelligence to disarticulate any possible form of localized warfare. CCP-47 Insufficient authority of international agencies. AOCH-35 Inserting a respectable world managerial system that privileges the whole new value system of humanity over any interest that favors only a part

GLOBAL CHALLENGES[3]	CONTINUOUS CRITICAL PROBLEMS[4]/ ACTIONS OVER CHALLENGES[5]
	of the world's population.
5. How can policymaking be made more sensitive to global long-term perspectives? "Challenge 5 will be addressed seriously when foresight functions are a routine part of most organizations and governments, when national SOFIs are used in at least 50 countries, when the consequences of high-risk projects are routinely considered before they are initiated, and when standing Committees for the Future exist in at least 50 national legislatures". (Glenn, J., Gordon, T., & Florescu, E., 2010, p.21) 5.1 "The BP oil spill and the cancellation of flights across Europe due to the volcano in Iceland expose the need for global, national, and local systems for resilience –the capacity to anticipate, respond, and recover from disasters while identifying future technological and social innovations and opportunities. Implementing resilience systems is one way to make policymaking more sensitive to global long-term perspectives". (Glenn, J., Gordon, T., & Florescu, E., 2010, p.20) 5.2 "Government future strategy units (see the CD Chapter 4.1) are being informally connected by Singapore's Future Strategy Unit to share best practices, compare research, and verify assumptions, just as the UN Strategic Planning Group connects 12 UN agency strategy units". (Glenn, J., Gordon, T., & Florescu, E., 2010, p.20) 5.3 "Foresight for development.org –in Africa- makes research documents, projects, scenarios, people, and blogs available to support African futures research". (Glenn, J., Gordon, T., & Florescu, E., 2010, p.21) 5.4 "Japan includes private-sector companies in its long-term strategic planning unit". (Glenn, J., Gordon, T., &	CCP-15 Generalized lack of agreed on alternatives to present trends. AOCH-18 Inserting the general practice of rigorously tested methodologies for attaining focused and structured dialog among people who need to take decisions which affect other people. (Flanagan, T. & Christakis, A., 2010). CCP-16 Widespread failure to stimulate man´s creative capacity to confront the future. AOCH-19 Creating and spreading a new theory of strategy which takes into account the relational nature of the human being, its new value system and the main trends observed in its environment. (Pérez, R. A., and Massoni, S., 2009). CCP- 18 Growing irrelevance of traditional values and continuing failure to evolve new value systems. AOCH-21 Establishing a value system that incorporates as guiding principles: world sustainable development, equity, peace, the well-being of children all over the world, love, gender equality, harmony and mutual respect for cultural differences. AOCH-55 Incorporating practices that lead to the gradual dismantling of the corruption existing in institutions all over the world. CCP-25 Generally inadequate and obsolete institutional arrangements. AOCH-30 Establishing a general law system that favors the conscious evolution of institutions and the continuous improvement of their practices. CCP-26 Limited understanding of what is feasible in the way of corrective measures. AOCH-18 Inserting the general practice of rigorously tested methodologies for attaining focused and structured dialog among people who need to take decisions which affect other people (Flanagan, T. R., and Christakis, A.N., 2010).

GLOBAL CHALLENGES[3]	CONTINUOUS CRITICAL PROBLEMS[4]/ ACTIONS OVER CHALLENGES[5]
Florescu, E., 2010, p.21) 5.5 "Forecasts of migrations from Asia and Africa are forcing Europe to reassess its future, as are the EU2020 strategy, Lisbon Strategy, emergence of China, and forecasts of public finances for social and health services for an aging population". (Glenn, J., Gordon, T., & Florescu, E., 2010, p.21) 5.6 "The rotating six-month EU presidency may have been necessary to enhance pan-European identification, but it makes long-term policy management difficult". (Glenn, J., Gordon, T., & Florescu, E., 2010, p.21) 5.7 "The 7th Framework Programme of the EU expands foresight support; the Institute for Prospective Technological Studies provides future studies for EU decision-making; the European Foresight Monitoring Network connects futurists; an annual European Futurists Conference is held in Switzerland; and the European Regional Foresight College improves future methods". (Glenn, J., Gordon, T., & Florescu, E., 2010, p.21) 5.8 "Yet futures approaches are ignored by the academic and mass media, which focus on urgent and confrontational issues over ideologies, unmet basic needs, growing inequality, and large economic groups that monopolize services". (Glenn, J., Gordon, T., & Florescu, E., 2010, p.21) 5.9 "The Global Millennium Prize was initiated in Mexico for students worldwide who have the best ideas for addressing global long-range challenges. Since the average age in Latin America is only 23, it is fundamental to incorporate the visions of the next generation". (Glenn, J., Gordon, T., & Florescu, E., 2010, p.21) 5.10 "There are increasing efforts to link academic research and future-oriented policymaking by special initiatives in	CCP-30 Inadequate and obsolete law enforcement and correctional practice. AOCH-33 Strengthening the law enforcement system with highly professionalized people who become, through their actions, the most respected people in their communities. CCP- 34 Fast obsolescing political structures and processes. AOCH-36 Strengthening the participation of the common citizens in the design of better political structures and also in the impartial evaluation of political processes. CCP-41 Inadequate participation of people at large in public decisions. AOCH-36 Strengthening the participation of the common citizens in the design of better political structures and also in the impartial evaluation of political processes.

GLOBAL CHALLENGES[3]	CONTINUOUS CRITICAL PROBLEMS[4]/ ACTIONS OVER CHALLENGES[5]
universities, think tanks, NGOs, and government departments". (Glenn, J., Gordon, T., & Florescu, E., 2010, p.21) 5.11 "Global perspectives in decision-making are emerging due to perpetual collaboration among different institutions and nations that has become the norm to address the increasing complexity and speed of global change". (Glenn, J., Gordon, T., & Florescu, E., 2010, p.21) 5.12 "Global long-term perspectives continue to be evident in the climate change policies of many local governments". (Glenn, J., Gordon, T., & Florescu, E., 2010, p.21)	
6. How can the global convergence of information and communications technologies work for everyone? "Challenge 6 will have been addressed seriously when Internet access and basic tele-education are free and available universally and when basic tele-medicine is commonplace everywhere". (Glenn, J., Gordon, T., & Florescu, E., 2010, p.23) 6.1 "Nearly 30% of humanity is connected to Internet, which has evolved from a passive information repository (Web 1.0) to a user-generated and participatory system (Web 2.0) and is morphing into Web 3.0, a more intelligent partner that has knowledge about the meaning of the information it stores and the ability to reason with that knowledge. (Glenn, J., Gordon, T., & Florescu, E., 2010, p.22) 6.2 "Today, mobile devices have become personal electronic companions, combining computer, GPS, telephone, camera, projector, music player, TV, and a library that is "aware" of its surroundings". (Glenn, J., Gordon, T., & Florescu, E., 2010, p.22) 6.3 "Self-organizing social networks are	CCP- 18 Growing irrelevance of traditional values and continuing failure to evolve new value systems. AOCH-21 Establishing a value system that incorporates as guiding principles: world sustainable development, equity, peace, the well-being of children all over the world, love, gender equality, harmony and mutual respect for cultural differences. AOCH-55 Incorporating practices that lead to the gradual dismantling of the corruption existing in institutions all over the world. CCP-28 Ideological fragmentation and semantic barriers to communication between individuals, groups and nations. AOCH-31 Building a consensual linguistic domain through the participation of individuals from different groups and nations in processes of Structured Dialogic Design (Christakis, A.N., and Bausch, K.C. 2006). CCP-37 Growing use of distorted information to influence and manipulate people. AOCH-39 Educating people to discern between types of information through the careful examination of

GLOBAL CHALLENGES[3]	CONTINUOUS CRITICAL PROBLEMS[4]/ ACTIONS OVER CHALLENGES[5]
augmenting hierarchical management of natural disasters, scientific research, and environmental monitoring. These new forms of transnational democracy are giving birth to unprecedented international conscience and action". (Glenn, J., Gordon, T., & Florescu, E., 2010, p.22) 6.4 "Open source software's non ownership model may become a significant element in the next economic system". (Glenn, J., Gordon, T., & Florescu, E., 2010, p.22) 6.5 "Real-time stream communications shorten the time it takes from situational awareness to decisions". (Glenn, J., Gordon, T., & Florescu, E., 2010, p.22) 6.6 "…growth of live streaming video puts stress on the Internet's capacities, requiring new approaches to keep up with bandwidth demand". (Glenn, J., Gordon, T., & Florescu, E., 2010, p.22) 6.7 "Businesses are building offices and holding meetings in Second Life and other cyber worlds that compete with conventional reality". (Glenn, J., Gordon, T., & Florescu, E., 2010, p.22) 6.8 "Wikipedia has become the world's encyclopedia, albeit with information reliability problems and struggles to counter disinformation campaigns…" (Glenn, J., Gordon, T., & Florescu, E., 2010, p.22) 6.9 "The Net has also created a new "virtual world" of a different type, blending into a single intercommunicating entertainment/image entity the domains of television, film, photography, music, and the visual Web (e.g. YouTube), so that images and performances flow freely among the various modalities. (There are also 14,000 Net "radio stations")". (Glenn, J., Gordon, T., & Florescu, E., 2010, p.22) 6.10 "It has also created an analogous intellectual world of information, linking newspapers, magazines, Web blogs and	the methods of production and presentation and the original intentions of its producers. AOCH-55 Incorporating practices that lead to the gradual dismantling of the corruption existing in institutions all over the world. CCP-39 Growing technological gaps and lags between developed and developing areas. AOCH-41 Establishing a new "intellectual property system" that fairly prizes original inventors and innovators whenever they honestly offer their knowledge on products and processes to anyone in the world through public media like internet. CCP-44 Growing tendency to be satisfied with technological solutions for every kind of problem. AOCH-44 Applying holistic systemic solutions for complex problems in world, regional, national and local situations, keeping sustainability in mind, and properly following up and periodically evaluating strategies.

GLOBAL CHALLENGES[3]	CONTINUOUS CRITICAL PROBLEMS[4]/ ACTIONS OVER CHALLENGES[5]
searches, TV news and information, and books and libraries". (Glenn, J., Gordon, T., & Florescu, E., 2010, p.22)	

6.11   "Issues of intellectual property are unresolved, however, and governments are wrestling with how to control harmful content". (Glenn, J., Gordon, T., & Florescu, E., 2010, p.22)

6.12   "Humanity, the built environment, and ubiquitous computing are becoming a continuum of consciousness and technology reflecting the full range of human behavior, from individual philanthropy to organized crime". (Glenn, J., Gordon, T., & Florescu, E., 2010, p.22)

6.13   "Low-cost computers are replacing high-cost weapons as an instrument of power in asymmetrical warfare". (Glenn, J., Gordon, T., & Florescu, E., 2010, p.22)

6.14   "Cyberspace is also becoming a battle zone among competing commercial interests and ideological adversaries as well as a key tool for extremists and a battleground between cybercriminals and law enforcement". (Glenn, J., Gordon, T., & Florescu, E., 2010, p.22)

6.15   "Meanwhile, Internet bases with wireless transmission are being constructed in remote villages; cell phones with Internet access are being designed for educational and business access by the lowest-income groups; and innovative programs are being created to connect the poorest 2 billion people to the evolving nervous system of civilization". (Glenn, J., Gordon, T., & Florescu, E., 2010, p.22)

6.16   "Social networking spurs the growth of political consciousness and popular power, and e-government systems allow citizens to receive valuable information from their leaders, provide feedback to them, and carry out needed transactions without time-consuming and possibly corrupt human intermediaries". (Glenn, J., Gordon, T., & Florescu, E., 2010, p.22)

GLOBAL CHALLENGES[3]	CONTINUOUS CRITICAL PROBLEMS[4]/ ACTIONS OVER CHALLENGES[5]
6.17 "...the UN has conducted comparative assessments of e-government status of its 191 member states since 2003". (Glenn, J., Gordon, T., & Florescu, E., 2010, p.22)	
7. **How can ethical market economies be encouraged to help reduce the gap between rich and poor?** "Challenge 7 will be addressed seriously when market economy abuses and corruption by companies and governments are intensively prosecuted and when the inequality gap –by all definitions- declines in 8 out of 10 years". (Glenn, J., Gordon, T., & Florescu, E., 2010, p.24) 7.1 "According to the IMF the world economy shrunk by 0.6% during 2009, per capita income fell about 2% to $10,500, and global unemployment reached 9%". (Glenn, J., Gordon, T., & Florescu, E., 2010, p.24) 7.2 "Nevertheless, the world still appears to be on track to halve the 1990 poverty rate (except in sub-Saharan Africa) by 2015". (Glenn, J., Gordon, T., & Florescu, E., 2010, p.24) 7.3 "The IMF estimates a 4.2% growth in 2010. Much of this recovery is led by the developing world, with expected growth of 6.3% in 2010 and 6.6% in 2011-13, compared with growth in advanced economies at 2.3% and 2.4% in those years". (Glenn, J., Gordon, T., & Florescu, E., 2010, p.24) 7.4 "The contribution of BRIC to world GDP in 2009 was over 23.5%, while a growing middle-class in developing countries opens new markets". (Glenn, J., Gordon, T., & Florescu, E., 2010, p.24) 7.5 "By 2015, the IMF expects unemployment to be 6.2% in advanced	CCP-1 Explosive population growth with consequent escalation of social, economic and other problems. AOCH-1 Achieving personal responsibility and commitment over reproduction processes among humans according to local circumstances, including job, health and educational capabilities. CCP-2 Widespread poverty throughout the world. AOCH-2 Creating combined financing and education programs that enhance productivity, long term self-sufficiency and amelioration of living conditions of poor communities. These programs are to be specifically chosen for each community, taking into account due respect for their cultural traditions and always looking for easiness of replication in other communities. CCP-5 Generalized and growing malnutrition. AOCH-49 Enriching all possible foods with proteins and vitamins which help stop malnutrition all over the world. CCP-8 Growing inequalities in the distribution of wealth throughout the world. AOCH-25 Inaugurating a global fair financial and salary system, transforming finance into a Global Commons and tightening the salary system to the satisfaction of all basic necessities in accordance to a global recognition of human rights. (A fair financial system implies: a) Stabilizing the value of national currencies and establishing a reliable global currency regime; b) Channeling savings into productive and sustainable investments that build real wealth; c) Managing fail-safe, transparent payment and settlement systems; d) Appropriate, dependable,

GLOBAL CHALLENGES[3]	CONTINUOUS CRITICAL PROBLEMS[4]/ ACTIONS OVER CHALLENGES[5]
economies and 5.4% in emerging and developing economies". (Glenn, J., Gordon, T., & Florescu, E., 2010, p.24) 7.6 "The World Bank estimates that the number of people living on less than $1.25 a day might be about 1 billion in 2015 and 826 million in 2020, while those living on less than $2 a day might be 2.06 billion and 1.92 billion respectively". (Glenn, J., Gordon, T., & Florescu, E., 2010, p.24) 7.7 "The 2009 net ODA from DAC countries was $120 billion and is expected to grow to $126 billion in 2010". (Glenn, J., Gordon, T., & Florescu, E., 2010, p.24) 7.8 "Remittances account for 20% of GDP in some countries. These fell by an estimated 6% in 2009, to about $317 billion, and are expected to grow by 2% in 2010". (Glenn, J., Gordon, T., & Florescu, E., 2010, p.24) 7.9 "UNCTAD forecasts FDI inflows to recover and grow from $1 trillion in 2009 to $1.8 trillion in 2011". (Glenn, J., Gordon, T., & Florescu, E., 2010, p.24) 7.10 "While FDI flows to developed countries continue to decline (falling 41% in 2009), FDI between developing countries (South-South) is growing rapidly". (Glenn, J., Gordon, T., & Florescu, E., 2010, p.24) 7.11 "The WTO forecasts world trade to grow 9.5% in 2010, after a 12.2% drop in 2009". (Glenn, J., Gordon, T., & Florescu, E., 2010, p.24) 7.12 "In 2011, the trade balance of emerging and developing economies might reach $663.5 billion, while that of advanced economies could further deteriorate to -$423.9 billion". (Glenn, J., Gordon, T., & Florescu, E., 2010, p.24) 7.13 "By 2015, the account balance of emerging and developing economies is expected to grow to $769 billion". (Glenn, J., Gordon, T., & Florescu, E., 2010, p.24)	transparent tools for managing financial risks and assuring that issuers, insurers and counterparties are accountable) (Henderson, H. in Gutierrez, L., 2010). CCP-12 Affluence and its unknown consequences. AOCH-15 Educating with a philosophy of happiness linked to the appreciation of human dignity and also linked to human rewards deeper than private property and accumulation. CCP-17 Continuing deterioration of inner-cities or slums. AOCH-20 Gradually installing of restoration programs to recuperate the dignity of inhabitable spaces within the cities. CCP-18 Growing irrelevance of traditional values and continuing failure to evolve new value systems. AOCH-21 Establishing a value system that incorporates as guiding principles: world sustainable development, equity, peace, the well-being of children all over the world, love, gender equality, harmony and mutual respect for cultural differences. AOCH-55 Incorporating practices that lead to the gradual dismantling of the corruption existing in institutions all over the world. CCP-19 Inadequate shelter and transportation. AOCH-22 Building ecological housing in rural and urban areas with complete water and energy systems, including water recycling facilities and all types of energy saving technologies. AOCH-23 Producing, distributing and operating ecology friendly transportation at accessible costs for the average inhabitant in every community. AOCH-24 Gradually increasing the capacity to work at home or near home. CCP-20 Obsolete and discriminatory income distribution system(s). AOCH-25 Inaugurating a global fair financial and salary system, transforming finance into a Global Commons and tightening the salary system to the satisfaction of all basic necessities in accordance to a global recognition of human rights. (A fair financial

GLOBAL CHALLENGES[3]	CONTINUOUS CRITICAL PROBLEMS[4]/ ACTIONS OVER CHALLENGES[5]
7.14 "The high tech-low wage conditions of China and India make it very difficult for other developing countries to compete; hence, developing countries should rethink their export-led growth strategies". (Glenn, J., Gordon, T., & Florescu, E., 2010, p.24) 7.15 "Although agriculture employs 37.5% of the labor force, its contribution to GDP is barely 6%". (Glenn, J., Gordon, T., & Florescu, E., 2010, p.24) 7.16 "Since 1976, microfinance institutions provided loans to over 113 million clients worldwide". (Glenn, J., Gordon, T., & Florescu, E., 2010, p.24) 7.17 "Financing to the private sector by the MDBs increased from less than $4 billion 20 years ago to $40 billion in 2009, while the IFC mobilized $14.5 billion in the new investments in private companies in developing countries". (Glenn, J., Gordon, T., & Florescu, E., 2010, p.24)	system implies: a) Stabilizing the value of national currencies and establishing a reliable global currency regime; b) Channeling savings into productive and sustainable investments that build real wealth; c) Managing fail-safe, transparent payment and settlement systems; d) Appropriate, dependable, transparent tools for managing financial risks and assuring that issuers, insurers and counterparties are accountable) (Henderson, H. in Gutierrez, L., 2010). CCP-31 Widespread unemployment and generalized under-employment. AOCH-34 Facilitating participants in non-structured economy legitimate activities the incorporation into a regulated structured economy, by offering them a fairer fiscal system and the minimum of restraints. CCP-38 Fragmented international monetary system. AOCH-40 Agreeing on an international globally accepted monetary system with the following functions: A) Fostering international monetary cooperation; B) Facilitating expansion and balanced growth of international trade; C) Encouraging money exchange stability; D) Contributing to the establishment of a multilateral paying system; E) Offering resources to participant countries with difficulties in their balance of payments (International Monetary System, Wikipedia, 2010). CCP-43 Irrational distribution of industry supported by policies that will strengthen the current patterns. AOCH-43 Gradually establishing a balanced division of labor which accounts for the advantages offered by different countries, recognizes the real strengths of the people involved, and also searches for the equitable participation of every single country. CCP-45 Obsolete system of world trade. AOCH-45 Gradually establishing a new world trade system that privileges the benefit of final consumers over particular interests of investors.
8. How can the threat of new and reemerging diseases and immune microorganisms be reduced?	CCP-5 Generalized and growing malnutrition. AOCH-49 Enriching all possible foods with proteins and vitamins which help stop malnutrition all over the world.

GLOBAL CHALLENGES[3]	CONTINUOUS CRITICAL PROBLEMS[4]/ ACTIONS OVER CHALLENGES[5]
"At the moment, the best ways to address infectious diseases remain early detection, accurate reporting, prompt isolation, transparency of information, increased investment in clean drinking water, sanitation, and hand washing. Also are WHO's eHealth systems, International Health Regulations to address SARS-like threats, immunization programs, and the Global Outbreak Alert and Response Network as global responses to this challenge. (Glenn, J., Gordon, T., & Florescu, E., 2010, pp. 26 and 27) 8.1 "Even though population is increasing, 30% fewer children under five died in 2008 than in 1990 and total mortality from infectious disease fell from 25% in 1998 to 16% in 2008". (Glenn, J., Gordon, T., & Florescu, E., 2010, p. 26) 8.2 "Vaccines supplied by UNICEF reach 55% of the world's children". (Glenn, J., Gordon, T., & Florescu, E., 2010, p. 26) 8.3 "Partnerships between the Global Alliance for Vaccines and Immunization and the Gates Foundation, WHO, UNICEF, and the World Bank have greatly improved global health cooperation over the past 10 years". (Glenn, J., Gordon, T., & Florescu, E., 2010, p. 26) 8.4 "Because the world is aging and increasingly sedentary, cardiovascular disease is now the leading cause of death in the developing as well as the industrial world; however infectious diseases are the second largest killer and cause about 67% of all preventable deaths of children under five (pneumonia, diarrhea, malaria and measles)". (Glenn, J., Gordon, T., & Florescu, E., 2010, p. 26) 8.5 "Urbanization, travel, trade, increased encroachment on animal territory, and concentrated livestock production move infectious organisms to more people in less time than ever before and could trigger new pandemics". (Glenn, J.,	CCP-9 Insufficient and irrationally organized medical care. AOCH-12 Gradually increasing organized medical care until it becomes a universally accessible service. AOCH-58 Dramatically increasing investments in research for developing effective, integral, preventive medicine that can be accessed in any country of the world. CCP-17 Continuing deterioration of inner-cities or slums. AOCH-20 Gradually installing of restoration programs to recuperate the dignity of inhabitable spaces within the cities. CCP-24 Major disturbances of the world´s physical ecology. AOCH-29 Gradually reversing global climate change. AOCH-50 Including in the international law system norms for protecting the world´s physical ecological balance. AOCH-52 Effectively increasing the use of alternative sources of clean energy. CCP-27 Unbalanced population distribution. AOCH-6 Creating new cities under a fair-regulated development plan. AOCH-7 Creating economic and political incentives for diminishing the concentration of population in few megacities. CCP-36 Irrational use of pesticides, chemical additives, insufficiently tested drugs, fertilizers, etc. AOCH-38 Producing organic food and prime materials. CCP-46 Ill conceived use of international agencies for national or sectoral ends. AOCH-46 Establishing an effective global Rule of Law.

GLOBAL CHALLENGES[3]	CONTINUOUS CRITICAL PROBLEMS[4]/ ACTIONS OVER CHALLENGES[5]
Gordon, T., & Florescu, E., 2010, p. 26)	
8.6 "The H1N1 virus (swine flu) infected millions of humans in all 214 countries and territories within a year, killing 18,000, and will be active another year. Although spreading very fast, the mortality was relatively low, causing WHO to review its decision to declare it a pandemic". (Glenn, J., Gordon, T., & Florescu, E., 2010, p. 26)	
8.7 "H5N1 (avian flu) killed half of the people infected, spread very slowly, has mutated three times in the last 15 years, and could mutate again, increasing its impact". (Glenn, J., Gordon, T., & Florescu, E., 2010, p. 26)	
8.8 "Over the past 40 years, 39 new infectious diseases have been discovered, 20 diseases are now drug-resistant, and old diseases have reappeared, such as cholera, yellow fever, plague, dengue fever, meningitis, hemorrhagic fever, and diphtheria. In the last five years, more than 1,100 epidemics have been verified. About 75% of emerging pathogens are zoonotic (they jump species)". (Glenn, J., Gordon, T., & Florescu, E., 2010, p. 26)	
8.9 "Some 33 million people are living with HIV/AIDS; 2.7 million were newly infected and 2 million died during 2009. The virus is unstable and mutates enough that $800 million of research has not produced a successful vaccine. So far, it cannot be cured, only stabilized, and it has become resistant to multiple drugs. While it appears that new cases peaked in the late 1990s and mortality peaked in 2004, predictions of 2.3 million new cases per year are likely to be true into the 2030s unless prevention is more successful. Sharing needles is thought to be three times more likely than sexual intercourse to transmit HIV; male circumcision may reduce infection by 50%; and since HIV crosses the placenta and breast milk to children, preventive	

GLOBAL CHALLENGES[3]	CONTINUOUS CRITICAL PROBLEMS[4]/ ACTIONS OVER CHALLENGES[5]
treatments are important". (Glenn, J., Gordon, T., & Florescu, E., 2010, p. 26)	

8.10　"While small numbers of people with Ebola and West Nile viruses have received (sic) media attention, the bigger health impacts are from schistosomiasis (200 million cases), dengue fever (50 million new cases a year), measles (30 million cases a year), onchocerciasis (18 million cases in Africa), typhoid and leishmaniasis (approximately 12 million each globally), rotavirus (600,000 child deaths per year), and shigella childhood diarrhea (600,000 deaths per year)". (Glenn, J., Gordon, T., & Florescu, E., 2010, p. 26)

8.11　"About half of the world's population is at risk of several endemic diseases". (Glenn, J., Gordon, T., & Florescu, E., 2010, p. 26)

8.12　"Climate change is altering insect and disease patterns. Vector reproduction, parasite development cycle, and byte frequency generally rise with temperature; therefore, malaria, tick-borne encephalitis, and dengue fever are expected to become increasingly widespread". (Glenn, J., Gordon, T., & Florescu, E., 2010, p. 26)

8.13　"Hepatitis B infects up to 2 billion people. There is more TB in the world now than ever before (2 million deaths, 9 million new infections in 2009), yet in the last 15 years 43 million TB cases have been treated and 36 million have been cured". (Glenn, J., Gordon, T., & Florescu, E., 2010, p. 26)

8.14　"There were 863,000 malaria deaths in 2009 (80% occurred in children younger than 5 in sub-Saharan Africa), yet 38 countries (9 in Africa) documented reductions of more than 50% in the number of malaria cases between 2000 and 2008". (Glenn, J., Gordon, T., & Florescu, E., 2010, p. 26)

GLOBAL CHALLENGES[3]	CONTINUOUS CRITICAL PROBLEMS[4]/ ACTIONS OVER CHALLENGES[5]
9. How can the capacity to decide be improved as the nature of work and institutions change? "Challenge 9 will be addressed seriously when the State of the Future Index or similar systems are used regularly in decision-making, when national corporate law is modified to recognize transinstitutional organizations, and when at least 50 countries require elected officials to be trained in decision-making". (Glenn, J., Gordon, T., & Florescu, E., 2010, p. 29) 9.1 "The number and complexity of choices seem to be growing beyond our abilities to analyze and make decisions". (Glenn, J., Gordon, T., & Florescu, E., 2010, p. 28) 9.2 "The acceleration of change reduces the time from recognition of the need to make a decision to completion of all the steps to make the right decision". (Glenn, J., Gordon, T., & Florescu, E., 2010, p. 28) 9.3 "The global challenges...show that the world is increasingly interdependent and intricate, requiring improved abilities for collaborative decision-making across institutional, political and cultural boundaries". (Glenn, J., Gordon, T., & Florescu, E., 2010, p. 28) 9.4 "Many of the world's decision-making processes are inefficient, slow, and ill informed". (Glenn, J., Gordon, T., & Florescu, E., 2010, p. 28) 9.5 "Previous economic models continue to mistakenly assume that human beings are well informed, rational decision makers in spite of research to the contrary". (Glenn, J., Gordon, T., & Florescu, E., 2010, p. 28) 9.6 "...relying on computer models for decisions proved unreliable in the financial crisis". (Glenn, J., Gordon, T., & Florescu, E., 2010, p. 28) 9.7 "The region's dependence (North	CCP-7 Expanding mechanization and bureaucratization of almost all human activity. AOCH-10 Reducing transactions (official procedures) all over the world, conveniently using the new Information and Communication Technologies with secure services that preserve the confidentiality of information. AOCH-11 Humanizing labor with the creativity necessary to efficiently solve every problem linked to human rights. CCP-15 Generalized lack of agreed on alternatives to present trends. AOCH-18 Inserting the general practice of rigorously tested methodologies for attaining focused and structured dialog among people who need to take decisions which affect other people (Flanagan, T. R., and Christakis, A.N., 2010). CCP-16 Widespread failure to stimulate man´s creative capacity to confront the future. AOCH-19 Creating and spreading a new theory of strategy which takes into account the relational nature of the human being, its new value system and the main trends observed in its environment (Pérez, R. A., and Massoni, S., 2009). CCP-20 Obsolete and discriminatory income distribution system(s). AOCH-25 Inaugurating a global fair financial and salary system, transforming finance into a Global Commons and tightening the salary system to the satisfaction of all basic necessities in accordance to a global recognition of human rights. (A fair financial system implies: a) Stabilizing the value of national currencies and establishing a reliable global currency regime; b) Channeling savings into productive and sustainable investments that build real wealth; c) Managing fail-safe, transparent payment and settlement systems; d) Appropriate, dependable, transparent tools for managing financial risks and

GLOBAL CHALLENGES[3]	CONTINUOUS CRITICAL PROBLEMS[4]/ ACTIONS OVER CHALLENGES[5]
America) on computer-augmented decision-making –from e-government to tele-business- creates new vulnerabilities to manipulation by organized crime, corruption, and cyber-terrorism…" (Glenn, J., Gordon, T., & Florescu, E., 2010, p. 29)	assuring that issuers, insurers and counterparties are accountable) (Henderson, H. in Gutierrez, L., 2010).
9.8 "More open systems, democratization, and interactive media are involving more people in decision-making, which further increases complexity". (Glenn, J., Gordon, T., & Florescu, E., 2010, p. 28)	CCP-25 Generally inadequate and obsolete institutional arrangements. AOCH-30 Establishing a general law system that favors the conscious evolution of institutions and the continuous improvement of their practices.
9.9 "DSS improves decisions by filtering out bias and providing a more objective assessment of facts and potential options". (Glenn, J., Gordon, T., & Florescu, E., 2010, p. 28)	CCP-26 Limited understanding of what is feasible in the way of corrective measures. AOCH-18 Inserting the general practice of rigorously tested methodologies for attaining focused and structured dialog among people who need to take decisions which affect other people. (Flanagan, T. R., and Christakis, A. N., 2010).
9.10 "Some software lets groups select criteria and rate options, some averages people's bets on future events, while others show how issues have alternative positions and how each is supported or refuted by research". (Glenn, J., Gordon, T., & Florescu, E., 2010, p. 28)	CCP-31 Widespread unemployment and generalized under-employment. AOCH-34 Facilitating participants in non-structured economy legitimate activities the incorporation into a regulated structured economy, by offering them a fairer fiscal system and the minimum of restraints.
9.11 "Self-organization of volunteers around the world via Web sites is increasing transparency and creating new forms of decision-making. Nearly half of the 200 million blogs were created from 2007 to 2009". (Glenn, J., Gordon, T., & Florescu, E., 2010, p. 28)	CCP-43 Irrational distribution of industry supported by policies that will strengthen the current patterns. AOCH-43 Gradually establishing a balanced division of labor which accounts for the advantages offered by different countries, recognizes the real strengths of the people involved, and also searches for the equitable participation of every single country.
9.12 "Issues-based information software in e-government allows decision-making to be more transparent and accountable". (Glenn, J., Gordon, T., & Florescu, E., 2010, p. 28)	CCP-47 Insufficient authority of international agencies. AOCH-35 Inserting a respectable world managerial system that privileges the whole new value system of humanity over any interest that favors only a part of the world's population.
9.13 "Unfortunately, we are still so flooded with so much trivial news that serious attention to serious issues gets little interest, and too much time is wasted going through useless information". (Glenn, J., Gordon, T., & Florescu, E., 2010, p. 28)	AOCH-47 Installing tested mechanisms for attaining democracy within international agencies and from the top to the bottom of every hierarchical system.
9.14 "Expert advice was most often the view of single individuals or very small groups, but now decision-making benefits	

GLOBAL CHALLENGES[3]	CONTINUOUS CRITICAL PROBLEMS[4]/ ACTIONS OVER CHALLENGES[5]
from online, open systems that invite broad and transparent participation". (Glenn, J., Gordon, T., & Florescu, E., 2010, p. 28) 9.15 "Ubiquitous computing will increase the number of decisions per day, constantly changing schedules and priorities". (Glenn, J., Gordon, T., & Florescu, E., 2010, p. 28)	
10. How can shared values and new security strategies reduce ethnic conflicts, terrorism, and the use of weapons of mass destruction? "Challenge 10 will be addressed seriously when arms sales and violent crimes decrease by 50% from their peak". (Glenn, J., Gordon, T., & Florescu, E., 2010, p. 31) 10.1 "Although the vast majority of the world is living in peace, half the world continues to be vulnerable to social instability and violence due to the global recession, to aging populations and decreasing water, food, and energy supplies per person, to climate change, and to increasing migrations due to political, environmental, and economic conditions". (Glenn, J., Gordon, T., & Florescu, E., 2010, p. 30) 10.2 "There were 14 conflicts with 1,000 or more deaths in 2010. These occurred in Africa (5), Asia (3), the Americas (2), and the Middle East (3), with 1 conflict classified as worldwide anti-extremism". (Glenn, J., Gordon, T., & Florescu, E., 2010, p. 30) 10.3 "The U.S. and Russia signed a nuclear arms reduction treaty, and the Cluster Munitions Convention will come into force in the fall of 2010". (Glenn, J., Gordon, T., & Florescu, E., 2010, p. 30) 10.4 "The Global Peace Index's rating of 144 countries' peacefulness again	CCP-3 Increase in the production, destructive capacity, and accessibility of all weapons of war. AOCH-21 Establishing a value system that incorporates as guiding principles: world sustainable development, equity, peace, the well –being of children all over the world, love, gender equality, harmony and mutual respect for cultural differences. AOCH-3 Destroying, under each country governmental responsibility, every arsenal of massive destruction weapons. AOCH-4 Hardening sanctions against arms traffickers. AOCH-5 Increasing intelligence against that crime (arms trafficking) with the highest technology at hand. CCP-10 Hardening discrimination against minorities. AOCH-13 Putting to work local Commissions of Human Rights all over the world. AOCH-14 Advancing legislative agendas that protect minorities against any type of discrimination. CCP-15 Generalized lack of agreed on alternatives to present trends. AOCH-18 Inserting the general practice of rigorously tested methodologies for attaining focused and structured dialog among people who need to take decisions which affect other people. (Flanagan, T. R., and Christakis, A. N., 2010).

GLOBAL CHALLENGES[3]	CONTINUOUS CRITICAL PROBLEMS[4]/ ACTIONS OVER CHALLENGES[5]
declined slightly, reflecting intensification of some conflicts and the economic crisis". (Glenn, J., Gordon, T., & Florescu, E., 2010, p. 30) 10.5 "In 2010, there are 124,000 UN peacekeepers from 115 countries in 16 operations". (Glenn, J., Gordon, T., & Florescu, E., 2010, p. 30) 10.6 "Total military expenditures are about $1.5 trillion per year. There are an estimated 8,100 active nuclear weapons, down from 20,000 in 2002 and 65,000 in 1985. However, there are approximately 1,700 tons of highly enriched uranium and 500 tons of separated plutonium that could produce nuclear weapons". (Glenn, J., Gordon, T., & Florescu, E., 2010, p. 30) 10.7 "Unmanned aircraft and robot land vehicles are increasingly being used". (Glenn, J., Gordon, T., & Florescu, E., 2010, p. 30) 10.8 "The nexus of transnational extremist violence is changing from complex organized plots to attacks by single individuals or small independent groups". (Glenn, J., Gordon, T., & Florescu, E., 2010, p. 30) 10.9 "Future desktop molecular and pharmaceutical manufacturing and organized crime's access to nuclear materials give single individuals the ability to make and use weapons of mass destruction –from biological weapons to low-level nuclear ("dirty") bombs". (Glenn, J., Gordon, T., & Florescu, E., 2010, p. 30) 10.10 "IAEA reports that between 1993 and the end of 2009, the Illicit Trafficking Database recorded 1,784 nuclear trafficking incidents (222 during 2009), ranging from illicit disposal efforts to nuclear material of unknown provenance". (Glenn, J., Gordon, T., & Florescu, E., 2010, p. 30) 10.11 "The ICRC has pointed out that the Geneva Convention needs to be modified	CCP- 18 Growing irrelevance of traditional values and continuing failure to evolve new value systems. AOCH-21 Establishing a value system that incorporates as guiding principles: world sustainable development, equity, peace, the well-being of children all over the world, love, gender equality, harmony and mutual respect for cultural differences. AOCH-55 Incorporating practices that lead to the gradual dismantling of the corruption existing in institutions all over the world. CCP-29 Increasing a-social and anti-social behavior and consequent rise in criminality. AOCH-32 Addressing the hopes of young people internationally for better living conditions and human development opportunities. AOCH-53 Gradually dismantling the local, national and international networks engaged in persons and drugs trafficking, using the most sophisticated intelligence and technology for detection of criminal activities. CCP-40 New modes of localized warfare. AOCH-42 Using higher forms of security intelligence to disarticulate any possible form of localized warfare. CCP-46 Ill conceived use of international agencies for national or sectoral ends. AOCH-46 Establishing an effective global Rule of Law. CCP-47 Insufficient authority of international agencies. AOCH-35 Inserting a respectable world managerial system that privileges the whole new value system of humanity over any interest that favors only a part of the world's population. AOCH-47 Installing tested mechanisms for attaining democracy within international agencies and from the top to the bottom of every hierarchical system. CCP-23 Generalized alienation of youth. AOCH-15 Educating with a philosophy of happiness linked to the appreciation of human dignity and also linked to human rewards deeper than private

GLOBAL CHALLENGES[3]	CONTINUOUS CRITICAL PROBLEMS[4]/ ACTIONS OVER CHALLENGES[5]
to cover intra-state conflicts". (Glenn, J., Gordon, T., & Florescu, E., 2010, p. 30)	property and accumulation. AOCH-21 Establishing a value system that incorporates as guiding principles: world sustainable development, equity, peace, the well-being of children all over the world, love, gender equality, harmony and mutual respect for cultural differences. AOCH-46 Establishing an effective global Rule of Law. AOCH-11 Humanizing labor with the creativity necessary to efficiently solve every problem linked to human rights. AOCH-54 Globally legalizing the personal consumption of the least human damaging drugs, and building in parallel an effective personalized control system for their sale.
11. How can the changing status of women help improve the human condition? "Challenge 11 will be addressed seriously when there is gender parity in school enrollment, literacy, and access to capital, when discriminatory laws are gone, when discrimination and violence against women is prosecuted, and when there are essentially equal numbers of men and women in policymaking positions". (Glenn, J., Gordon, T., & Florescu, E., 2010, p. 32) 11.1 "The ratio of women in national parliaments has increased from 13.8% in 2000 to 18.9% in 2010, while the current ratio of women in ministerial positions is 29% in health, 26% in culture, 25% in education, and 4% in defense, while 5% are heads of government. Some 100 countries have mandatory or voluntary gender quotas for their legislatures". (Glenn, J., Gordon, T., & Florescu, E., 2010, p. 32) 11.2 "The Gender Equity Index 2009 computed by Social Watch shows that in most countries the gender gap is not closing and progress is largely dependent on the gender discrimination status in the	CCP- 18 Growing irrelevance of traditional values and continuing failure to evolve new value systems. AOCH-21 Establishing a value system that incorporates as guiding principles world sustainable development, equity, peace, the well-being of children all over the world, love, gender equality, harmony and mutual respect for cultural differences. AOCH-11 Humanizing labor with the creativity necessary to efficiently solve every problem linked to human rights. AOCH-13 Putting to work local Commissions of Human Rights all over the world. AOCH-15 Educating with a philosophy of happiness linked to the appreciation of human dignity and also linked to human rewards deeper than private property and accumulation. AOCH-32 Addressing the hopes of young people internationally for better living conditions and human development opportunities. AOCH-46 Establishing an effective global Rule of Law. AOCH-53 Gradually dismantling the local, national and international networks engaged in persons and drugs trafficking, using the most sophisticated intelligence and technology for detection of criminal activities.

GLOBAL CHALLENGES[3]	CONTINUOUS CRITICAL PROBLEMS[4]/ ACTIONS OVER CHALLENGES[5]
country, and not on the region or economic development. The index decreased from 35% in 2008 to 34.5% in 2009, with setbacks in 51% of the countries that were already in the worse relative situation, while 77% of those in a comparatively better situation made progress". (Glenn, J., Gordon, T., & Florescu, E., 2010, p. 32) 11.3 "Most progress was made in achieving universal primary education. Of the estimated 72 million primary-age children who are not in school, girls only slightly outnumber boys. However, only 53% of countries achieved gender parity in both primary and secondary education, with the gap for secondary schooling widening in some regions". (Glenn, J., Gordon, T., & Florescu, E., 2010, p. 32) 11.4 "Around 126 million children are still involved in hazardous work, and the economic crisis threatens the education status of a whole generation of children". (Glenn, J., Gordon, T., & Florescu, E., 2010, p. 32) 11.5 "Meanwhile, 50% of university students worldwide are women, and in many countries they outnumber men". (Glenn, J., Gordon, T., & Florescu, E., 2010, p. 32) 11.6 "Women account for over 40% of the world's workforce but earn less than 25% of the wages. In developing countries, they represent over 60% of all unpaid family workers, typically with no job security and benefits". (Glenn, J., Gordon, T., & Florescu, E., 2010, p. 32) 11.7 "Environmental disasters, food and financial crises, armed conflicts, and forced displacement further increase vulnerabilities and generate new forms of disadvantages for women and children". (Glenn, J., Gordon, T., & Florescu, E., 2010, p. 32) 11.8 "...women control over 70% of global consumer spending and by 2015 might	AOCH-55 Incorporating practices that lead to the gradual dismantling of the corruption existing in institutions all over the world. CCP-20 Obsolete and discriminatory income distribution system(s). AOCH-25 Inaugurating a global fair financial and salary system, transforming finance into a Global Commons and tightening the salary system to the satisfaction of all basic necessities in accordance to a global recognition of human rights. (A fair financial system implies: a) Stabilizing the value of national currencies and establishing a reliable global currency regime; b) Channeling savings into productive and sustainable investments that build real wealth; c) Managing fail-safe, transparent payment and settlement systems; d) Appropriate, dependable, transparent tools for managing financial risks and assuring that issuers, insurers and counterparties are accountable) (Henderson, H. in Gutierrez, L., 2010). CCP-29 Increasing a-social and anti-social behavior and consequent rise in criminality. AOCH-32 Addressing the hopes of young people internationally for better living conditions and human development opportunities. AOCH-59 Hardening sanctions against criminals who attempt to injure any person through physical violence, sexual abuse, rape, kidnapping, torture, persons trafficking or any behavior based on discrimination, or just accentuated because of a state of defenselessness of the victim.

GLOBAL CHALLENGES[3]	CONTINUOUS CRITICAL PROBLEMS[4]/ ACTIONS OVER CHALLENGES[5]
generate 70% of the global household income growth". (Glenn, J., Gordon, T., & Florescu, E., 2010, p. 32) 11.9 "Some religious and patriarchal structures continue to impede women's liberty and access to family planning in many cultures. Unsafe and illegal abortions cause some 5.3 million disabilities and 68,000 deaths each year. Of the more than 500,000 maternal deaths per year, 99% happen in developing countries, with the highest prevalence in Africa and Asia due to high fertility rates and weak health systems". (Glenn, J., Gordon, T., & Florescu, E., 2010, p. 32) 11.10 "At the current rate of improvement, the UN goal to reduce maternal mortality to 120 deaths per 100,000 live births by 2015 will not be achieved". (Glenn, J., Gordon, T., & Florescu, E., 2010, p. 32) 11.11 "About 2.5 million people from 127 different countries are being trafficked around the world, out of which approximately 70% are women and girls and up to 50% are minors, the "largest slave trade in history"". (Glenn, J., Gordon, T., & Florescu, E., 2010, p. 32) 11.12 "The Protocol to Prevent, Suppress and Punish Trafficking in Persons, especially Women and Children, has 137 parties and 117 signatories, but it has yet to be adopted and enforced by some key countries". (Glenn, J., Gordon, T., & Florescu, E., 2010, p. 32) 11.13 "Despite significant progress in setting international mechanisms to eradicate all forms of violence against women, about half of the countries have no legislation to stop gender-based discrimination, and crimes against women continue to be perpetrated with impunity". (Glenn, J., Gordon, T., & Florescu, E., 2010, p. 32) 11.14 "About one-third of women suffer gender-based violence during their lives,	

GLOBAL CHALLENGES[3]	CONTINUOUS CRITICAL PROBLEMS[4]/ ACTIONS OVER CHALLENGES[5]
and one in five has been a victim of rape or attempted rape, especially during armed conflicts". (Glenn, J., Gordon, T., & Florescu, E., 2010, p. 32)	
12. How can transnational organized crime networks be stopped from becoming more powerful and sophisticated global enterprises? "Challenge 12 will be seriously addressed when money laundering and crime income sources drop by 75% from their peak". (Glenn, J., Gordon, T., & Florescu, E., 2010, p. 34) 12.1 "Havocscope.com estimates world illicit trade to be just over $1 trillion per year, with counterfeiting and intellectual property piracy accounting for $300 billion to $1 trillion, the global drug trade at $386 billion, trade in environmental goods at $63 billion, human trafficking and prostitution at $141 billion, smuggling at $96 billion, and weapons trade at $12 billion". (Glenn, J., Gordon, T., & Florescu, E., 2010, p. 34) 12.2 "The FBI estimates that online fraud cost U.S. businesses and consumers $560 million in 2009, up from $265 million in 2008. These figures do not include extortion or organized crime's part of the $1 trillion in bribes that the World Bank estimates are paid annually or its part of the estimated $1.5-6.5 trillion in laundered money". (Glenn, J., Gordon, T., & Florescu, E., 2010, p. 34) 12.3 "Hence the total income could be $2-3 trillion —about twice as big as all the military budgets in the world". (Glenn, J., Gordon, T., & Florescu, E., 2010, p. 34) 12.4 "The financial crisis and bankrupt financial institutions have opened new filtration routes for TOC crime". (Glenn, J., Gordon, T., & Florescu, E., 2010, p. 34)	CCP-1 Explosive population growth with consequent escalation of social, economic and other problems. AOCH-1 Achieving personal responsibility and commitment over reproduction processes among humans according to local circumstances, including job, health and educational capabilities. CCP-3 Increase in the production, destructive capacity, and accessibility of all weapons of war. AOCH-21 Establishing a value system that incorporates as guiding principles: world sustainable development, equity, peace, the well-being of children all over the world, love, gender equality, harmony and mutual respect for cultural differences. AOCH-3 Destroying, under each country governmental responsibility, every arsenal of massive destruction weapons. AOCH-4 Hardening sanctions against arms traffickers. AOCH-5 Increasing intelligence against that crime (arms trafficking) with the highest technology at hand. CCP-29 Increasing a-social and anti-social behavior and consequent rise in criminality. AOCH-32 Addressing the hopes of young people internationally for better living conditions and human development opportunities. AOCH-53 Gradually dismantling the local, national and international networks engaged in persons and drugs trafficking, using the most sophisticated intelligence and technology for detection of criminal activities. AOCH-59 Hardening sanctions against criminals who attempt to injure any person through physical

GLOBAL CHALLENGES[3]	CONTINUOUS CRITICAL PROBLEMS[4]/ ACTIONS OVER CHALLENGES[5]
12.5 "The world recession has increased human trafficking and smuggling. Human body parts for transplantation are a new element in TOC. There are up to 27 million people being held in slavery today (the vast majority in Asia), more than during the peak of the African slave trade. UNICEF estimates that 1.2 million children are trafficked every year". (Glenn, J., Gordon, T., & Florescu, E., 2010, p. 34) 12.6 "The online market in illegally obtained data and tools for committing data theft and other cybercrimes continues to grow, and criminal organizations are offering online hosting of illegal applications". (Glenn, J., Gordon, T., & Florescu, E., 2010, p. 34) 12.7 "Computer transfers of $2 trillion per day make tempting targets for international cybercriminals". (Glenn, J., Gordon, T., & Florescu, E., 2010, p. 34)	violence, sexual abuse, rape, kidnapping, torture, persons trafficking or any behavior based on discrimination, or just accentuated because of a state of defenselessness of the victim. CCP-40 New modes of localized warfare. AOCH-42 Using higher forms of security intelligence to disarticulate any possible form of localized warfare. CCP-46 Ill conceived use of international agencies for national or sectoral ends. AOCH-46 Establishing an effective global Rule of Law. CCP-23 Generalized alienation of youth. AOCH-15 Educating with a philosophy of happiness linked to the appreciation of human dignity and also linked to human rewards deeper than private property and accumulation. AOCH-21 Establishing a value system that incorporates as guiding principles: world sustainable development, equity, peace, the well-being of children all over the world, love, gender equality, harmony and mutual respect for cultural differences. AOCH-46 Establishing an effective global Rule of Law. AOCH-11 Humanizing labor with the creativity necessary to efficiently solve every problem linked to human rights. AOCH-54 Globally legalizing the personal consumption of the least human damaging drugs, and building in parallel an effective personalized control system for their sale.
13. How can growing energy demands be met safely and efficiently? "Challenge 13 will have been addressed seriously when the total energy production from environmentally benign processes surpasses other sources for five years in a row and when atmospheric CO_2 additions drop for at least five years". (Glenn, J., Gordon, T., & Florescu, E., 2010, p. 36)	 CCP-21 Accelerating wastage and exhaustion of natural resources. AOCH-26 Progressively diminishing wastage and the actual levels of natural resources exploitation. AOCH-27 Increasing recycling of organic and inorganic chemicals that can be income-producing. AOCH-52 Effectively increasing the use of alternative

GLOBAL CHALLENGES[3]	CONTINUOUS CRITICAL PROBLEMS[4]/ ACTIONS OVER CHALLENGES[5]
13.1 "World energy demand is expected to increase by between 40% to 50% over the next 25 years, with the vast majority of the increase being in China and India". (Glenn, J., Gordon, T., & Florescu, E., 2010, p. 36) 13.2 "Without major policy and technological changes (which could be triggered by the BP oil spill), fossil fuels will dominate energy sources, making large-scale carbon capture, storage, and/or reuse a top priority to reduce climate change". (Glenn, J., Gordon, T., & Florescu, E., 2010, p. 36) 13.3 "The total global renewable energy investment for 2010 is estimated at $200 billion, up nearly 50% from 2009. To meet total energy demand, an annual $1.1 trillion (1.4% of global GDP) is needed, and an additional $10.5-trillion investment by 2030 will be necessary if the world is to meet the goal of keeping atmospheric CO_2 concentration below 450ppm". (Glenn, J., Gordon, T., & Florescu, E., 2010, p. 36) 13.4 "…the world spends more than $310 billion on energy subsidies every year. G20 leaders pledged to phase out fossil fuel subsidies in the medium term. Eliminating subsidies could lead to a 10% reduction of GHG emissions by 2050". (Glenn, J., Gordon, T., & Florescu, E., 2010, p. 36) 13.5 "In 2008, for the first time, the majority of US and EU increases in the production of electricity came from renewable sources instead of fossil or nuclear sources". (Glenn, J., Gordon, T., & Florescu, E., 2010, p. 36) 13.6 "Meanwhile, 1.5 billion people have no access to electricity and 3 billion still rely on traditional biomass for cooking and heating". (Glenn, J., Gordon, T., & Florescu, E., 2010, p. 36) 13.7 "In the IEA reference scenario, the	sources of clean energy. CCP-20 Obsolete and discriminatory income distribution system(s). AOCH-25 Inaugurating a global fair financial and salary system, transforming finance into a Global Commons and tightening the salary system to the satisfaction of all basic necessities in accordance to a global recognition of human rights. (A fair financial system implies: a) Stabilizing the value of national currencies and establishing a reliable global currency regime; b) Channeling savings into productive and sustainable investments that build real wealth; c) Managing fail-safe, transparent payment and settlement systems; d) Appropriate, dependable, transparent tools for managing financial risks and assuring that issuers, insurers and counterparties are accountable) (Henderson, H. in Gutierrez, L., 2010). CCP-24 Major disturbances of the world´s physical ecology. AOCH-29 Gradually reversing global climate change. AOCH-50 Including in the international law system norms for protecting the world´s physical ecological balance. AOCH-52 Effectively increasing the use of alternative sources of clean energy.

GLOBAL CHALLENGES[3]	CONTINUOUS CRITICAL PROBLEMS[4]/ ACTIONS OVER CHALLENGES[5]
number of people lacking access to electricity drops by only 200 million by 2030 and the number actually increases in Africa". (Glenn, J., Gordon, T., & Florescu, E., 2010, p. 36) 13.8 "The World Bank estimates that countries with underperforming energy systems may lose up to 1-2% of growth potential every year, while billions of gallons of petroleum are wasted in traffic jams around the world". (Glenn, J., Gordon, T., & Florescu, E., 2010, p. 36)	
14. How can scientific and technological breakthroughs be accelerated to improve the human condition? "Challenge 14 will have been addressed seriously when the funding of R&D for societal needs reaches parity with funding for weapons and when an international science and technology organization is established that routinely connects world S&T knowledge for use in R&D priority setting and legislation". (Glenn, J., Gordon, T., & Florescu, E., 2010, p. 39) 14.1 "The ability to invent life has been demonstrated. The J. Craig Venter Institute synthesized a 1.08-million base pair chromosome to construct the bacterial cell *Mycoplasma mycoides JCVI-syn1.0,* the first self-replicating synthetic cell". (Glenn, J., Gordon, T., & Florescu, E., 2010, p. 38) 14.2 "Synthetic neurobiologists are creating "co-processors" for the brain to cure blindness or make us more intelligent. The lab-created Isx-9 molecule can make nerve stem cells mature into brain cells, leading the way to brain regeneration". (Glenn, J., Gordon, T., & Florescu, E., 2010, p. 38) 14.3 "IBM plans to have the Sequoia 20-petaflops computer ready for DOE by	CCP- 18 Growing irrelevance of traditional values and continuing failure to evolve new value systems. AOCH-21 Establishing a value system that incorporates as guiding principles: world sustainable development, equity, peace, the well-being of children all over the world, love, gender equality, harmony and mutual respect for cultural differences. AOCH-55 Incorporating practices that lead to the gradual dismantling of the corruption existing in institutions all over the world. CCP-19 Inadequate shelter and transportation. AOCH-22 Building ecological housing in rural and urban areas with complete water and energy systems, including water recycling facilities and all types of energy saving technologies. AOCH-23 Producing, distributing and operating ecology friendly transportation at accessible costs for the average inhabitant in every community. AOCH-24 Gradually increasing the capacity to work at home or near home. CCP-20 Obsolete and discriminatory income distribution systems. AOCH-25 Inaugurating a global fair financial and salary system, transforming finance into a Global Commons and tightening the salary system to the satisfaction of all basic necessities in accordance to a

GLOBAL CHALLENGES[3]	CONTINUOUS CRITICAL PROBLEMS[4]/ ACTIONS OVER CHALLENGES[5]
2012, which is estimated to be the first computer with the processing power of a human brain". (Glenn, J., Gordon, T., & Florescu, E., 2010, p. 38) 14.4 "A transistor has been built from seven atoms". (Glenn, J., Gordon, T., & Florescu, E., 2010, p. 38) 14.5 "There are already machines that can be controlled by thought alone". (Glenn, J., Gordon, T., & Florescu, E., 2010, p. 38) 14.6 "The acceleration of S&T innovations from improved instrumentation, communications among scientists, and synergies among nanotechnology, biotechnology, information technology, cognitive science, and quantum technology continues to fundamentally change the prospects for civilization". (Glenn, J., Gordon, T., & Florescu, E., 2010, p. 38) 14.7 "Millions of people passively volunteer their computers' excess capacity to run data analysis programs to help speed up research in biomedicine, mathematics, artificial intelligence, and cancer. Over 50 million volunteer citizen scientists gather and analyze data, dramatically expanding the capacity of scientific research around the world". (Glenn, J., Gordon, T., & Florescu, E., 2010, p. 38) 14.8 "Patients with rare diseases share real-time clinical data to assist doctors". (Glenn, J., Gordon, T., & Florescu, E., 2010, p. 38) 14.9 "Free university courses, curricula, and tools in science and technology are increasing on the Web to share extraordinary breakthroughs". (Glenn, J., Gordon, T., & Florescu, E., 2010, p. 38) 14.10 "Scanning electron microscopes can see 0.01 nanometers (the distance between a hydrogen nucleus and its electron), and the Hubble telescope has seen 13.2 billion light-years away". (Glenn, J., Gordon, T., & Florescu, E.,	global recognition of human rights. (A fair financial system implies: a) Stabilizing the value of national currencies and establishing a reliable global currency regime; b) Channeling savings into productive and sustainable investments that build real wealth; c) Managing fail-safe, transparent payment and settlement systems; d) Appropriate, dependable, transparent tools for managing financial risks and assuring that issuers, insurers and counterparties are accountable) (Henderson, H. in Gutierrez, L., 2010). CCP-26 Limited understanding of what is feasible in the way of corrective measures. AOCH-18 Inserting the general practice of rigorously tested methodologies for attaining focused and structured dialog among people who need to take decisions which affect other people. (Flanagan T. R., and Christakis, A. N., 2010). CCP-39 Growing technological gaps and lags between developed and developing areas. AOCH-41 Establishing a new "intellectual property system" that fairly prizes original inventors and innovators whenever they honestly offer their knowledge on products and processes to anyone in the world through public media like internet. CCP-44 Growing tendency to be satisfied with technological solutions for every kind of problem. AOCH-44 Applying holistic systemic solutions for complex problems in world, regional, national and local situations, keeping sustainability in mind, and properly following up and periodically evaluating strategies. AOCH-60 Installing international online co-laboratories among trans-disciplinarian groups of experts, that are opened to general public access and its selective collaboration, in order to make science and technology progress, evaluate each one of the breakthroughs and try to harmonize them with a vision of the universe, supported by the new value system and the new philosophy of happiness.

GLOBAL CHALLENGES[3]	CONTINUOUS CRITICAL PROBLEMS[4]/ ACTIONS OVER CHALLENGES[5]
2010, p. 38)	
14.11 "The Large Hadron Collider is exploring the nature of dark energy". (Glenn, J., Gordon, T., & Florescu, E., 2010, p. 38)	
14.12 "Photons have been slowed and accelerated, and four photons have been precisely controlled on a silicon chip to learn how to create optical computers". (Glenn, J., Gordon, T., & Florescu, E., 2010, p. 38)	
14.13 "Over 450 planets have been discovered orbiting other stars". (Glenn, J., Gordon, T., & Florescu, E., 2010, p. 38)	
14.14 "A record five photons have been entangled (quantum entanglement is the simultaneous change of entangled objects separated in space) to explore futuristic communications, security, simple teleportation, and the transport of energy". (Glenn, J., Gordon, T., & Florescu, E., 2010, p. 38)	
14.15 "External light can be concentrated inside the body for photodynamic therapy and to power implanted devices". (Glenn, J., Gordon, T., & Florescu, E., 2010, p. 38)	
14.16 "MRI brain imaging shows primitive pictures of real-time thought processes". (Glenn, J., Gordon, T., & Florescu, E., 2010, p. 38)	
14.17 "Magnetic signals from a single electron buried inside a solid sample have been detected". (Glenn, J., Gordon, T., & Florescu, E., 2010, p. 38)	
14.18 "A new sensor can detect over 2,000 viruses and about 900 bacteria within 24 hours". (Glenn, J., Gordon, T., & Florescu, E., 2010, p. 38)	
14.19 "Extinct mammoth's blood now lives using ancient DNA". (Glenn, J., Gordon, T., & Florescu, E., 2010, p. 38)	
14.20 "Nanotechnology-based products have grown by 25% in the last year to over 800 items today for the release of medicine in the body, thin-film	

GLOBAL CHALLENGES[3]	CONTINUOUS CRITICAL PROBLEMS[4]/ ACTIONS OVER CHALLENGES[5]
photovoltaic, super hard surfaces, and many lightweight strong objects". (Glenn, J., Gordon, T., & Florescu, E., 2010, p. 38) 14.21 "DNA scans open the possibility of customized medicine and eliminating inherited diseases". (Glenn, J., Gordon, T., & Florescu, E., 2010, p. 38) 14.22 "Viruses have been used to help build efficient batteries that are half the size of a human cell". (Glenn, J., Gordon, T., & Florescu, E., 2010, p. 38) 14.23 "Transistors measuring 10-by-1 atoms have been produced out of graphene, a material just 1 atom thick –the thinnest material in the world-. Graphene may ultimately replace silicon in many nano-electronic applications". (Glenn, J., Gordon, T., & Florescu, E., 2010, p. 38) 14.24 "Over 12 million robots do everything from routine surgery to building cars and managing farms, even marrying couples in Japan". (Glenn, J., Gordon, T., & Florescu, E., 2010, p. 38)	
15. How can ethical considerations become more routinely incorporated into global decisions? "Challenge 15 will be addressed seriously when corruption decreases by 50% from the World Bank estimates of 2006, when ethical business standards are internationally practiced and regularly audited, when essentially all students receive education in ethics and responsible citizenship, and when there is a general acknowledgement that global ethics transcends religion and nationality". (Glenn, J., Gordon, T., & Florescu, E., 2010, p. 41) 15.1 "The global financial crisis demonstrated the interdependence of economics and ethics. While quick fixes have pulled the world out of recession, it is not clear that ethics have been	CCP-10 Hardening discrimination against minorities. AOCH-13 Putting to work local Commissions of Human Rights all over the world. AOCH-14 Advancing legislative agendas that protect minorities against any type of discrimination. CCP-11 Hardening prejudices against differing cultures. AOCH-21 Establishing a value system that incorporates as guiding principles: world sustainable development, equity, peace, the well-being of children all over the world, love, gender equality, harmony and mutual respect for cultural differences. CCP- 18 Growing irrelevance of traditional values and continuing failure to evolve new value systems. AOCH-21 Establishing a value system that

GLOBAL CHALLENGES[3]	CONTINUOUS CRITICAL PROBLEMS[4]/ ACTIONS OVER CHALLENGES[5]
addressed sufficiently to prevent future crises". (Glenn, J., Gordon, T., & Florescu, E., 2010, p. 40) 15.2 "International meetings of the G-20 and other forums are trying to reach agreements about how to improve systems in order to increase integrity, financial transparency, and accountability". (Glenn, J., Gordon, T., & Florescu, E., 2010, p. 40) 15.3 "At the same time, 12-27 million people are slaves today, more than at the height of the nineteenth century slave trade". (Glenn, J., Gordon, T., & Florescu, E., 2010, p. 40) 15.4 "The World Bank estimates over $1 trillion are paid each year in bribes". (Glenn, J., Gordon, T., & Florescu, E., 2010, p. 40) 15.5 "...organized crime takes in $2-3 trillion annually". (Glenn, J., Gordon, T., & Florescu, E., 2010, p. 40) 15.6 "Concerns are also growing about ties between organized crime and terrorism threatening the future of democracy". (Glenn, J., Gordon, T., & Florescu, E., 2010, p. 40) 15.7 "Meanwhile, trivial news and entertainment flood people's minds with unneeded products and unethical behavior". (Glenn, J., Gordon, T., & Florescu, E., 2010, p. 40) 15.8 "Some experts speculate that the world is heading for a "singularity"-a time in which technological change is so fast and significant that people today are incapable of conceiving what life might be like beyond 2025. This acceleration of technological change seems beyond the ability of most people and institutions to comprehend, leading to ethical uncertainties". (Glenn, J., Gordon, T., & Florescu, E., 2010, p. 40) 15.9 "Individuals can now experiment with genetics to create new life forms in home labs without the safeguards of	incorporates as guiding principles: world sustainable development, equity, peace, the well-being of children all over the world, love, gender equality, harmony and mutual respect for cultural differences. AOCH-55 Incorporating practices that lead to the gradual dismantling of the corruption existing in institutions all over the world. CCP-20 Obsolete and discriminatory income distribution system(s). AOCH-25 Inaugurating a global fair financial and salary system, transforming finance into a Global Commons and tightening the salary system to the satisfaction of all basic necessities in accordance to a global recognition of human rights. (A fair financial system implies: a) Stabilizing the value of national currencies and establishing a reliable global currency regime; b) Channeling savings into productive and sustainable investments that build real wealth; c) Managing fail-safe, transparent payment and settlement systems; d) Appropriate, dependable, transparent tools for managing financial risks and assuring that issuers, insurers and counterparties are accountable) (Henderson, H. in Gutierrez, L., 2010). CCP-28 Ideological fragmentation and semantic barriers to communication between individuals, groups and nations. AOCH-31 Building a consensual linguistic domain through the participation of individuals from different groups and nations in processes of Structured Dialogic Design (Christakis A.N., and Bausch K. C., 2006). CCP- 32 Spreading "discontent" throughout most classes of society. AOCH-31 Building a consensual linguistic domain through the participation of individuals from different groups and nations in processes of Structured Dialogic Design (Christakis A.N., and Bausch K. C., 2006). AOCH-21 Establishing a value system that incorporates as guiding principles: world sustainable development, equity, peace, the well-being of children all over the world, love, gender equality, harmony and mutual respect for cultural differences.

GLOBAL CHALLENGES[3]	CONTINUOUS CRITICAL PROBLEMS[4]/ ACTIONS OVER CHALLENGES[5]
government and commercial laboratories". (Glenn, J., Gordon, T., & Florescu, E., 2010, p. 40) 15.10 "Globalization and advanced technology allow fewer people to do more damage and in less time, so that possibly one day a single individual may be able to make and deploy a weapon of mass destruction". (Glenn, J., Gordon, T., & Florescu, E., 2010, p. 40) 15.11 "New technologies also allow more people to do more good than ever before, such as single individuals organizing worldwide actions around specific ethical issues via the Internet". (Glenn, J., Gordon, T., & Florescu, E., 2010, p. 40) 15.12 "The moral will to act in collaboration across national, institutional, religious, and ideological boundaries that is necessary to address today's global challenges requires global ethics". (Glenn, J., Gordon, T., & Florescu, E., 2010, p. 40) 15.13 "Public morality based on religious metaphysics is challenged daily by growing secularism, leaving many unsure about the moral basis for decision-making". (Glenn, J., Gordon, T., & Florescu, E., 2010, p. 40) 15.14 "Unfortunately, religions and ideologies that claim moral superiority give rise to "we-they" splits". (Glenn, J., Gordon, T., & Florescu, E., 2010, p. 40)	AOCH-44 Applying holistic systemic solutions for complex problems in world, regional, national and local situations, keeping sustainability in mind, and properly following up and periodically evaluating strategies. AOCH-18 Inserting the general practice of rigorously tested methodologies for attaining focused and structured dialog among people who need to take decisions which affect other people. (Flanagan, T. R., and Christakis, A. N., 2010). AOCH-46 Establishing an effective global Rule of Law. AOCH-32 Addressing the hopes of young people internationally for better living conditions and human development opportunities. AOCH-11 Humanizing labor with the creativity necessary to efficiently solve every problem linked to human rights. AOCH-15 Educating with a philosophy of happiness linked to the appreciation of human dignity and also linked to human rewards deeper than private property and accumulation. AOCH-13 Putting to work local Commissions of Human Rights all over the world. CCP-42 Unimaginative conceptions of world-order and the rule of law. AOCH-21 Establishing a value system that incorporates as guiding principles: world sustainable development, equity, peace, the well-being of children all over the world, love, gender equality, harmony and mutual respect for cultural differences. AOCH-44 Applying holistic systemic solutions for complex problems in world, regional, national and local situations, keeping sustainability in mind, and properly following up and periodically evaluating strategies. AOCH-46 Establishing an effective global Rule of Law. CCP-47 Insufficient authority of international agencies. AOCH-35 Inserting a respectable world managerial system that privileges the whole new value system of humanity over any interest that favors only a part of the world's population.

GLOBAL CHALLENGES[3]	CONTINUOUS CRITICAL PROBLEMS[4]/ ACTIONS OVER CHALLENGES[5]
	AOCH-47 Installing tested mechanisms for attaining democracy within international agencies and from the top to the bottom of every hierarchical system.
For the whole set of global challenges. "Ethics in the post-crisis world must be rooted in placing the common good above individual ambition; in ensuring a government's right to regulate the economy and to provide basic services for all; and in promoting infinite benefits, such as spiritual ones, over the consumption of finite, material goods. The ethics of a new project for civilization must incorporate environmental preservation into the concept of sustainable development, value solidarity economy and fair trade networks, and strengthen civil society as a regulator of government action" (Frey Betto, 2010, p. 21, in World Economic Forum *"Faith and the Global Agenda: Values for the Post-Crisis Economy"*)	CCP-49 Insufficient understanding of Continuous Critical Problems, of their nature, their interactions and of the future consequences both they and current solutions to them are generating. AOCH-44 Applying holistic systemic solutions for complex problems in world, regional, national and local situations, keeping sustainability in mind, and properly following up and periodically evaluating strategies. AOCH-18 Inserting the general practice of rigorously tested methodologies for attaining focused and structured dialog among people who need to take decisions which affect other people. (Flanagan, T. R., and Christakis, A. N., 2010). AOCH-35 Inserting a respectable world managerial system that privileges the whole new value system of humanity over any interest that favors only a part of the world's population. AOCH-47 Installing tested mechanisms for attaining democracy within international agencies and from the top to the bottom of every hierarchical system. CCP-50 An absence of individuals with appropriate and sufficient psychological formation (Bausch, K. C., 2010). AOCH-51 Educating in the appropriate balance between the feminine and masculine polarities existing in every human being no matter its gender, with especial attention during infancy and adolescence (Gutiérrez, L., 2010).

---

[3] It refers to the 15 Global Challenges published in "2010 State of the Future" of the Millennium Project, by Glenn, J., Gordon, T., & Florescu, E., (2010).

[4] The first 49 continuous critical problems (CCP) come from an illustrative list that grounds the *problematique* created by Hasan Ozbekhan (1970). Only CCP 50 referes to a different proposal made by Ken Bausch (2010).

[5] The actions to cope with the challenges have been designed by the authors of the present monograph

Figure 3: **Map of Actions to successfully cope with the Global Challenges of the Millennium Project.**

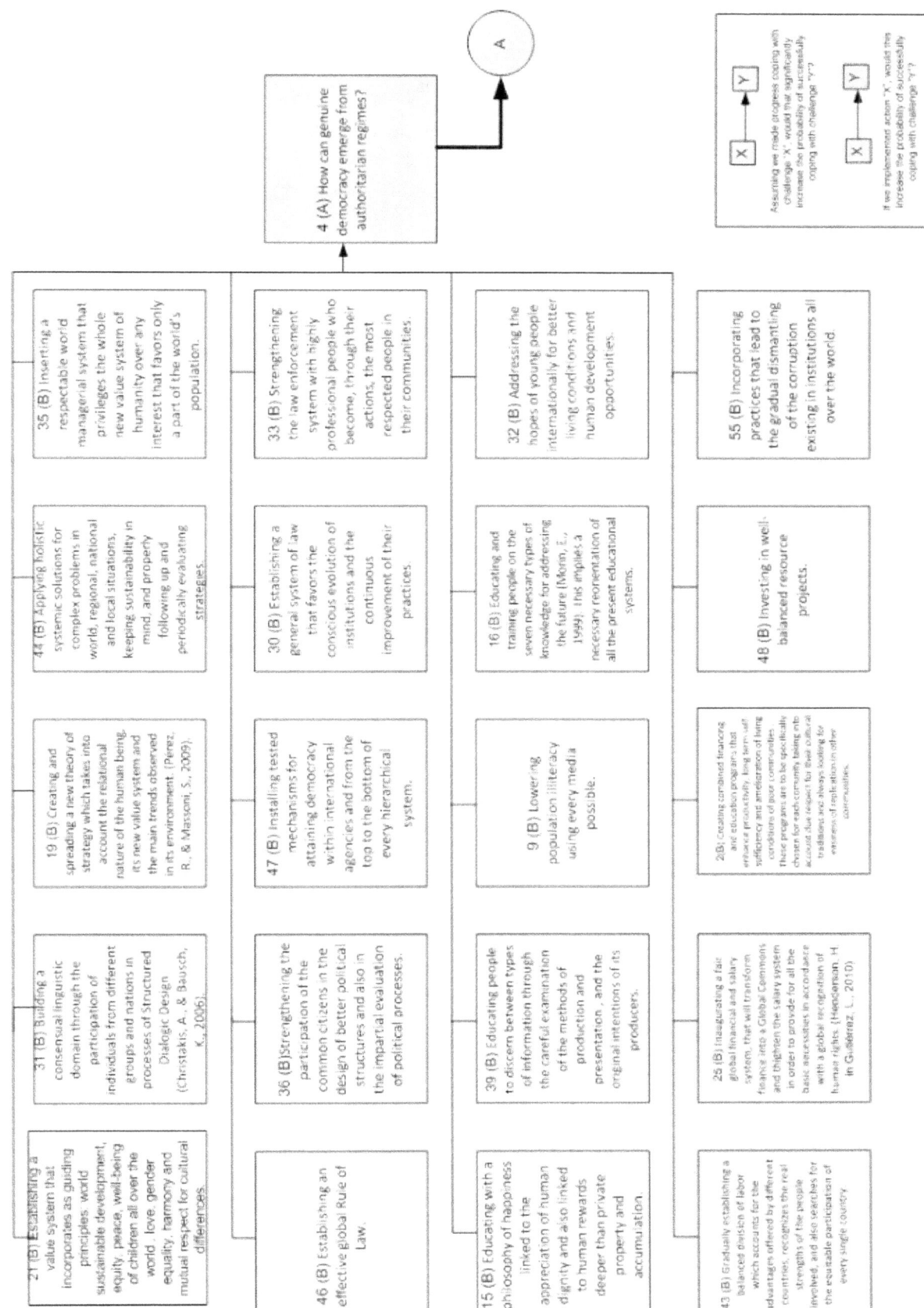

X

4 (A) How can genuine democracy emerge from authoritarian regimes?

A

Assuming we made progress coping with challenge "X", would that significantly increase the probability of successfully coping with challenge "Y"?

If we implement action "X", would this increase the probability of successfully coping with challenge "Y"?

21 (B) Establishing a value system that incorporates as guiding principles, world sustainable development, equality, peace, well-being of children all over the world, love, gender equality, harmony and mutual respect for cultural differences.

31 (B) Building a consensual linguistic domain through the participation of individuals from different groups and nations in processes of Structured Dialogic Design (Christakis, A. & Bausch, K., 2006).

19 (B) Creating and spreading a new theory of strategy which takes into account the relational nature of the human being, its new value system and the main trends observed in its environment. (Perez, R. & Massoni, S., 2009).

44 (B) Applying holistic systemic solutions for complex problems in world, regional, national and local situations, keeping sustainability in mind, and properly following up and periodically evaluating strategies.

35 (B) Inserting a respectable world managerial system that privileges the whole new value system of humanity over any interest that favors only a part of the world's population.

46 (B) Establishing an effective global Rule of Law.

36 (B) Strengthening the participation of the common citizens in the design of better political structures and also in the impartial evaluation of political processes.

47 (B) Installing tested mechanisms for attaining democracy within international agencies and from the top to the bottom of every hierarchical system.

30 (B) Establishing a general system of law that favors the conscious evolution of institutions and the continuous improvement of their practices.

33 (B) Strengthening the law enforcement system with highly professional people who become, through their actions, the most respected people in their communities.

15 (B) Educating with a philosophy of happiness linked to the appreciation of human dignity and also linked to human rewards deeper than private property and accumulation.

39 (B) Educating people to discern between types of information through the careful examination of the methods of production and presentation, and the original intentions of its producers.

9 (B) Lowering population illiteracy using every media possible.

16 (B) Educating and training people on the seven necessary types of knowledge for addressing the future (Morin, E., 1999). This implies a necessary reorientation of all the present educational systems.

32 (B) Addressing the hopes of young people internationally for better living conditions and human development opportunities.

43 (B) Gradually establishing a balanced division of labor which accounts for the advantages offered by different countries, recognizes the real strengths of the people involved, and also searches for the equitable participation of every single country.

25 (B) Inaugurating a fair global financial and salary system, that will transform finance into a Global Commons and heighten the salary system in order to provide for all the basic universalism in accordance with a global recognition of human rights. (Henderson, H. in Gutierrez, L., 2010)

2(B) Creating combined financing and education programs that enhance productivity, long-term self sufficiency and amelioration of living conditions of poor communities. These programs are to be specifically chosen for each community, taking into account due respect for their cultural traditions and always looking for extension of replication in other communities.

55 (B) Incorporating practices that lead to the gradual dismantling of the corruption existing in institutions all over the world.

48 (B) Investing in well-balanced resource projects.

123

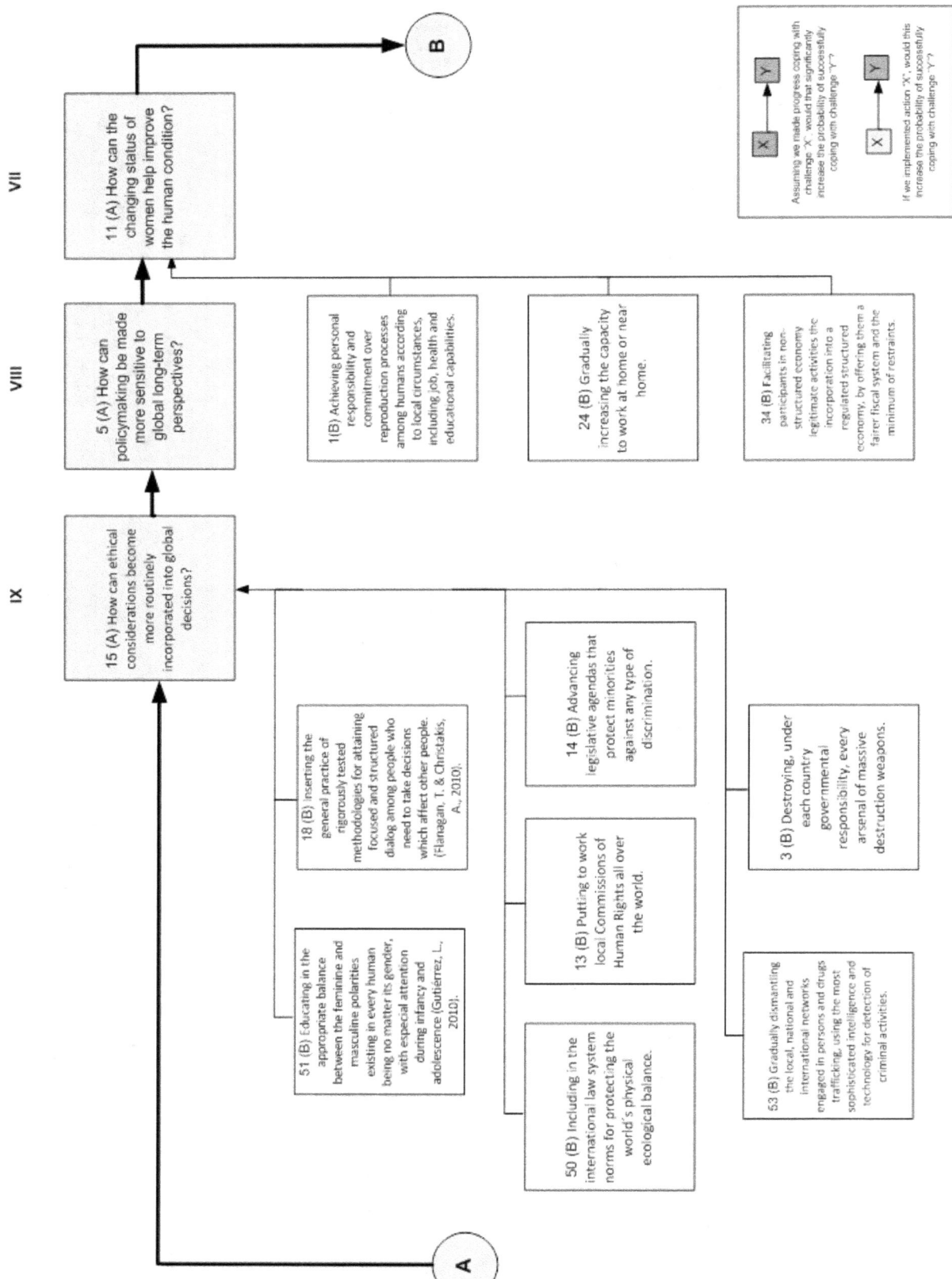

VII

VIII

IX

11 (A) How can the changing status of women help improve the human condition?

5 (A) How can policymaking be made more sensitive to global long-term perspectives?

15 (A) How can ethical considerations become more routinely incorporated into global decisions?

B

1(B) Achieving personal responsibility and commitment over reproduction processes among humans according to local circumstances, including job, health and educational capabilities.

24 (B) Gradually increasing the capacity to work at home or near home.

34 (B) Facilitating participants in non-structured economy legitimate activities the incorporation into a regulated structured economy, by offering them a fairer fiscal system and the minimum of restraints.

18 (B) Inserting the general practice of rigorously tested methodologies for attaining focused and structured dialog among people who need to take decisions which affect other people. (Flanagan, T. & Christakis, A., 2010).

14 (B) Advancing legislative agendas that protect minorities against any type of discrimination.

3 (B) Destroying, under each country governmental responsibility, every arsenal of massive destruction weapons.

51 (B) Educating in the appropriate balance between the feminine and masculine polarities existing in every human being no matter its gender, with especial attention during infancy and adolescence (Gutiérrez, L., 2010).

13 (B) Putting to work local Commissions of Human Rights all over the world.

50 (B) Including in the international law system norms for protecting the world's physical ecological balance.

53 (B) Gradually dismantling the local, national and international networks engaged in persons and drugs trafficking, using the most sophisticated intelligence and technology for detection of criminal activities.

A

Assuming we made progress coping with challenge "X", would that significantly increase the probability of successfully coping with challenge "Y"?

If we implemented action "X", would this increase the probability of successfully coping with challenge "Y"?

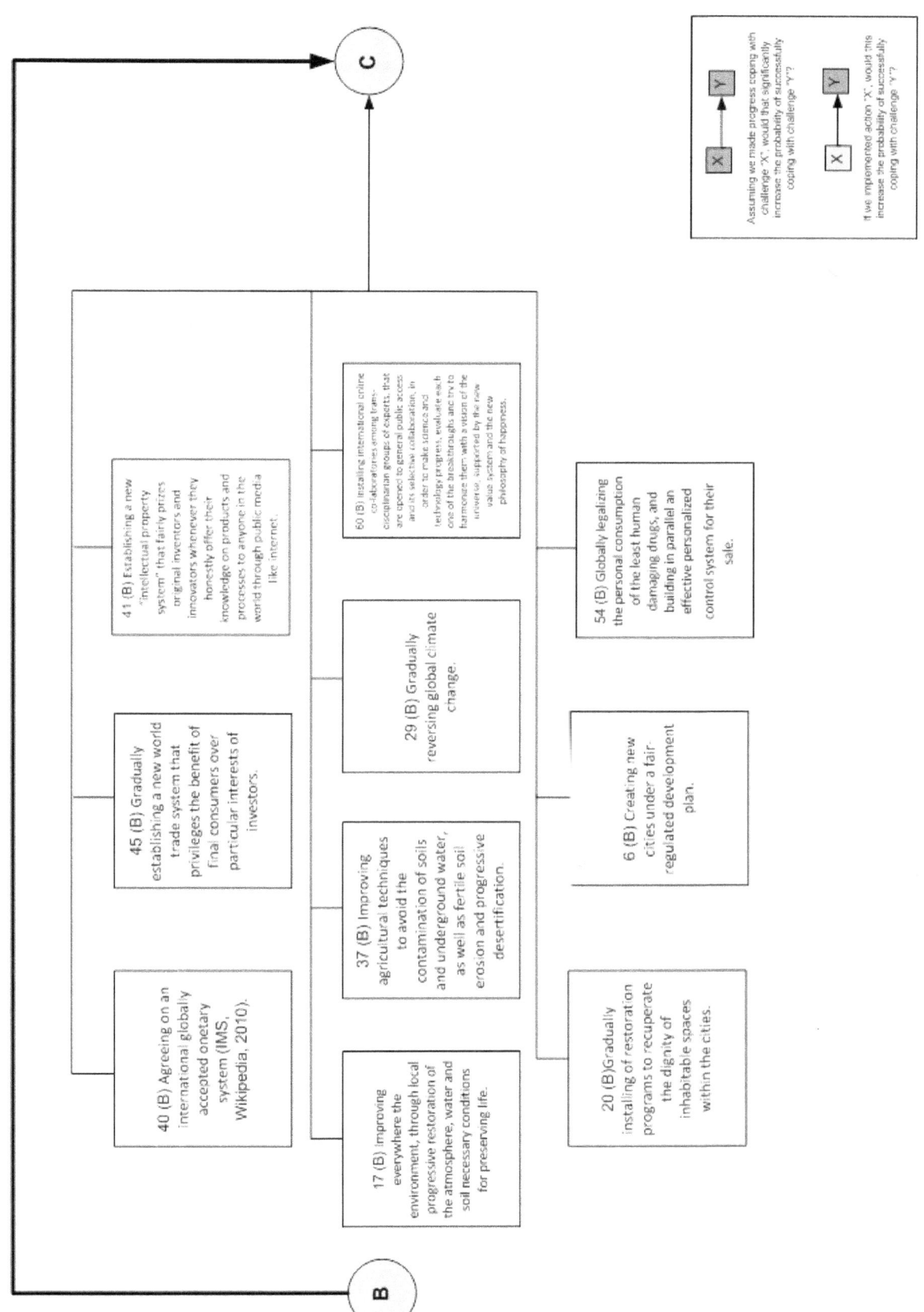

B

40 (B) Agreeing on an international globally accepted onetary system (IMS, Wikipedia, 2010).

45 (B) Gradually establishing a new world trade system that privileges the benefit of final consumers over particular interests of investors.

41 (B) Establishing a new "intellectual property system" that fairly prizes original inventors and innovators whenever they honestly offer their knowledge on products and processes to anyone in the world through public media like internet.

17 (B) Improving everywhere the environment, through local progressive restoration of the atmosphere, water and soil necessary conditions for preserving life.

37 (B) Improving agricultural techniques to avoid the contamination of soils and underground water, as well as fertile soil erosion and progressive desertification.

29 (B) Gradually reversing global climate change.

60 (B) Installing international online co-laboratories among trans-disciplinarian groups of experts, that are opened to general public access and its selective collaboration, in order to make science and technology progress, evaluate each one of the breakthroughs and try to harmonize them with a vision of the universe supported by the new value system and the new philosophy of happiness.

20 (B)Gradually installing of restoration programs to recuperate the dignity of inhabitable spaces within the cities.

6 (B) Creating new cities under a fair-regulated development plan.

54 (B) Globally legalizing the personal consumption of the least human damaging drugs, and building in parallel an effective personalized control system for their sale.

C

Assuming we made progress coping with challenge "X", would that significantly increase the probability of successfully coping with challenge "Y"?

If we implemented action "X", would this increase the probability of successfully coping with challenge "Y"?

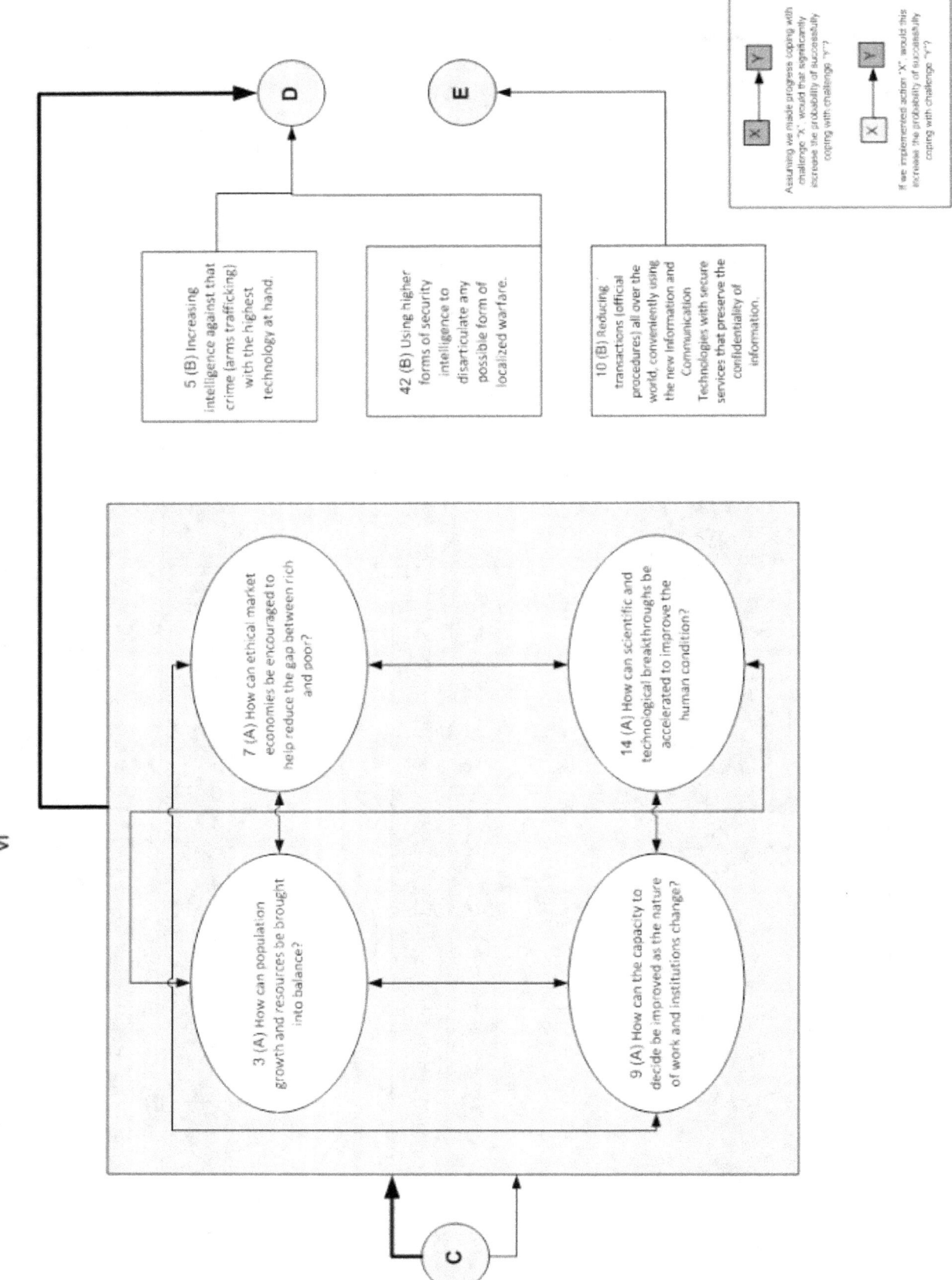

VI

5 (B) Increasing intelligence against that crime (arms trafficking) with the highest technology at hand.

42 (B) Using higher forms of security intelligence to disarticulate any possible form of localized warfare.

10 (B) Reducing transactions (official procedures) all over the world, conveniently using the new Information and Communication Technologies with secure services that preserve the confidentiality of information.

D

E

7 (A) How can ethical market economies be encouraged to help reduce the gap between rich and poor?

14 (A) How can scientific and technological breakthroughs be accelerated to improve the human condition?

3 (A) How can population growth and resources be brought into balance?

9 (A) How can the capacity to decide be improved as the nature of work and institutions change?

C

Assuming we made progress coping with challenge "X" would that significantly increase the probability of successfully coping with challenge "Y"?

If we implemented action "X" would this increase the probability of successfully coping with challenge "Y"?

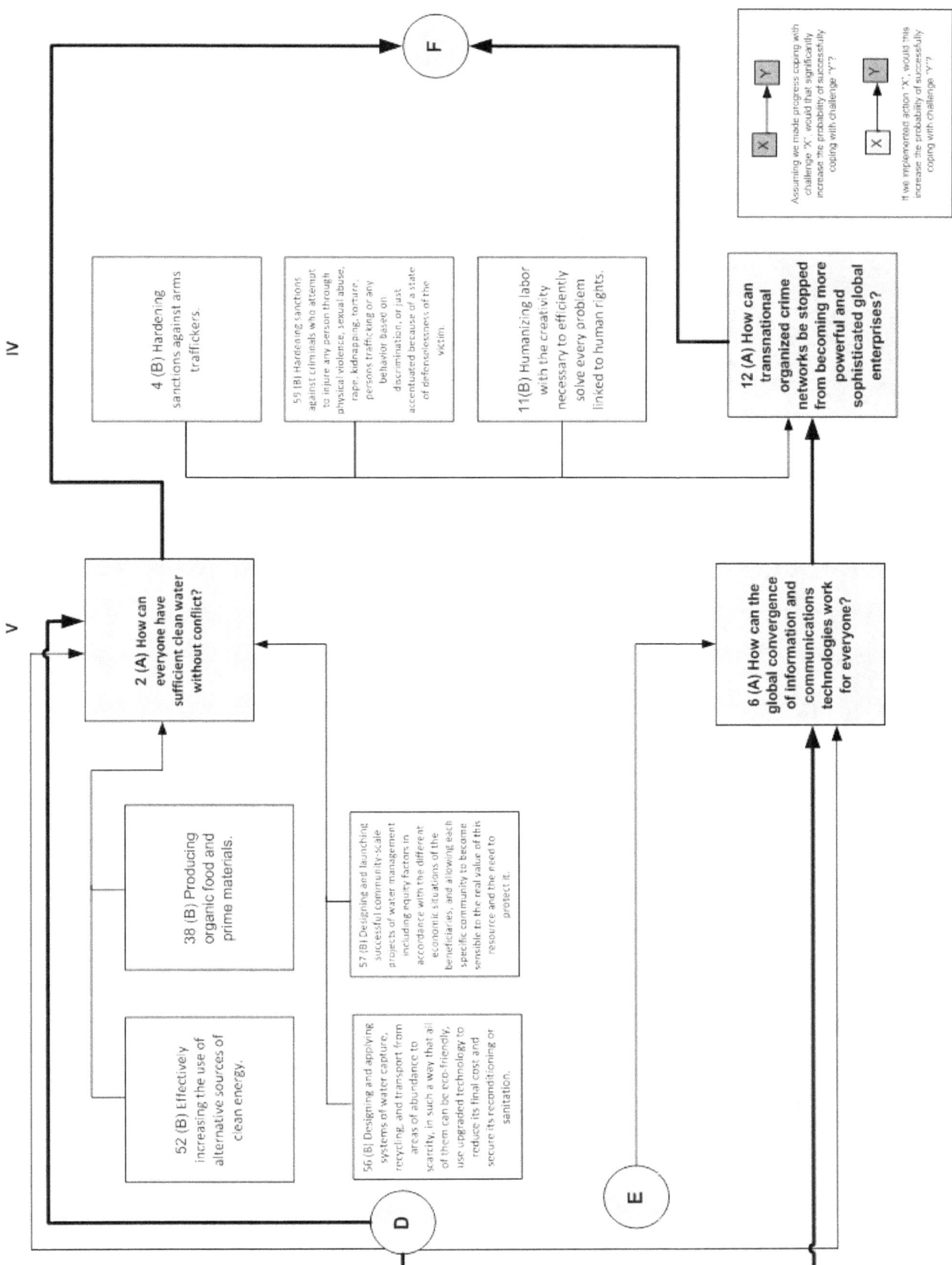

IV

V

4 (B) Hardening sanctions against arms traffickers.

59 (B) Hardening sanctions against criminals who attempt to injure any person through physical violence, sexual abuse, rape, kidnapping, torture, persons trafficking or any behavior based on discrimination, or just accentuated because of a state of defenselessness of the victim.

11 (B) Humanizing labor with the creativity necessary to efficiently solve every problem linked to human rights.

12 (A) How can transnational organized crime networks be stopped from becoming more powerful and sophisticated global enterprises?

2 (A) How can everyone have sufficient clean water without conflict?

6 (A) How can the global convergence of information and communications technologies work for everyone?

38 (B) Producing organic food and prime materials.

57 (B) Designing and launching successful community-scale projects of water management including equity factors in accordance with the different economic situations of the beneficiaries, and allowing each specific community to become sensible to the real value of this resource and the need to protect it.

52 (B) Effectively increasing the use of alternative sources of clean energy.

56 (B) Designing and applying systems of water capture, recycling, and transport from areas of abundance to areas of scarcity, in such a way that all of them can be eco-friendly, use upgraded technology to reduce its final cost and secure its reconditioning or sanitation.

F

D

E

X → Y

Assuming we made progress coping with challenge 'X', would that significantly increase the probability of successfully coping with challenge 'Y'?

X → Y

If we implemented action 'X', would this increase the probability of successfully coping with challenge 'Y'?

127

III

F

G

10 (A) How can shared values and new security strategies reduce ethnic conflicts, terrorism, and the use of weapons of mass destruction?

13 (A) How can growing energy demands be met safely and efficiently?

7 (B) Creating economic and political incentives for diminishing the concentration of population in few megacities.

12 (B) Gradually increasing organized medical care until it becomes a universally accessible service.

22 (B) Building ecological housing in rural and urban areas with complete water and energy systems, including water recycling facilities and all types of energy saving technologies.

58 (B) Dramatically increasing investments in research for developing effective, integral, preventive medicine that can be accessed in any country of the world.

28 (B) Gradually reducing environmental pollution.

49 (B) Enriching all possible foods with proteins and vitamins which help stop malnutrition all over the world.

X → Y
Assuming we made progress coping with challenge "X", would that significantly increase the probability of successfully coping with challenge "Y"?

X → Y
If we implemented action "X", would this increase the probability of successfully coping with challenge "Y"?

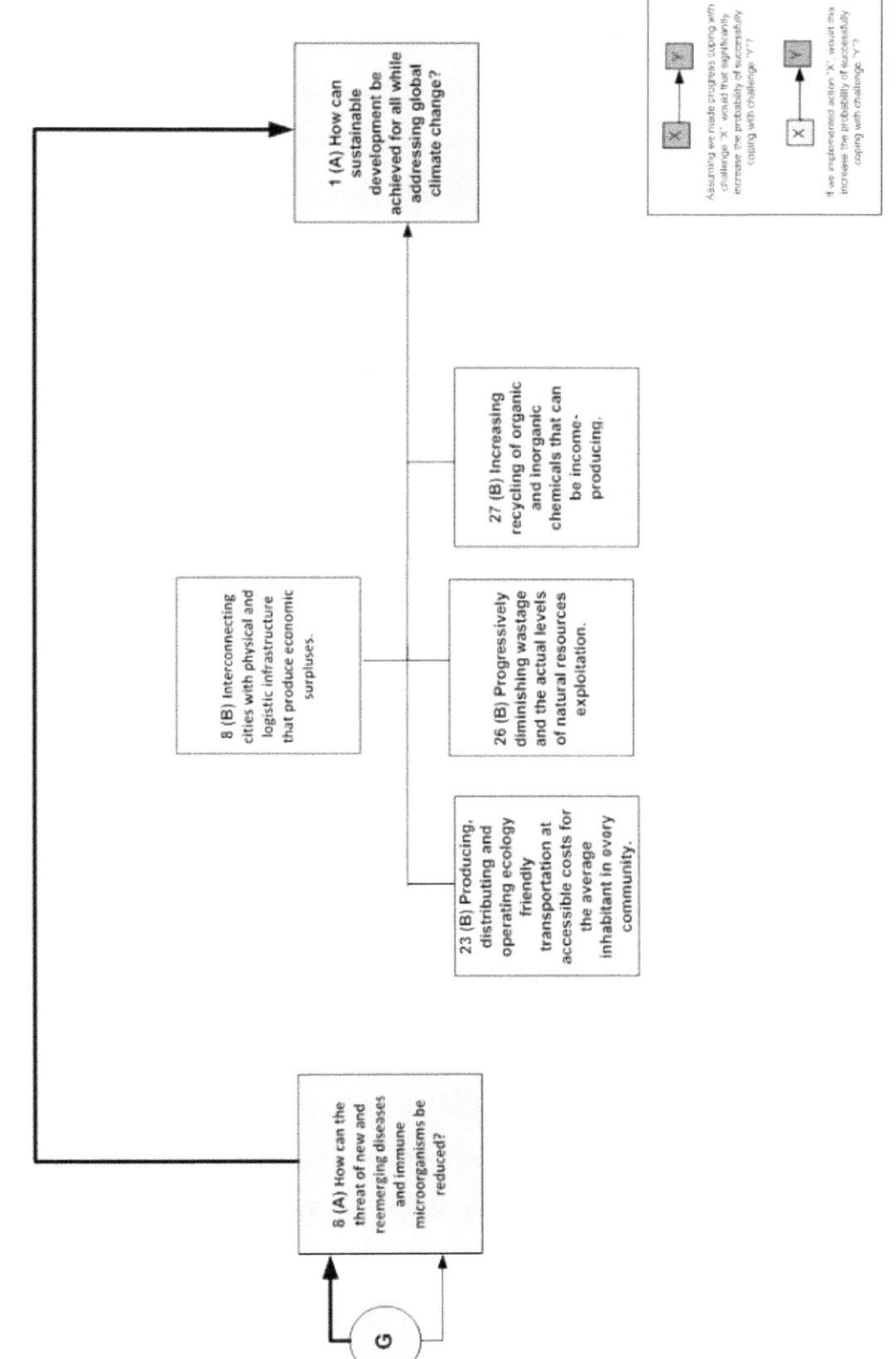

I

1 (A) How can sustainable development be achieved for all while addressing global climate change?

8 (B) Interconnecting cities with physical and logistic infrastructure that produce economic surpluses.

27 (B) Increasing recycling of organic and inorganic chemicals that can be income-producing.

26 (B) Progressively diminishing wastage and the actual levels of natural resources exploitation.

23 (B) Producing, distributing and operating ecology friendly transportation at accessible costs for the average inhabitant in every community.

II

8 (A) How can the threat of new and reemerging diseases and immune microorganisms be reduced?

G

Assuming we made progress coping with challenge "X" would that significantly increase the probability of successfully coping with challenge "Y"?

If we implemented action "X" would this increase the probability of successfully coping with challenge "Y"?

129

6 INTERPRETATION OF RESULTS

The two research matrices and the two maps produced are the core parts of the present research. Now they will become interpreted and some remarks will be added as corollaries. From 6.1 to 6.4 a meta-interpretation will be shown, i.e. an interpretation of results as Explanative Models. From 6.5 on, the contents of those models will be interpreted in a preliminary approach.

6.1. The Systemic Map of the 15 Millennium Project Global Challenges.

We quote Ozbekhan (1970):

"It seems reasonable…to postulate that the fragmentation of reality into closed and well-bounded problems creates a new problem whose solution is clearly beyond the scope of the concepts we customarily employ. It is this generalized meta-problem (or meta-system of problems) which we have called and shall continue to call the "problematique" that inheres in our situation" (p.13).

Over time the concept of *"problematique"*, contributed by Ozbekhan (1970), as a set of closely interrelated problems, became the accepted name of the maps that would be built based on the property of transitivity. These systemic maps did not exist in 1970. They came into existence through the methodology of interactive management invented by John Warfield and Alexander Christakis. A refined version of this methodology, Structured Dialogic Design was used in this present project.

The *"aggravation"* that some problems exert over other problems is the basis of this methodology. In our work we refer to this as an influence relation. We asked: If Situation X were already significantly overcome, would that increase the probability that Problem Y could be successfully confronted, the X, Y, Z… standing, in our case, for each of the Global Challenges. Using a sequence of these questions and their transitive relationship, we established a map that can properly be called the *"great-problematique"* of our Age.

That Map can also be interpreted as follows: Challenge 4 on level X significantly aggravates Challenge 15 on level IX; Challenge 15 significantly aggravates Challenge 5 on level VIII, and so on. By *"aggravation"* we should understand that the existence of a challenge "X" significantly increases the magnitude or the complexity, or both, of a challenge "Y", making it more difficult to confront, and making it more difficult to bring the situation to a satisfactory solution. Inversely, the successful overcoming of a challenge "X" (reduction of its magnitude or complexity, or its eventual disappearance) significantly facilitates or contributes to the successful confrontation of a challenge "Y". Transitivity, incorporated in the software, allows us to contemplate the challenges as a whole and in their interrelationships in less time than if we had to examine, for example, 15 x 14, i.e., 210 pairs of challenges in interrelation. The property of transitivity is understood as follows:

$$\text{If X} \rightarrow \text{Y, and Y} \rightarrow \text{Z; then X} \rightarrow \text{Z.}$$

The previous disquisition leads us to grasp in a very intuitive manner the relationships of influence exerted by some challenges over other challenges in the totality of the Map. When cycles emerge (two in this case, one in level VI with four challenges, and another in level III with two challenges) it becomes clear that the influence interrelationships are reciprocal (they go and come between the challenges). This is the reason for the special representation of those challenges by including them in two big light gray rectangles.

Detailed observation of the Systemic Map of the 15 Global Challenges shows us that the Map is not a linear representation of how the challenges should be addressed in time but how, knowing that some challenges depend on other challenges regarding the ease or difficulty involved in confronting them, a Global Strategy can be designed that effectively overcomes the barriers implied. If we could overcome the lack of democracy in the world, it would be easier to overcome the lack of ethics in global decisions; it would also be easier to overcome the lack of long-term perspectives in global decisions; it would heighten considerations respecting women's rights by equalizing them with men's rights, and so on. The challenge, which influences all of the rest, is Challenge 4, which invites us to overcome the lack of democracy everywhere. That does not mean, however, that the other challenges should wait for a turn to be addressed. All and each one of them must be addressed as soon as possible, since the survival of the Earth as our habitat and the habitat of many future generations depends on that successful task. The Map is only a useful guide for designing a fitter Global Strategy.

The linear chaining of various challenges speaks of bottlenecks to sustainable development of the planet. The chaining of challenges 4, 15, 5, and 11 is the first bottleneck. The linear chaining of Challenges 6 and 12 is another bottleneck as is the chaining of Challenges 8 and 1. We can imagine how the relative overcoming of any these challenges or bottlenecks could affect other challenges or bottlenecks. Changes beyond their desired effects would produce collateral results and new risk factors into the socio-demographic, economic, physical-chemical and biological subsystems, etc.

On the other hand, the chaining of challenges 3, 7, 9, and 14 produces a virtuous cycle that enables fluidity and the incorporation of favorable factors that could evolve to attain the intended objective of sustainable development for the Earth. This cycle provides alternate paths for addressing the next challenge.

As will be later understood, the confrontation of all and each of the Challenges will demand the intervention of many international organizations, of treaties and agreements between the governments, of many political wills at the national and local levels, of many civilian, scientific and religious organizations. It will also require massive communications media support, and joint work of many groups of well-disposed citizens. All this cooperative effort striving for sustainable development for the Earth will be required. Every subsystem of the Web has to participate and perform to make the Global Strategy effective.

The Systemic Map of the Challenges is not the Map of the Subsystems of the Web. It is not a map that identifies distinct interactions existing between the subsystems. It is not a tool for observing how performance factors proper to subsystems combine themselves. Looking retrospectively, the Systemic Map of the Global Challenges is only an abstract interpretative model of how the Web actually becomes involved in our need to overcome the 15 Global Challenges. It provides a generalized map we can travel if we human beings decide that the most important thing is for us to tune ourselves to the Web's auto-evolution in order to achieve its sustainable development.

6.2. **Research Matrix 1**

The distribution of the Continuous Critical Problems among the Global Challenges initially followed an intuitive common sense criterion based on past experiences of the authors. The purpose was to examine which problems would specifically correspond to each challenge and which problems contributed in fact to produce and reinforce the challenges.

Before we produced the second map, i.e. the Map of Superposition of Actions on the Global Challenges, that procedure required us to assign certain problems to certain categories in anticipation.

After the second map was produced, we observed some assignment mistakes. Some problems were assigned improperly to a specific Global challenge, and other problems should have been assigned to it, but they were not taken into account because they were not anticipated from the beginning of the task. Upon consideration we concluded that information overload, our unawareness of the interrelationships that the designed Actions exerted over the Challenges, plus the complexities inherent in the Web were responsible for these flaws in the distribution reached. The later study of the Map of Actions allowed us to add some problems not considered before. We decided, however, to maintain the initial assignations of problems as they were in the matrix. Because of this decision, we invite readers who appreciate our analytical and synthetic processes to examine the whole document, and then undertake the task of eliminating in the Matrix any badly assigned problems.

Each one of the Continuous Critical Problems represents one or more risk factors derived from the bad performance of one or various subsystems in the Web or derived from its environment. Against the risk factors pointed out in the matrix we tried to design actions that would incorporate stimulation, inhibition, dissuasion, attraction, rejection and coalition factors. These factors in random combinations at different times might overcome a Global Challenge by dissolving bottlenecks, forming virtuous cycles, or eliminating vicious cycles.

We think that the Global Challenges are an accumulation of risk factors in the evolution process, whose random combinations have created the undesirable characteristics in the subsystems and in the Web. That accumulation is not equivalent to the concept of mathematical addition. It results rather from the intertwining of different factors in different proportions.

In Research Matrix 1 we can see that some of the Continuous Critical Problems are assigned to many challenges, even though they do not directly affect those challenges. However, we can see with more scrutiny that a CCP may indirectly affect them because it can exacerbate interrelated problems and influence their size and characteristics.

Our research is a preliminary study that could be enriched with contributions from experts and with intra, inter, and trans-disciplinary work. It does not affirm dogmatic truths of any kind. It is just a guide for deeper investigation of the Global Problematique that can help us develop a Global Strategy that responds to constant observation and feedback. We adhere in this document to an open position that goes back over this great complex situation and remakes its contents if necessary. A better comprehension and a better design can emerge from it. We do not think that our effort is astray but we do consider that any of its statements might become improved in the future.

6.3. Research Matrix 2

Some Actions in Research Matrix 2 are reactive and some are Proactive. Reactive Actions counter risk factors that need to be overcome. Examples of risk factors that demand "reactive" Actions are:
- The international presence of organized crime,
- The inadequate procurement of justice in the whole world,
- Corruption,
- Child and adult malnutrition,

- The employment of contaminating energy sources,
- Arms and persons trafficking,
- The accumulation of wealth in very few hands and its consequences, and
- The manipulation of information.

All of these factors demand immediate actions of a dissuasive or coactive nature.

Meanwhile, other Actions push an indirect but effective process for changing the actual status. These Actions are considered *"proactive"*. They include actions that affect our mentality, attitude, or ethical positioning as human beings within society and lead us to face the Web as a whole. The most iconic action is *"establishing a value system that incorporates as guiding principles world sustainable development, equity, peace, the well-being of children all over the world, love, gender equality, harmony and mutual respect for cultural differences"*.

As we scrutinize the Actions included in Research Matrix 2, we see that many of them require a broader description, which could be developed by experts within each one of the issues involved.

These Actions also require programs of implementation that should be subject to agreement between many institutions, different organizations or individuals possessing authority in the world. The authors at this time limit themselves to synthetic descriptions, except in a few cases where a semantic confusion around its contents could occur. We are nevertheless aware that very scrupulous follow-up work is demanded, to better delimit each Action and its implementation program.

Any such program should make clear the need for international, national, or local management that can pass judgment on its feasibility and viability. Nevertheless, we believe that all the Actions proposed are relevant, perhaps necessary, if the Predicament of Mankind as expressed by Ozbekhan is to be solved. Precise observation of every implementation program deployed will make possible improved forms of coping with the Global Challenges as they are changing.

Research Matrix 2 includes Actions that introduce processes for harmonizing many factors. Bringing them into play at the right time and place will produce a tuning effect in such a way that properties highly usable in and for the Web would emerge (emergent properties). Readers should grasp why these Actions affecting different subsystems in the Web are located as possible means for successfully coping with subsystems inside each of the Challenges.

We exhort readers to widen their information base around some of the actions which are addressed in books like *"How People Harness their Collective Wisdom and Power to Construct the Future in Co-Laboratories of Democracy"* by Alexander N. Christakis and Kenneth C. Bausch (2006); *"Toward a General Theory of Planning"* by Hasan Ozbekhan (1968); *"Hacia una Teoría General de la Estrategia"* by Rafael Alberto Pérez and Sandra Massoni (2009); *"A Science of Generic Design"* by John Warfield (1990), and *"The Talking Point"* by Thomas Flanagan and Alexander N. Christakis (2010).

Research Matrix 2 is actually a tool that we can follow by using it as a Platform for Reflection.

6.4. Map of Superposition of Actions to Successfully Cope with the Millennium Project Global Challenges

Because of its extension and complexity this map is presented in section 5 in seven successive pages using interconnecting symbols like gray circles with letters in alphabetical order. In this map levels with roman numerals are maintained as in the first Systemic Map of the Global Challenges, and these ones are inscribed in light gray rectangles to facilitate the localization of its components. Actions, which constitute the Global Strategy as a set, are inscribed in white rectangles to differentiate them from the Global Challenges. The meaning of the arrows that connect the components appears on each one of the pages for fast access and consultation.

The Map of Superposition is the most valuable result of the whole research, not only because of the architecture of its contents, but also because of the broadness of the information provided to readers. It is the synthesis of the Global Strategy and offers a holistic view and also a detailed account of its components.

One of the particular things that amazed the authors was finding that the Global Challenge 5 did not have any actions superimposed in order to cope with it. The probable answer to this observation lies in the nature of this challenge in level VIII, because we believe that it could be subsumed in Global Challenge 15 in level IX, since designing sensible public policies for the long-term is also an ethical consideration, i.e., something to be accounted for within ethical considerations in public decisions.

Hasan Ozbekhan (1970) leads us to reflect about constructing a model like the Map of Superposition:

"The primary aim of modeling is to give the subject a shape, a structure, a configuration that is determined by an objective which, itself, is external to the subject. Hence the clarifications of insights that might be obtained from a successful modeling effort are never reached in terms of the subject (i.e., a problem or a situation) but in terms of the external objective to satisfy which the modeling was undertaken in the first place. Such an objective always entails a value, and the setting of it must therefore create the particular value-base that gives meaning and direction to the whole endeavor". (p. 21).

"A value-base explicitly stipulates certain assumptions about what is "good" and what "bad". In the past, it was not always necessary to make such a stipulation because a problem could be recognized clearly and singularly as a problem and therefore fell automatically into a negative value category. This is not the case nowadays when we must deal with the problematique of a whole world-wide situation. In so extended and complex a problem area the value premises reveal themselves as being so confused that it becomes imperative to define a value-base that will govern the work from the very outset" (p. 21).

"…we are confronted with a problematique which is eco-systemic in character. The normative statement that describes the value-content of any eco-system is "ecological balance". Consequently it is the idea of ecological balance that can, and will, be taken as the underlying value-base of the study; for in the terms dictated by our situation the "good" is self-evidently and most generally capable of being defined as the re-establishment of that many-dimensional dynamic balance that seems to have been lost in the modern world" (p. 23).

We fully agree in our present case with this last discourse about modeling. In fact, we think that it describes our new vision of the Web. This vision shows our Global Strategy leading us through unbroken steps to achieve the last Global Challenge at the right end of the Map. That last challenge is to install the "ecological balance" necessary to support the sustainability of the planet we are dwelling in.

With the concept of "sustainability" we intend to "transcend" the equilibrium installed in the environment of different ecological subsystems by generating interactions among living beings that protect and preserve life. With this term, we want to imply the need for making the whole planet hospitable to every interaction possible between its different subsystems so that it is continuously developing as a harmonious whole.

An indispensable question after looking at the Map is: How can organized human beings install "harmony" in the set of subsystems to reach global ecological balance (understood as the expected behavior of the whole in movement that the Web represents)?

6.5. Better comprehension of the complexity of the Web

After this research had advanced various steps, we developed the objective of understanding that Earth, the familiar planet we dwell in, is a Web. In other words, it is a very complex network with subsystems functioning, in apparent disharmony, where interactions are thwarted by bottlenecks and vicious cycles threatening its existence and the existence of mankind. We believed that cataloguing the global challenges would help humanity overcome acute situations afflicting the Web, which arise due to our not addressing the Continuous Critical Problems. Since their identification by Hasan Ozbekhan and their presentation (*"The Predicament of Mankind"*) to the Club of Rome in 1970, they prevail and generate risk factors which we now visualize as not only isolated but in a worrying togetherness. Understanding such risk factors leads us to a better comprehension of the Web as an Open System that demands a global ecological balance to support its own evolutionary process.

The human species cannot continue looking only at itself. It must realize that it forms part of a complex totality affected in many ways and in different intensities by its behavior. Mankind needs to subject itself to the judgment (already perceived) of future generations, which will have to solve the after-pains produced by our present generations because we do not address their anticipated claims.

It is imperative that we consider the Earth as the habitat of both our species and the other species of living beings. We need to care for the physical-chemical subsystems, the essential life-supporting substrate that is necessary to sustain life. We must behave properly and contribute wisely to the survival of this living Earth. Many people might be thinking that if man has already conquered part of sidereal space, he can in the future get out of Earth to live in other environments, not yet defined, "Why the heck are we worried about this?" However, we all must tremble if we make a cost analysis of what that really means for the species.

6.6. Better comprehension of the complexity of the subsystems in the Web

The list of subsystems implicated in the Web determines the levels of complexity involved. Taking into account not only the subsystems mentioned but also their performance and interactive behavior, one can understand that the specific functions attributed to them overlap. Interactions multiply in the same way the intervening factors do, and effects are re-distributed to transform themselves into new factors in interrelation. The evolutions of the Web and its subsystems are not linear. For that reason, we never intended here to produce a linear strategy as if there were a recipe to be followed step by step.

We wanted to understand, initiating with the description of the Global Challenges and of the Continuous Critical Problems pertaining to them, which actions would be most effective in addressing them; which actions would better hit the targets; and which ones would be more likely to change them from their relatively permanent original state into a state that reduces their bad effects, or much better, eventually cancels them. The Continuous Critical Problems, before being identified, constituted risk factors present in subsystems and their interactions. They had not yet been examined to design defined global strategies against them. Their clustering inside the Global Challenges allows us to consider how they impact the main subsystems. Also, their level of influence is just now being identified.

6.7. The Articulation of Global Challenges

As is declared in the book *"2010, State of the Future,"* the Global Challenges are interdependent. Thus their articulation in a Map of Influence that shows how influential the challenges are in relation to each other is much to be desired. Our map shows how progress made coping with one of them might affect other challenges. It shows which challenges are the most influential and which ones are influenced.

The Map of the Global Challenges does not restrain strategists in the sense of prescribing that some Challenges should not be addressed first. It does not stop them from addressing the rest of the challenges while the most influential ones are being addressed. It does, however, give greater weight to actions that combine stimulation, inhibition and dissuasion, influence, rejection, attraction, coalition and other likely factors that can address the most influential challenges. These combinations can diminish or adequately confront the risk factors, dissolving the bottlenecks to propagating beneficial effects, installing virtuous cycles, and impeding formation of vicious cycles within the Web and its subsystems.

6.8. A more detailed characterization of the Global Challenges taking into account the Continuous Critical Problems

The description of the Millennium Project Global Challenges contains a large set of highly diversified indicators showing the nature, breadth, penetration, and intensity of each particular Challenge. This list might suggest our taking actions to attack specific phenomena without considering the simultaneous or intermittent possible influences over other challenges. The list of the 49 Continuous Critical Problems prevailing from 1970 till today allows us to combine the Challenges and Problems by inserting the problems selectively into the different global challenges. This insertion is done on the basis of intuition to give us a workable hypothesis detailing likely influences of aggravation among the challenges, which are introduced by specific sets of those problems. This new characterization of the Global Challenges increases our options for coping with them by coming at them from different angles.

6.9. Interpretation of the contents of the Global Strategy

The first thing jumping into our sight on the Map of Superposition of Actions over the Global Challenges is the accumulation of 20 actions of the 60 designed (33.33%), which address Global Challenge 4 (the absence of democracy in the world and the deficiency of democracy in a large number of countries). This accumulation calls to our attention that these actions are of a relatively different nature. Each one of them, however, would help us move from authoritarian regimes toward true democracy.

Just after finishing the construction of the Map, using the CogniScope II software, we found ourselves with 20 Actions to deal with Global Challenge 4 without an organization between them. After some careful scrutiny and an ulterior synthesis, some similarities allowed grouping them in four clusters of five Actions each. The leading action of the first cluster is the necessity of making a reliable value realm effective for everyone. The leading action for the second cluster had to do much more with legality and the procurement of justice subjected to the permanent scrutiny of citizens. The third one places hopes for change upon the impact of education considered as an inalienable right that can produce knowledge, skills, and values strongly linked to the ethical global subsystem. The fourth action focuses on production factors, mainly finance and labor as well as the material resources that can stimulate the inclusion of every human being in development, thanks to the cancelation of poverty and the restraining of corruption. All these efforts work to overcome this specific Challenge because (now it seems obvious why) the administration, distribution and influence of political power are determinant in our actual world organization based in the concept of nation-state. Political power has granted large fields of influence to economic power. Some say that this distribution of power is designed just to make rich agents win, while the vast majority of dwellers in the world lose – and the Earth with them also.

Addressing Challenge 4 would greatly contribute to the dissolution of the bottleneck implied by its connection to Challenges 15, 5 and 11 in levels IX, VIII and VII on the Map. Obviously, democracy is interpreted here as an activity that embraces the whole field of human activity in society. That is to say, democracy is not limited to citizen action in elections of functionaries, but it also involves a re-organization of society under political structures and political processes that serve people.

At level IX, the Actions that confront Challenge 15 support ethical social and economic structures all over the world. Respect for the human rights of individuals and social minorities and the provision of instruments to guarantee those rights are vital. Recognition by the powerful that they will always be limited by a superior attraction factor which is the global ecological balance is necessary. The most terrible dangers leading to the extinction of the Earth comes from abuse of power. With a genuine and effective democracy this risk factor is enormously diminished.

The existence of arsenals of massive destruction goes against common sense. Their eventual use would eliminate any benefits of a social peace attained by force. Their use would be a defeat for the survival of Earth as habitat for living beings and descendants. The dismantling of those arsenals by every country possessing them would be a solidarity gesture toward the sustainability of the planet. It would be the main symbol that a quantum leap has been achieved in the conscious evolution of humanity.

Human slavery and trafficking in it within modern slavery regimes is the greatest opprobrium in our world civilization. Slavery is neither an isolated event nor the product of local mafias. Our information and communication technologies have facilitated an iniquity business that deeply erodes its victim's sense of existence and definitively destroys the notion of human dignity in the people doing the violence. This scourge has been potentiated in our globalization era, where the laws of supply and demand, operating anonymously and without nationality, have prostituted human beings and demeaned them as just pieces of merchandise.

The status of women obviously needs to be denounced with an international ethical standard based on the new proposed value system. Society as society, the way we live this reality in the whole world, has imposed roles that do not consider the existence of a feminine/masculine polarity in every human being independently of their genital characteristics. Society regulates through law and customs how each one of us has to look at the person of the opposite sex. There is, however, no social role that could not become interchangeable, with the exception perhaps of the one differentiating the biological capacities for procreation.

Until today, the preparation of a new baby to assume his (her) relational nature as a component of society lies under the responsibility of the woman who carries it in her womb before liberating it to the world. That intimate contact possesses a mystery that prepares boys and girls to understand their place in society. The male might share during the pregnancy some feelings, plays, hopes, and utopias with his female partner, but the true social subtleties of the human being are fundamentally provided by the woman. This does not mean that the mother transfers to the children the feminine sensibility in an exclusive manner, or that the father cannot impede it. The feminine sensibility is already present in parents, both man and woman, as it is in every human being.

When should a man liberate a feminine behavior and a woman a masculine behavior? Exhibitions of such liberation are many times incomprehensible for society. Nevertheless, this liberation is linked to our proper human nature and has nothing to do with genitals. Society has not recognized its inadequate portrayal of men and women. This inadequacy is transposed to the field of social roles. As a result, society discriminates people according to ungrounded motives.

Because of this discrimination, a woman who is the head of a family is never made equal to a man who is head of a family, and because of that, she receives less salary in a job that is perfectly equivalent. She is obliged to take pregnancy tests before she can sign a job contract; she is considered less capable of traveling than a man; she is sent to the end of the row whenever new personal is to be hired; she is sexually harassed and often abused in labor circumstances; she is fired without any remorse whenever a man aspires to replace her in her job, etc. All these prejudices emerge whenever a criterion of supply-demand rules without consideration for fundamental values. An enlightened policy would move employers innovatively towards a new social re-organization to foster productivity. Gradually increasing the capacity for both men and women to work at home or near home could offer economic solutions, which avoid other problems and not only discrimination against women. Such a reorganization of work could be favorable for everyone. The decisions regarding procreation should be shared by men and women. They should be grounded in a wider consideration of their descendants' real opportunities for development, which could be abundant if the informal producers of goods and services could be incorporated in a better structured economy.

The following cluster of Actions aims to cope with Global Challenges 3, 7, 9, and 14, in level VI. They are systemic factors (different factors in combination) representing revolutionary modes of looking at the socio-demographic, economic, institutional, and technical-scientific subsystems. These actions can establish a more intensive synergy among other proposed Actions. Each these Actions affects a different key component of the mentioned subsystems. In concrete terms, they re-structure the operational ways actually given to provide them with more organic and communicative conditions for establishing virtuous cycles. The economy, society, the environment including agro and urban locations, and a social relaxation atmosphere would all collaborate and facilitate work and the progressive development of individual and group capacities and skills. It should not be forgotten here, that all the Actions (in levels X, IX. and VIII) work to make Actions in level VI fructify in tune with them.

The organization of the main inputs of every system, i.e. information, energy and material resources, like water for example, represented by Actions over Global Challenges 2 and 6 in level V, are intimately connected with the maintenance of peace and security in the world.

It is a paradox that modern information technologies can show windows and back rooms behind stores at the same time. Only the virtual world could bring forth this new ambiguity to the real world. It is so easy to confuse others and ourselves in a world where "me" and the "not me of the same me" are distributed in diverse proportions. This ambiguity enables us to cheat, attack, defame, extort, steal, afflict, corrupt and impoverish others under a cover of immunity. We have recently begun to understand why the disclosure of our own personal data might become a knife of two cutting edges. A regulation directed to establish order in the internet world without falling into censorship would be much better than scoring the victory goal in a football world championship.

The information technology released in the last decades of the 20th Century and dawn of the new millennium offers enormous capabilities for making any set of systems synergic between themselves. We wish that its power were given to collaborating attitudes toward sustainable development. Instead this power is being used to extend economic dominance over communities and nations at the expense of their weaknesses. Today on the Internet the most dirty human inclinations derived from the lack of personal individual satisfaction are prevailing. Gossip, obsessive games, aggressiveness, harassment, insults, the search and worship of easy pleasure, emulation, superfluous goods consumption, cheating, and disorganized information are spreading in cyberspace and overload our mental capacities. Time liberated to each individual for undertaking creative and productive work has been superseded by banal entertainment with no intended service to anybody. This fills our psyche with just informative trash.

Against this deplorable situation, the use of the Internet to facilitate decision making would make every human institution a real power for achieving and managing knowledge, interchanging skills, and accelerating the improvement of goods and services. This would bring forth a revolution in the use of time by the human species. Communication, as the broth of the Global Strategy, would allow coordinated labor, easily followed up, monitored by every involved agent, criticized because of its weaknesses, corrected for deviations, and nurtured by the best and most opportune innovations. The condition of possibility for this beautiful utopia lies, however, in a swelling of global communication in an atmosphere that does not provoke fear of any kind; and that has security incorporated in the management of the tool. Every human being would realize that leading anyone else to error would be delaying the sustainability of the Web, stopping what should be value regulated, and accumulating trash. Fluid interchange in many directions should be a reliable fact that gives us the golden opportunity to run along a path to make us stronger in our relational capacity and uncountable fruits.

Scarcity of clean water will be a misfortune for humanity. An important question will be: Will human beings in communities possessing clean water make common cause with human beings in places where water scarcity exists, or will mad hunger and sicknesses spread to ruin life for all of them? Without this precious resource living beings die sooner or later. Of every factor making life and sustainability possible water is the most important. The protection of watersheds in the whole world should be a shared commitment. Purification of water needs to be a shared task. Recycling of water to avoid its waste, and to support the natural cycles of recovering the liquid, is also a shared responsibility. Technological advances should have as a main focus the production of clean water. New urban development plans need to consider the existence of sources of water as the main factor of development. A renewal of agricultural practices to diminish the consumption of fresh water should be in the minds of every researcher in the food production field.

Two Actions on level IV are reactive (4 and 59) and one is pro-active (11). Unfortunately we have to take into account the three of them, because there are individuals in our actual world who overlook the survival of the Web and the dignity of every human being and pursue their personal desires. The reason why drugs trafficking, arms-trafficking and the manipulation of human beings as sexual slaves continue is the acquisition of easy money. In our free market economy, these activities bear within themselves the germ of their own reproduction. There is no better way to stop these calamities than the humanization of labor.

As humble a task or service might be, labor will always possess a dignity when it contributes to the harmonization of the Web. Recognition of the dignity of labor will only occur when each one of us can see our basic human rights like liberty, subsistence, health, shelter and self-development reinforced through the contribution of our work to the wellbeing of communities. Only with this in mind, can we think of achieving progressive access to a better life. Actually, it is not true that the so declared minimum wage provides human beings with the satisfaction of all their basic human needs. Again, it is not true that existing institutions provide labor conditions that respect and protect all those basic rights.

Affluence concentrated in just very few hands in the world, as it is impudently proclaimed each year in Forbes list of multi-millionaires (see http://www.forbes.com/lists/), testifies to the existence of exploiters and exploited people. This disparity also demonstrates the absence of coordination between subsystems, and the absence of coordination among the majority of people investing their time, efforts, and intelligence without the fair reward deserved. The economic predominance of just a few over the rest of humanity is infamous.

Intelligence applied to amassing money cannot deserve the continuous huge surpluses, for example in the incomes of financiers and corporate tax accountants, since more brilliant minds are surely dispersed in the zoological human group. As soon as the wealth has accumulated the now rich recipients resist making proactive decisions favoring humanity. Their general ethos does not allow them to deploy their money and intelligence for any more wisely productive resources for the rest of humanity. The actual global finance system automatically reproduces their money not because of their own efforts but because of the efforts and intelligence of the majority of human beings. The megawealthy people are thus transformed into unproductive drones for the survival of the Earth. It is essential that a democratically regulated world management system be born very soon, which will begin redistributing resources to ameliorate the wages and living conditions of the majorities.

The present political structures inside nation-states have are obsolescent entelechies that do not favor good management for the world.

The Global Challenges in levels III, II and I are strongly linked together. The proposed Actions in the Global Strategy to cope with them display a close interdependence.

The demand and supply of energy is clearly an international issue. It is not now subject to free market forces because of a 5 mega Oil company cartel. Therefore, energy supply needs to be regulated. Also its distribution needs to involve cooperation of some countries with other countries.

After Fukushima we are now aware that the production of usable energy based upon the disintegration of atoms is an issue concerning the whole world (Francois, J., 2011) http://www.dgcs.unam.mx/boletin/bdboletin/2011_169.html). The immediate reactions of countries like Germany, France and the United States has been cautionary, but also obstinate on the part of nuclear advocates. The nuclear catastrophe in Japan – paradoxically a country that has located in space a satellite pilot station concentrating solar energy to be delivered as usable energy to the Earth (Glenn, J., Gordon, T., and Florescu, E., 2010, p. 36) – shows that the construction and dismantling of nuclear plants are such complex and acute situations that should not to be trusted to the government of just one country. The international Rule of Law must intervene to regulate decisions like this that affect all living beings in the world. After the earthquake in Japan, on March 11, 2011, many extremely painful lessons are in sight. Hopefully, a shared ethic for global sustainability will lead us toward pro-active responses, and help us avoid disastrous energy wars.

The health factor supplies sensitive and accurate indicators of the value of sustainability. This value is related to many factors in the technical-scientific subsystem related to health, such as:
- the integration and operation of a global preventive medicine subsystem,
- care for the physical-chemical and biological substrate of the Web (water and natural resources),

- relief of mega-city demographic concentrations,
- scrupulous planning of new human settlements of manageable intermediate size,
- the employment of clean energy sources,
- a dignified way of living within necessary shelter without excesses,
- the preservation of local environments,
- a transport and communication subsystem ecologically and logistically designed for productivity,
- the provision of essential daily nutriments for all human beings, and
- the recycling of usable prime materials through technological and non contaminant procedures.

All of these factors are directly related to health, and are indirectly but strongly related to the sustainable development of the Earth and its communities. Hansen, R., (2011), an archeologist, is reported to have discovered the cause for the collapse the Mayan civilization (c. 150 A.D.) in the exaggerated destruction of forest trees and the excessive exploitation of natural resources (see http://www.eluniversal.com.mx/articulos/63343.html).

The Map of Superposition of Actions over Global Challenges identifies a set of issues that need to be researched and brought into tune with reality. A trans-disciplinary collaboration is essential. The Science of Dialogic Design could offer us a range of products derived from this Map that would help us understand better from time to time the complexity of the Web. Now, the integration of public policies following the proposed Global Strategy might help us change the face of the world in a notable way.

7. PENDING TASKS

There is yet too much to think, to say, and to do concerning the present research, the methodology employed, and the systemic integration of all the concepts involved. Here is a short summary:

7.1. Methodological clarifications and suggestions for the future

Our use of the CogniScope II software program was made outside its habitual context that involves groups with preferably more than 12 and less than 30 participants (this last maximum number recommended by one of the authors who is a certified international practitioner). The participants would preferably come from different walks of life and jobs, as well as different academic trajectories. This diversity of participants helps the process to provide sufficient diversity of observations, concepts, and categories. The goal is to harness the best collective intelligence resources.

Two excellent sources provided us with sufficient, high quality diversity: First, a very broad consultancy generated the Global Challenges of the Millennium Project. Second, are the 49 Continuous Critical Problems identified by Hasan Ozbekhan (1970), which have withstood the test of time.

Nevertheless, we think that another trial or trials might be run with new stakeholder/participants who might have different expertise and knowledge. Ideally, we would convene a group of expert university teachers or postgraduate students from different disciplines, together with a group of executives who have made decisions and designed policies for international organizations and countries. We would recommend that this elite group go through the dialog processes from different points of departure chosen by the same participants.

Again, the authors consider that a gathering of citizens from different countries and continents into this conversation would be most desirable. The validity of the results of the present research would be subjected in this way to a process of high discernment. We expect that some people in the world would be drawn to this systemic thinking and consider it as an actual demand of the Web and of populations around the globe. Follow-up will require the specific assignation of resources that can trigger the shared final Global Strategy.

During the construction of the Map of the 15 Global Challenges, no problems emerged in relation with the software program CogniScope II. However, that was not exactly the case when we tried the construction of the Map of Superposition. In generating the interrelations between 55 Actions over 15 Global Challenges, our use of CogniScopeII yielded 5 misplaced Actions that had to be re-localized after we attained a visual analytic examination of the whole. The Actions were: 18, 50, 13, 14, and 10. It is very likely that the two researchers involved in producing this Map suffered from information overload and this unconsciously motivated our mistaken voting responses. However, it is also likely that the software program cannot handle such a big number of ideas (observations) and hence yields untrustworthy results during its operation. The most probable reason could be that the mental fatigue of the researchers produced these flaws. None the less, this slip in applying the methodology warns of the need to check positions inside the Map once the whole of it is produced. This thoughtful check is an acknowledgment that software is only a helping tool, and not a substitute for the intelligence of the participants.

We have said that the first integration included only 55 Actions instead of the 60 Actions appearing on the Map. We need to make clear that Actions 56 to 60 were designed afterwards, i.e. after we acknowledged suggestions that *"2010, State of the Future"* made for addressing some of the Challenges. These last 5 Actions were significantly different from the 55 already designed. We thought that the identified specific factors enhanced the Global Strategy in a remarkable way. We used common sense and intuition to place them on the Map. We consider that this procedure did not significantly alter the results previously achieved and, on the contrary, it seems to enrich the product. Readers must judge for themselves.

7.2. Systemic integration of concepts

Many new researches are still pending. It would be highly satisfactory to generate a Map showing the interrelationships of Actions, to better understand if some of them might be favorable for putting other Actions into practice. It would also be helpful to give more thought to developing adequate timing for launching the Actions. Besides, each proposed Action must be examined in detail by specialists that can certify its feasibility and viability, and also to see what will be a factor's effect when it is launched into the Web. We will also need to ascertain, preferably through a pre-programmed follow- up procedure, what an Action's primary and collateral (both desirable and undesirable) effects would be.

A job that cannot wait any longer is the design of indicators for the Global Strategy's follow-up phase. We also have to design optimal ways of sharing these indicators as we go along in order to generate modifications and new proposals. Whenever we see that the contents of a Strategy are relevant we should put them to work. We need continuous feedback and feed-forward from thinkers and agents of social change (thinkers and doers). We consider this to be an unending process to enrich our comprehension of the Web and of ways to address its large problematique.

On the other hand, we need to create a Map of the Interrelationships within Subsystems of the Web. Actions within those Subsystems can be physical-chemical, biological, psychical, ethical, religious, socio-demographic, economic, technical-scientific, political, and juridical-legal. They can address issues of justice procurement, of communication, of culture, and ecology. To address these issues effectively we need a better comprehension of the Web.

As a suggestion, we might begin the preliminary mapping of the interactions with a triggering question focused on the interactions between only two subsystems. When those interactions have been mapped and evaluated, we would employ a similar question on the next pair of subsystems. And so on. This would show us the most relevant functions which each subsystem contributes to the survival of the Web.

Later integration would interrogate if the interactions might also be predicated as existing between any one subsystem and the rest of the subsystems. In each discovered interaction one might try to differentiate factors incorporated according to their nature. For example, the exponential growth of the world's population in relationship with the socio-demographic subsystem might be conceived:
- as an inhibition factor of economic global growth that pertains to the economic subsystem;
- as a factor of reproduction (stimulation) of poverty pertaining to the socio-demographic and economic subsystems,
- as a factor of influence for the growing secularism pertaining to the religious subsystem;
- as a risk factor for flaring up global climate change;
- as a factor of influence that intensifies natural resource exploitation, which intensifies resource depletion as a major risk factor pertaining to the physical-chemical, biologic and ecological subsystems;

- as a risk factor that dangerously increases the inequities already present in the distribution of wealth, that pertains to the ethical procurement of justice, and economic subsystems;
- as a factor polarizing the dispersion-concentration pattern of the population in different territories of the five continents, allowing big concentrations of population in very few mega-cities and low concentration in rural areas without services and infrastructure for their development. This pertains to the socio-demographic subsystem and the economic subsystem, etc.

The ethical commitment of being responsible for procreation according to local circumstances might be a factor opposed to exponential demographic growth. Its analysis would also need to put into perspective the ethical subsystem and the socio-demographic subsystem.

All along our research trajectory we have become aware that in dealing with complex social systems we are pressed to address boundary conditions between subsystems, and between a system and its environment. Our approach to this situation is what we call trans-boundarism.

In general, every dialogic step utilizes a boundary-spanning process among participants, since it is in this way that it is possible to have reciprocal enrichment. Once a subsystem crosses over the boundaries of others through information, energy or materials, an interchange occurs between the parts of the systems in contact. After some stage of this encounter, readjustments in the original subsystems happen and boundaries of all of them expand, even though the boundaries of each one differentiate from each other again, after the assimilation process has ended. In a certain way, this process is similar to the acquisition of superior abstract notions by a conscious system developing itself, like Piaget (1967) and Vygotski (1988) espouse in their theories about the development of cognitive functions. The conscious systems for these psychologists were the minds of children and adolescents in the process of comprehending more complex phenomena.

When we comprehend the notion of the sum of unities we can catch the phenomena of multiplication and raising to a power in mathematics. We can also catch the inverse phenomena of division and extraction of roots. In our process, acknowledging the roles of factors in the Web lets us go beyond statements of determinist cause and effect, toward statements of multi-factors entering in random combinations. It lets us expand on our multi-effects principle. Hence, we anticipate that some effects might become emergent properties of great value for the performance and ulterior development of the subsystems and the whole system.

In summary, the development of a biological system and its interaction with other subsystems might achieve its emergence as a psyche with profitable functions of sensibility and respect for the environment. It might emerge with representative and creative imaginative processes and be capable of organizing once dispersed unities and formulating concepts necessary for initiating superior syntheses, etc. When primitive man knew how to control the fire he himself had produced the grounds of a new civilization were established. When his grunts, grimaces, and gestures were the communication media at hand, the replication of symbols began to be constructed in practice, and language appeared. With these tools, our interpersonal communications began to save energy, and we learned to prefer words over the more strenuous grunts and gestures. Later this progress became potentiated with cave paintings and written language. Every learning process bears within it a trans-boundary process that returns to increase the capabilities of the original systems.

The inductive and deductive, analytic and synthetic and retroductive (abductive, in words of Charles Sanders Peirce, 1931-1958) procedures need to be accounted for in the whole process of systemic integration. Further study will surely open new channels for research. The design of ever more adequate strategies for the benefit of the Web, for its survival and healthy evolution will never end.

8. CONCLUSIONS

The present research provides us with a holistic perspective for comprehending the Web from the perspective of the Global Challenges described by the team of the Millennium Project. Other systemic properties of the Web can be worked with the holistic approach, from other angles such as the proper functions of the Web's subsystems, or their collateral (non-intended) effects.

The methodology employed is reproducible in its fundamental procedures. However, it might be enriched through a structured dialogic process, which fosters boundary-spanning processes and encourages collective intelligence, intra, multi and trans-discipline perspectives, and the emergence of progressive and more embracing insights.

The design of a Global Strategy cannot remain inside the established frontiers given in this research. New design efforts should go beyond these results and give free play to uncountable questions such as the
- "motivational why",
- the "transformational what for", and most importantly to
- the "how, where, for whom, with whom, in spite of what obstacles, with which resources,
- what are the departing points, what resources might be added in intermediate stages,
- what indicators and detection systems might be employed to evaluate and ponder progress and possible achievements,
- what sub-products or collateral effects emerge,
- what values are shared all along the implementation process,
- how often the monitoring is required and, also,
- what emergent properties might become usable to improve, accelerate or decelerate according to new necessities, or possibly, to change the route after the learning obtained.

One cannot conclude that a Strategy of the dimensions here articulated will be deployed without the contributions of additional systems for detecting errors and deviations. Many actual events (Fukushima and other nuclear plants in the world, the civil war in Libya, Haiti and the scourging poverty of its inhabitants) call us to continue reflecting over the Web itself and our interventions in it. The price of not doing this is the increased burdens we levy on future generations, and possibly the irreversible decline of the Web.

Nevertheless, the possibility of a suitable Global Strategy raises the hopes of mankind for new ways to reach the harmonization of subsystems with the Web, and the harmonization of the Web with its environment and in its evolutionary process. The main objective of the present research is to lay out a trajectory for progress toward sustainability. Testing results after implementing Actions is another arc of the trajectory. Should those results be favorable, we would walk further arcs with persistence and we might just create a sustainable world that humanity would enjoy.

9. EPILOGUE

The Archanesian Geometry as the frame to review the report:

STRATEGIC ARTICULATION OF ACTIONS TO COPE WITH THE HUGE

CHALLENGES OF OUR WORLD TODAY

A Platform for Reflection

Reynaldo Treviño Cisneros and Bethania Arango Hisijara

I think this report has made a magnificent contribution in terms of the utilization of the "Archanesian geometry" to perform multiple mappings of various aspects of the Global Problematique, as conceptualized over the last forty years by different observers, e.g., Hasan Ozbekhan, Jerome Glenn, and others. I am sure that if Ozbekhan and Warfield were still with us, they would be very appreciative of this work. They would be the first to congratulate Reynaldo and Bethania.

In order to make my commentary on the significance of this contribution by the two authors, I must first explain the meaning of the Archanesian geometry. I think this geometry is the appropriate frame for understanding the languaging prevalent in this report.

During the 20 years I worked as the CEO of the CWA Ltd. consultancy (www.CWALtd.wetpaint.com), i.e., from 1989 till 2009, I had the good fortune to collaborate with some very distinguished systems scientists, such as Ken Bausch, Kevin Dye, Tom Flanagan, Reynaldo Trevino, Bela Banathy, and many others, all of whom have had distinguished careers in research and development organizations. One of the most inquiring colleagues at the time happened to be Kevin Dye. I remember spending many sleepless nights in my home in Philadelphia, and in hotels, with Kevin discussing various questions, such as:

Are there alternative ways of designing and conducting discourse on complex socio-political issues among observers, and if so how can we human beings select the most appropriate alternative? Is it conceivable to think of an alternative for languaging as an "axiomatic construct" such as the Euclidean or Riemannian geometries? Can we envision the evolution of observations and explanations constructed through languaging among a set of observers to be substantially different depending on the geometry they adopted for constructing their observations? Are there alternative geometries that are more suitable for languaging in certain linguistic domains, as for example the Euclidean geometry is suitable for classical mechanics and not suitable for relativistic mechanics? Is it possible for human beings to make a transition to a new geometry for languaging in socio-political domains, just as they did one hundred years ago when they accepted the transition from the observations made in the domain of Newtonian physics, which is based on Euclidean geometry languaging, to the observations in the domain of Einstein's theory of relativity, which is based on Riemannian geometry languaging? Is the use of modern Information Technology in languaging an oxymoron?

It is well known that geometry treats of ontological entities which are denoted by the words straight line, point, pattern, field, etc., and that these entities do not take for granted any knowledge or intuition whatsoever, but they presuppose only the validity of the axioms on which they are founded. The seven axioms of Dialogic Design Science (DDS), for those interested to view them, are presented in: http://dialogicdesignscience.wikispaces.com/Axioms+%287%29

These seven axioms are to be taken initially in a purely formal sense, i.e., as void of all content of intuition or experience. The science of dialogic design postulates the axioms and proceeds to derive ontological entities for its geometry that are suitable for languaging in the context of the science.

I have chosen to name the geometry of dialogic design science "Archanesian," in honor of my village in Crete that has 6,000 years of history of languaging, going back to the Minoan culture. Just like the "Euclidean geometry" was instrumental in the development of the science of classical physics, and the "Riemannian geometry" was instrumental in developing and validating the science of relativistic physics, the Archanesian geometry, as demonstrated by the report of Reynaldo and Bethania very rigorously, has been instrumental in the development and validation of the science of dialogic design. The validation of the science should always occur in the evolutionary context of the Domain of Science Model (DOSM) of John Warfield, as discussed in:

http://dialogicdesignscience.wikispaces.com/file/view/DDSontoDOSM.pdf .

On the foundation of the seven axioms of the science of dialogic design, the following ontological entities of the Archanesian geometry are derived:

- **Nodes** – Observations of trends, events, issues, action options, challenges and choices;
- **Classifications** – Categorical Schema and inductive clusters involving observations;
- **Links** – Observed interdependencies amongst nodes constructed abductively;
- **Field** – Ordered set of categories;
- **Profile** – Selections of observations in a field;
- **Maps** – Nodes and their interdependencies (links);
- **Pathways** – A walk of links;
- **Superposition** – Links from a profile to a map.

One consequence of the adoption of the Archanesian geometry was the discovery and validation, by my colleague Kevin Dye, of the "Erroneous Priorities Effect." The articulation of this effect has major implications in designing social systems and in public policy-making (Christakis & Bausch, 2006):

"Erroneous Priorities Effect"

➢ Issues with highest awareness or popularity among participants may not be those with the most influence on other issues, often leading to erroneous priorities

➢ Effective priorities emerge ONLY after evolutionary, democratic, and authentic inquiry of the interdependencies among the ideas– the next stage, influence mapping, minimizes the risk of erroneous priorities

Failure to take into consideration the distinction between preferences in voting on relative importance among a set of ideas by a group of stakeholders, as compared to the results obtained when the same group of stakeholders is engaged in determining and voting on the influences among the same set of ideas, leads to erroneous priorities and ineffective actions for a social system designing situation.

By using the Archanesian geometry and taking advantage of its power of languaging and representation, Reynaldo and Bethania produced a set of mappings that enhances the transparency of the complexity of the Global Problematique, while at the same time avoids the trap of the Erroneous Priorities Effect Their report is really a masterpiece of linguistic transparency that it would have been impossible to produce and communicate with other inquirers and students of the Global Problematique by using normal language instead of utilizing the Archanesian geometry for languaging.

Alexander N. Christakis is the co-author of
Colaboratories of Democracy with Ken Bausch,
and of *The Talking Point* with Tom Flanagan.
President of ISSS (www.ISSS.org) from 2002 to 2003
Founded the Institute for 21st Century Agoras (www.globalagoras.org) in 2002.
He studied physics at Princeton University,
and earned a PhD in theoretical physics from Yale University in 1964.

10. BIBLIOGRAPHY

1. Bausch, K. (2010). "Body Wisdom: interplay of body and ego". USA: Ongoing Emergence Press.
2. Christakis, A. (1996). A People Science: The CogniScope system approach. Systems: Journal of Transdisciplinary Systems Sciences. Vol. 1, No 1, pp.18-25
3. Christakis, A. and Flanagan, T. (2011). "Referential transparency for Dialogic Design Science". Institute for 21st Century Agoras.
4. Christakis, A., and Bausch, K. (2006) "How people harness their collective wisdom and power to construct the future in co-laboratories of democracy". U.S.A.: Information Age Publishing Inc.
5. Flanagan, T. and Christakis, A. (2010). "The Talking Point: creating an environment for exploring complex meaning". USA: Information Age Publishing, Inc.
6. Flanagan, T. and Bausch, K. (2011). "A democratic approach to sustainable futures". Institute for 21st Century Agoras.
7. Flanagan, T. et. al. (2011). "An online course in sustainable democracy: a group decision making process".
8. Forbes (2011) "Listis". Recuperado el 25 de Marzo del 2011 de: http://www.forbes.com/lists/
9. François, J., (2011) "Alarma en Fukushima, no es desastre nuclear" Recuperado el 23 de marzo del 2011 de: http://www.dgcs.unam.mx/boletin/bdboletin/2011_169.html
10. Glenn, J., Gordon, T. and Florescu, E. (2009). "State of the future". U.S.A: The Millennium Project.
11. Glenn, J., Gordon, T. and Florescu, E. (2010). "State of the future". U.S.A: The Millennium Project.
12. Gutiérrez, L. (2010). "Going forward after the UN MDG summit" Recuperado el 4 de octubre, 2010 de: http://www.pelicanweb.org/solisustv06n10page1.html
13. Gutiérrez, L. (2010). "The root cause of unsustainable development". Recuperado el 2 de noviembre, 2010 de: http://www.pelicanweb.org/solisustv06n11page1.html
14. Henderson, H., (1992) "Paradigms in progress: life beyond economics". U.S.A.: Knowledge Systems, Inc.
15. Hansen, R. (2011) "Mayas sucumbieron por colapso ambiental". Recuperado el 16 de marzo del 2011 de: http://www.eluniversal.com.mx/articulos/63343.html
16. Institute for 21st Century Agoras (2010). Recuperado el 8 de septiembre del 2010 de: http://www.globalagoras.com/
17. Morin, E. (1999). "Los siete saberes necesarios para la educación del futuro". París, Francia: UNESCO.
18. Ozbekhan, H. (1968). "Passages from toward a general theory of planning". Recuperado el 12 de enero del 2011 de: http://www.panarchy.org/ozbekhan/planning.1968.html
19. Ozbekhan, H. (1970). "The predicament of mankind". Recuperado el 19 de Octubre del 2010 de: http://sunsite.utk.edu/FINS/loversofdemocracy/Predicament.PTI.pdf
20. Pérez, R. y Massoni, S. (2009). "Hacia una Teoría General de la Estrategia: el cambio de paradigma en el comportamiento humano, la sociedad y las instituciones". España: Ariel.
21. Piaget, J. (1967). "Biología y conocimiento". México: Siglo veintiuno editores.
22. Peirce, C. (1931-1958). "Collected Papers of Charles Sanders Peirce". Vol. 1-8. C. Hartshorne, P. Weiss y A. W. Burks (Eds). Cambridge, MA: Harvard University Press.
23. The Millennium Project (2011). "15 Global Challenges: Videos en lista de reproducción". Recuperado el 6 de enero del 2011 de: http://www.youtube.com/view_play_list?p=2C7D2B78000F1C2D
24. Vygotski, L. (1988). "El desarrollo de los procesos psicológicos superiores". Barcelona: Grijalbo.
25. Warfield, J., (1990) "A Science of Generic Design: Managing Complexity through Systems Design" Vol. I. U.S.A.: Intersystems Publications.
26. Wikipedia (2010) "Sistema Monerario Internacional". Recuperado el 5 de octubre del 2010 de: http://es.wikipedia.org/wiki/Sistema_Monetario_Internacional
27. Wikipedia (2011) "Era Cenozoica". Recuperado el 10 de

marzo del 2011 de: http://es.wikipedia.org/wiki/Era_Cenozoica

28. World Economic Forum (2010). "Faith and the Global Agenda: values for the post-crisis economy". Ginebra, Suiza.

COMMENTARIES

Problems with Problematiques

By Patricia Kambitsch
Graphic facilitator and multidisciplinary artist
Explores and promotes tools for dialogue available
Through the visual arts, theatre, creative movement, and dance.

The world, our world, is in a mess.

A big, complicated mess of messes.

Each mess is tangled up in all the other messes.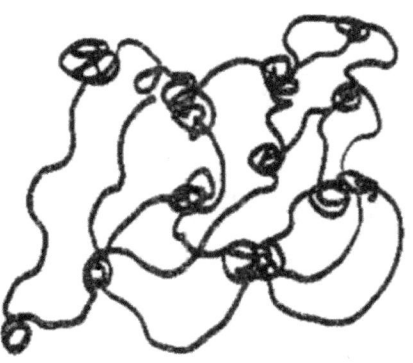

As in any living system,

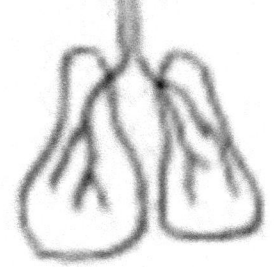

ONE SYSTEM IS NO MORE IMPORTANT THAN THE OTHER.

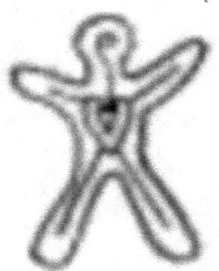

EACH INFLUENCES THE WHOLE.

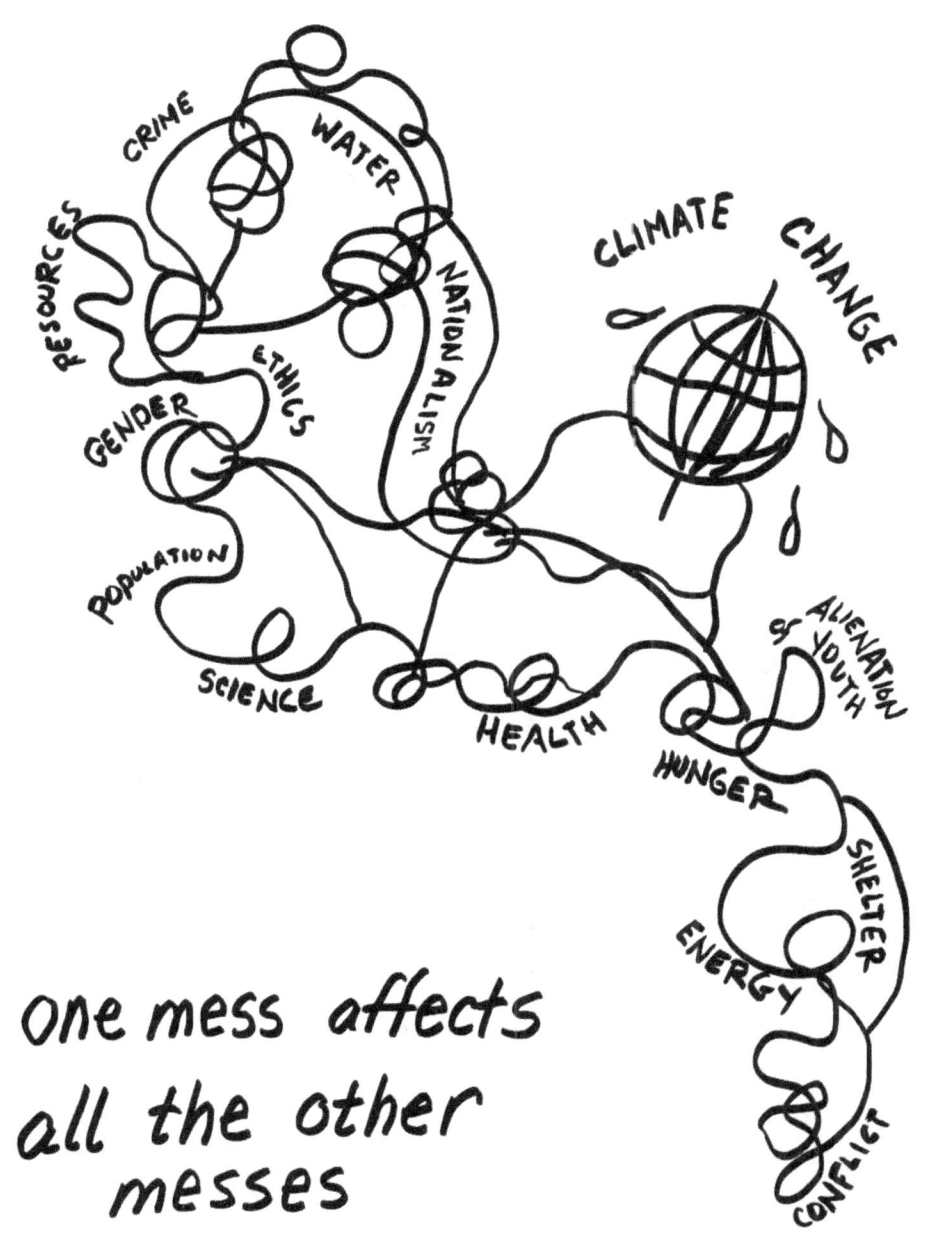

CRIME
RESOURCES
WATER
NATIONALISM
CLIMATE CHANGE
ETHICS
GENDER
POPULATION
SCIENCE
HEALTH
HUNGER
ALIENATION of YOUTH
SHELTER
ENERGY
CONFLICT

one mess affects
all the other
messes

Each CHALLENGE
IS COMPLEX

WITH ITS OWN CHALLENGES
at LOCAL
NATIONAL
and
GLOBAL LEVELS

WHAT MIGHT WE DO TOGETHER

THAT WE CAN'T DO ALONE?

WHAT ARE THE MOST CRITICAL CHALLENGES?

DOES OUR WORK WITH ONE MESS COMPLICATE ANOTHER?

HOW MIGHT WE TALK ABOUT THESE MESSES AND WORK TOGETHER?

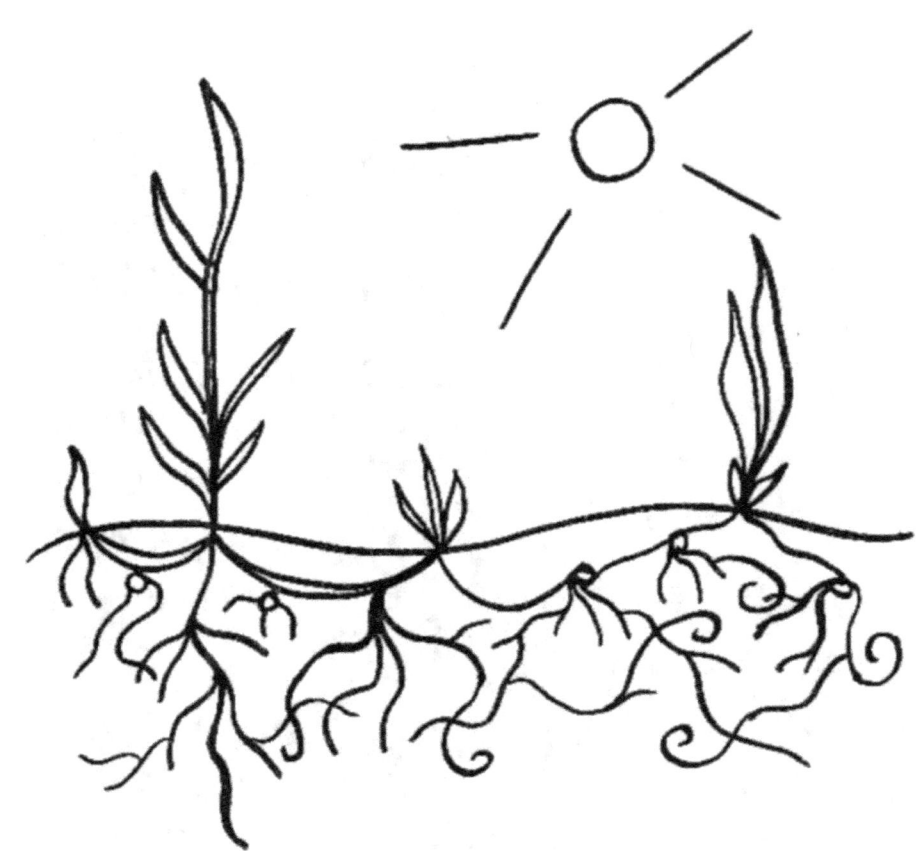

ENTANGLED SYSTEMS
CAN BE HEALTHY, TOO.

Representation of Systems Views in the Science of Dialogic Design

The thought piece, '*Strategic Articulation of Actions to Cope with the Huge Challenges of Our World Today*' illustrates a rigorous use of the Interpretive Structural Modeling (ISM) technique introduced by John N. Warfield and brought into the social arena by John and Alexander N. Christakis shortly thereafter. Readers who are familiar with Structured Dialogic Design (SDD) and its progenitor practices recognize the central role that ISM plays in capturing and reflecting systems understandings generated in stakeholder dialogue. ISM has, of course, been used by engineering teams in many applications that do not actively involve stakeholders. What makes Reynaldo and Bethania's application of ISM particularly relevant is its potential for catalyzing a critical stakeholder use of ISM to explore the challenges of global sustainability. Global studies currently lack a robust stakeholder engagement process that can generate results necessary for our future survival. Reynaldo and Bethania provide a window into a methodology that can have profound relevance for global systems research.

Reynaldo and Bethania faced a challenge in communicating their findings. How could they make it easier for their audience to interpret the acyclic directed graph (the map) that results from ISM? When ISM was pioneered, early engineering users in military organizations found the new graphic language difficult to grasp. Practitioners familiar with SDD might find this point surprising. Engineers thoroughly skilled in reading systems maps might still find the ISM map difficult. Given the engineers' difficulty, practitioners can be sympathetic to non-engineering audiences who are confronted with an ISM map.

One of the forward- going challenges for SDD is to find ever improved means to communicate output from structured dialogue events. In this context, Patricia Kambitsch has contributed an illustration of graphic narrative representation for aspects of Reynaldo and Bethania's work. Patricia's work uses the ISM map as a design brief upon which she launches a graphic interpretation. I have previously called this approach "scripting a collaborative narrative" (Flanagan, 2008). Carrying interpretations of ISM maps to community members who have not experienced the SDD event itself does present some risks of misunderstandings. If the ISM map – or a featured portion of such a map – is included in narrative interpretations of the map, then the narrative carries a piece of the "whole cloth" with it.

Facilitating accurate understandings of situations revealed in ISM maps is a formidable challenge that is driven by the urgency to have information to guide collective action when citizens individually and collectively have increasingly narrow bandwidths for engaging complex situations. Overly simplistic interpretations which are not anchored in transparently shared deeply reasoned systems thinking are dangerous shards of fact. Reynaldo and Bethania's approach for assembling a backlog of data upon which relevant systems perspectives reside eases the information management and communication task. This said, the task is formidable. The consequences of avoiding the task, however, are more formidable still.

This first issue of the monograph series launched by Kenneth C. Bausch provides insights into a key challenge in the arena of practice, and through these insights it provides a means for practitioners to speak to theorists in efforts to evolve new refinements to the practice. The monograph series thus plays a critical role in facilitating the flow of information from the arena into the corpus of the science in the cyclic pattern John Warfield described in the Domain of Science Model (Warfield, 1986, 1987; Bausch and Flanagan, 2013).

REFERENCES

Bausch, KC and TR Flanagan, 2013. A Confluence of Third-Phase Science and Dialogic Design Science. *Systems Research and Behavioral Science* (in press).

Flanagan, TR, 2008. Scripting a Collaborative Narrative: An Approach for Spanning Boundaries. *Design Management Review*, 19(3):80-86.

Warfield, JN, 1986. The Domain of Science Model: Evolution and Design, Proc. 30th Annual Mtg., Society for General Systems Research, Salinas: Intersystems, 1986, H46-H59.

Warfield, JN, 1987. The Domain of Science Model: Extensions and Restrictions. George Mason University white paper, John N. Warfield Collection 35.14
http://digilib.gmu.edu:8080/xmlui/bitstream/1920/3303/1/Warfield_35_14_A1b.pdf

Thomas R Flanagan, Ph.D., MBA.
Coordinator The New Narratives Project, New Bedford, MA.
Co-author *The Talking Point, A Democratic Approach to Sustainable Futures,* and *Body Wisdom in Dialogue.*

A Mission Impossible

or the Needed Critical Piece of the Puzzle?

This project launched by Reynaldo Treviño Cisneros and Bethania Arango Hisijara could be characterized as "mission impossible;" and the authors are aware of it, but press on. They envision a viable alternative to the competing drastic alternatives offered today for our world's huge challenges.

Some argue that we just need to reduce the world population drastically; the densities and pressures will be less, and so we could muddle through as usual. In this case, they believe we can re-start from square one with a healthy sustainable civilization by just reducing "numbers" but inflicting unprecedented suffering. Others believe in swarm intelligence and simulations, which would use and capitalize on all available data, information and knowledge. Such a "Global Earth Simulator" would then create out of all the "mess" and "noise" the blue-print for policy development and crisis management. The amount of suffering involved, the loss of individual and cultural autonomy are mind-staggering. We would lose our stake for a democratic harmonious development. We would be forced to stumble down the delusional path of "unrealistic optimism."[1]

I have known proponents of many extremes and wonder why, for example, population-reduction fans have not studied harmonious life-styles, and sustainable civilizations through the ages, where different attitudes towards the Earth secured much larger population-densities - even when that should not be desirable. I wonder on the other hand how "trend extrapolators" can assume that the noise and rubbish of complexity run amok can be modeled and molded by a "super-intelligent" system. Will machines generate humane, value based policies for the best of all humankind? Discussions about the value of models, scenarios, and symptoms have raged for 40 years ever since the first Club of Rome World Models. Has no one followed these discussions?

Treviño and Arango were walking into a terra incognita marked by a welter of outcomes proposed by different objectives, perspectives, expertise, and degrees of synthesis. People more famous than they had foundered in the global problematique. They began with an awareness of the 49 Continuous Critical Problems (CCPs) identified by Hasan Ozbekhan in 1970, and the 15 Challenges to Humanity identified by the Millennium Project. Then they were on their way to making sense of the global mind-boggling mess using the Structured Dialogic Design (SDD) methodology formulated by Alexander Christakis and others. Congratulations for this trail-blazing effort.

We all agree that problem spaces have "exploded" and leave us with unpredictable repercussions. We have numerous lists of problems, but the question is: How are they connected? Can we identify root-causes with leverage-points[2], places where we can intervene in systems to make a difference for the better instead of staring at all the tipping points where earth-systems dynamics get out of control?[2]

We also agree that all stakeholders cannot be brought to one room at one time to uncover the deep meanings that people are typically not aware of, or to anticipate future consequences. So what to do? Make more embryonic steps like the one commented here.

What is our future as futurists? Are we to continue doing business as usual expecting newer technology to create more positive results? What of new approaches that work with broad participation, rich definitions, abductive reasoning, and structured dialogue? Can they find their rightful place in the local, national, and global dialogue? What can we do to advance this new approach?

There a numerous signs that many of us have a heightened interest in global/local issues of climate change, hunger, population, water availability, ethics, and alienation. There is an intense desire to find root causes for these complex and interrelated issues.[3] Some examples:

- The charter of the Millennium Development Goals asks us to address root causes and come to "win, win, win" situations so that solving one problem will help us solve others. The ability of ISM to map influence relations among issues and find root causes fits that requirement.
- The Millennium Project has amassed an immense store of information and is setting up 15 groups of caretakers to give the ultimate test to the standard methods of problem assessment.
- Organizations such as the ONLIFE Think Tank[4] of the Digital Futures Task Force of the European Commission have placed great focus on the need to re-imagine the concept of democracy, along with other concepts such as distributed responsibility, privacy etc.

We have numerous opportunities to provide and publicize SDD interventions, in addition to this one, that will demonstrate SDD's greater utility at a cost of minus 2 orders of magnitude.

Some notable applications of SDD in the public sector are: the Third Iberoamerican Encounter about Communication Strategies (Mexico)[5]; and the work done by Christakis with the US Federal Drug Administration, and the World Health Organization[6].

----

1. How unrealistic optimism is maintained in the face of reality. Shrot T, Korn CW, Dolan RJ. Source Welcome Trust Centre for Neuroimaging, University College London, Nat Neurosci. 2011 www.ncbi.nlm.nih.gov/pubmed/21983684
2. Leverage Points: Places to Intervene in a System, Donella Meadows . http://www.sustainer.org/pubs/Leverage_Points.pdf
3. I recommend the International Encyclopedia of Systems and Cybernetics and the presentation by the founding editor when introducing the 2nd edition: benking.de/systems/encyclopedia/concepts-and-models.htm
4. ONLIFEec.europa.eu/digital-agenda/en/onlife-original-outcome www.futureworlds.eu/wiki/Reinventing_democracy and CARDIAC cardiac-eu.org
5. III Encuentro Iberoamericano sobre Estrategias de Comunicación, México, 2005: www.fisecforo.org/index.php#
6. Christakis AN and Bausch KC 2006. *How People Harness Their Collective Wisdom and Power to Construct the Future in Co-Laboratories of Democracy.* Greenwich: Information Age Publishing

Heiner Benking
Council on Global Issues, Toronto/Berlin

A New Strategic Theory for Democratization Implies
A New Communications Theory for Structured Dialogic Design

By Kevin Dye

In the preface, the authors (Reynaldo Treviño Cisneros and Bethania Arango Hisijara) cite the 2009 book *Toward a General Theory of Strategy* (1) as the inspiration and "seed of this peculiar research." In that 2009 work, Rafael Alberto Pérez and Sandra Massoni depict a "New Strategic Theory" (NST) summarized as seven proposals for "drastic changes" regarding the future of strategy. Pérez claims (2) that the conception of NST began as a surprise – even to himself, the "revealing of a secret", a "breaking proposal" = as he penned page 672 of his 2001 book *Communication Strategies* (3). In *Communication Strategies* Pérez critiqued the logical-analytic paradigm of planning and came to suggest a change in orientation from one based in rationality to one based in complexity.

Pérez expressed the "need" for a new theory of strategy as a set of "pragmatic intentions":

- to regain the human being as opposed to economic constructs of people as rational actors, voters, consumers, or game players;
- to move away from conflictual models of game theory towards negotiative models with cognitive and valuative processes;
- to encourage empathy in participants through the formation of a dialogic, negotiative, cooperative and consensual orientation;
- to move towards narrative means of managing discourse rather than following paradigmatic rules;
- and to restate strategy from a communications standpoint rather than solely from an economic and informational perspective.

A decade after publication of *Communication Strategies,* in reviewing the State-of-the-Art of Strategy (4), Pérez reported seeing progress in the world on communication strategies such as the increased use of dialogue, the ramping up of participatory communication, and the proliferation of social networks. That's the good news. The bad news is that this increased use of dialogue may not yet be having a substantial effect on the world's problems. One of his observations was brought to his attention through the 2011 analysis by our own authors, Treviño & Arango (5), and their views of the world's interdependent problems. While the academic foundations and communicative infrastructure for communication strategies have advanced substantially, it seems that the New Strategic Theory is not yet well diffused in the social change practitioner community. Treviño & Arango call for exactly this diffusion in nominating one of the sixty actions to address the system of Global Challenges:

> Action to Successfully Cope with Global Challenges #19 - Creating and spreading a new strategic theory which takes into account the relational nature of human beings, our new value system, and the main trends observed in our environment (Pérez, R., and Massoni, S., 2009)

Treviño & Arango further assert that Action #19, as proposed by Pérez, can exert great leverage in addressing what they discern to be the deepest driver of the Global Challenges:

> Millennium Project Global Challenge #4 - How can genuine democracy emerge from authoritarian regimes?

A key foundation of Pérez's proposal for a New Strategic Theory, which pertains to democratic transformations, is an underlying theory of communication forged during just such a transformation. The communication theory underlying Pérez's proposal is *La Mediación Social* (*Social Mediation*).

Pérez's collaborator on *Communication Strategies*, Manuel Martín Serrano, influenced him in the expression of the "need" for "a less geometric and more hermeneutic new strategic theory, less rational and more relational" (6). Serrano, a Spaniard, is a man of letters, a sociologist, and a philosopher. He developed *Social Mediation,* as a comprehensive theory of communication and the media, over several decades. *Social Mediation* started as a PhD Thesis, (in France), studying the influence of the mass media, and television in particular. It developed through a phenomenological approach to become one of the most influential new foundations for communication theory in the Spanish speaking world over the last thirty years. Development of the first book began during 1969-1975. Towards the end of this incubation period there was a move towards a modest liberalization of the authoritarian Franco regime in Spain. In December of 1973, the hard-line Prime Minister Admiral Luis Carrero Blanco was assassinated. On February 12, 1974 the newly appointed Prime Minister of Spain, Carlos Arias Navarro, "a classic liberal reformer," announced *aperturismo,* 'an opening'.(8) The call for *aperturismo* spurred demand for improving the quality of journalism which in turn created demand for research and a search for theoretical foundations – especially regarding communication theory.

This call for openness reflected an international movement at that time which called for increasing attention to the role of communications and media in culture and politics in the developing world. Emblematic of this concern was the clamor, which led to the creation by UNESCO of The International Commission for the Study of Communication Problems in 1977, which led to the controversial publication of *Many Voices One World*. The first Spanish university communications departments were just starting in the 1970's so they were in a good position for a fresh start on communications theory. The timing was such that communications theorists could draw on previous Anglo-Saxon developments in journalism, but they also drew on developments in European Semiotics. Serrano especially drew inspiration from the phenomenologists. He was positioned historically and geo-politically (9) to cultivate a theory of communication largely independent of the theory of communication of Structured Dialogic Design. In addition, Social Mediation includes the role of the media – which has never really been addressed in the theoretical foundations informing the methodology of Structured Dialogic Design.

In the first paragraph of the preface to the 30th Anniversary Edition *of Social Mediatio*n (10), Serrano recalls the abundance of forecasts of social change, during the writing of the first edition. He characterizes most of them on both the left and on the right, as being wrongheaded continuations of the old paradigm, dominated by the perspective of the already-developed-world and resistant to the spirit and desire of the social movements, which had as their hallmark the May Revolution (inspired by critical theories). Serrano highlights one such forecast as emblematic of the forecasts he disdains – the Club of Rome endeavor which led to the Limits to Growth Report. This is the very one our authors, Treviño & Arango, seek to redress, recompose, and transform by revisiting its original premise as espoused by Hasan Ozbekhan et al. Now, they, and the Structured Dialogic Design community, can take advantage of the new foundations in communication theory offered b*y Social Mediation.* We ought to leverage it.

Leveraging Social Mediation implies at least four directives for the Structured Dialogic Design (SDD) community of practice.

- The role of the media should be carefully considered in design of SDD engagements.
- The communication theory underlying the practice of SDD should be revisited and reworked following Social Mediation and the evolution of communication theories.
- The tools of Structural Modeling employed in SDD should be leveraged in understanding social networks and power relationships.

- The approach to science of Social Mediation and communication theories should be considered in enriching the grounding of SDD in the Domain of Science Mode and Third Phase Science.

In SDD applications that are instruments of a broader democratic process, the media should probably always be presumed to be a stakeholder. The inclusion of the media as participants should be evaluated because they will also be part of the logistics management for the event. They will be employed in announcing an SDD event, or inviting participation, or reporting on it. In these ways, media are necessary and could even be considered as part of the event's design and facilitation team. This dual role as participant and facilitation team member is problematic – still we must figure out models of how to deal with this.

An acknowledgement of how media have already framed positions on a situation, constructed rhetoric, and influenced people's mental models should be part of the preliminary fact-finding in an SDD engagement. Media are not just players, but in many cases have already cultivated substantive content, which will be invoked, even unknowingly, by other participants. We have thus a very sensitive dilemma: the authentic voice of a participant may not be immediately discerned in their utterances. Participants' expression of "their opinion" may be, indeed is likely to be, strongly *mediated,* framed, and conditioned by the media. So, the results of an engagement may also be mediated. SDD engagement designers should consider how this is handled. SDD teams must consider in addition to media involvement in the problematic situation itself, the power asymmetry of the media with respect to their influence in planning events, stakeholder identification, participation, representation, and framing the content prior to and after events. Indeed, an SDD event on the future of Cyprus discerned exactly this concern. Media were seen as deep drivers hindering the peace-building efforts there (11). To accommodate media within the practice of SDD requires us to reexamine our theories of power and generate more sophisticated stakeholder analysis techniques, while designing the overall intervention of which a SDD event is a part. It is not sufficient to merely ameliorate the influence of power within the dialogue event as is already accomplished within SDD. We cannot keep the media at-a-distance; they are already inside the situation and event in many ways. A new theory of communication, especially one that addresses power asymmetries, is needed to direct the practice of the SDD community of practice.

The most influential communication theorist in the early development of SDD in the 1970's was Harold Lasswell. Lasswell was trained in sociology and political science at the University of Chicago, in the decade following World War I. At that time, the Chicago faculty fostered a call for quantification of social and political phenomena. Lasswell completed his thesis on the use of propaganda and its influence on political behavior in 1927. He invented systematic content analysis, which came to be employed in the study of propaganda in World War II. He formulated a model of communication in the second quarter of the 20th century with a major work on the topic published in 1948 (12). His model is characterized by some as a "transmission model" of communication similar to that which became prevalent in information science and cybernetics in the 1950s and 1960's. He coined the phrase "policy sciences" in the 1950's and turned his interest to how groups could engage large amounts of information about a situation – proposing notions such as "decision seminars," "urban planetariums", and "prelegislatures" as mechanisms to accomplish this.

Lasswell came to influence John N. Warfield, one of the co-founders of the methodology of Structured Dialogic Design. Warfield was trained as an Electrical Engineer, specializing in communications, which in the 1950's & 60's meant a focus on networks and information theory. Lasswell and Warfield both favored an information-theoretic treatment of communication. In his 1976 book *Societal Systems,* Warfield drew on Lasswell more than any other author except Herbert Simon – an economist and information scientist. Warfield addressed Lasswell's later concerns by developing better infrastructure to ameliorate the behavioral pathologies of groups and enhance their information processing capacity. The infrastructure included the design of the meeting room, computer support, and displays. The development of what came to be known as "observatoriums" as an aid to communication followed from this as a major contribution to the practice of Structured Dialogic Design.

Lasswell had also encouraged the use of diagrams to assist communication. The diagrammatic representations of what was being communicated are perhaps Lasswell's most direct inspiration to a product which is very characteristic of Structured Dialogic Design engagements – that is the "Problematique". An example of a problematique appears in Figure 2 of Treviño & Arango's monograph above. In *The Handbook of Interactive Management*, Warfield tells the story of Lasswell's formative experience in group work in a Peruvian mountain village. The project on restoring the viability of their community was having difficulty with communication until they started using "a graphics language that was developed on the spot, using chalk drawings on the wall of a cave" (pg 109-110).

The use of diagrams as a communication aid very much appealed to Warfield in that he had a deep appreciation for particular kinds of diagrams – that is networks. Warfield became involved in planning very large-scale projects which employed matrices as well as networks and he also was getting engaged in computer programming. In seeking a way to integrate these representations and find a way to leverage them with computers, Warfield developed a relationship with Frank Harary, a mathematician considered a father of Graph Theory. Harary, a professor at the University of Michigan, was known for his good communication skills. He promoted applications of Graph Theory in physics, psychology, sociology, and even anthropology. Already by the 1950's people were starting to apply techniques from the emerging field of graph theory in understanding the nature of power relationships in families, organizations, and politics, such as in the use of sociograms.

In 1953, Harary co-authored a paper on the Theory of Relations with Irving Copi, a philosopher and logician familiar with the work of Charles Sanders Peirce. This is probably the path by which Warfield became aware of Peirce, a polymath most especially a logician. In *Societal Systems*, (pg 202) Warfield cites Copi's 1948 paper which acknowledges the 1870 work of Peirce "wedding logic to matrices apparently aimed in the direction of a theory of structural modeling." Peirce employed diagrams to represent logic and argument along with abductive inference of relations in the diagrams as key tools in his approach to semiotics. This linking of logic to diagrams appealed to Warfield's mindset. Thus Warfield came to tie together Boolean logic, matrices, algebra, and digraphs along with an abductive inquiry process, in the spirit of Peircean diagramming. This formed the semiotic motif of Structured Dialogic Design. Over the three decades following Warfield's first citation of work by Peirce he increasingly called for people to pay attention to Peirce's work especially Peirce's pragmaticism. It supplied the model for science that Warfield employed to evolve the methodology that he helped to create.

Although Peirce and Ferdinand de Saussure advanced the field of semiotics in the early 20th century, it was not until the 1960's that semiotics began to be institutionalized. While Warfield found inspiration, and sought legitimacy in Peirce's work, he did not draw very deeply on Peirce's contributions. (One reason may be that Peirce's work was not very accessible and Peircean scholarship was still very young.) Nor did Warfield follow the emerging field of semiotics – at least not in a fashion that he translated into methodology. Still he put out the call for us to pay attention to Peirce and, albeit implicitly, to semiotics. Treviño & Arango provide an important lead in this regard. It was mentioned above that many of the Spanish and European communication theorists engaged semiotics (Sausserian semiology and structuralism). However, Serrano himself was not known as a semiotician. Serrano trained under Abraham Moles, an Electrical Engineer and systems scientist, who had his own model of communication, (one that included the media). But Serrano's most outstanding disciple was Jesus Martín-Barbero who did become a semiotician and a leading communication theorist in Latin America.

In 1987 Martín-Barbero described the formation of a new paradigm of communication in Latin America as starting "at the end of the 1960's when Lasswell's model from an epistemological background of psychological behaviorism was poured into the theoretical mould of structuralist semiology, making possible its "conversion"(13). Martín-Barbero describes a second major "conversion" in the 1970's as moving away from what he called the 'scientism of information theoretic models' and away from the functionalism of Lasswell (by the majority of communication theorists.). This was driven by "stubborn social processes" in Latin America of the period. Martín-Barbero notes, "The field of studies in communication in Latin America derives from the interplay of two different paradigms: the information/instrumentalism of North American research and the ideological criticism of Latin American social sciences. Between the two, and modulating them, stands French semiotic structuralism" (14). Thus was forged a much richer theory of communication accommodating politics, culture, conflict, ideology, power, transnationalization, processes of collective behavior, markets, the media, and consumption. Today in Latin America half of the professors of Communication Theory claim to not ascribe to a dominant model with the next 30% drawing primarily on Critical Theory, Constructivism, Structuralism, and Phenomenology. Now fewer than one in five focus on models from the previous paradigm – Behaviorism, Functionalism, Informationalism, and Systems theory.

Peirce went from treating semiotics as a science of signs to treating semiotics as a basis for his philosophy of science itself, his "pragmaticism". There are intimations that Martír-Barbero posits communication theory turning from a field that draws on many different disciplines to becoming a scientific platform underpinning other sciences. So too, Serrano views the frontiers of knowledge to be at the points of human intervention – the very loci of his theory of communication – Social Mediation. Here is one insight regarding what that might mean for Structured Dialogic Design's Domain of Science Model – which has been based on Peircean Pragmaticism and De Zeeuw's Third Phase Science. As one of its motifs, Social Mediation theory posits that in order to develop a plan for intervention in the world, one begins with a world view that is framed to a large extent by the media, and more generally by "mediators", all with power and special interests. Envisioned actions may also be so conditioned. Furthermore, the social mobilization required for the envisioned transformations will also require the media and be "mediated." Therefore, in planning interventions our model of the situation must include the intended action and express the embedded context in which it will operate. It must express the intent of the action and describe how action and model are mediated. It must also accommodate the ways various interests will characterize the negotiations and describe the relations among the actors.

The first part of this, the inclusion of the intended action within the model of the situation, sounds very much like Gerard De Zeeuw's self-constructed object notion of Third Phase Science (15) – but was developed and published two decades earlier than De Zeeuw's working paper. Social Mediation theory goes far beyond self-constructed objects. How might Social Mediation theory affect the evolution of Structured Dialogic Design if we were to embrace it? Let's think about that. Treviño & Arango draw us, the practitioners of Structured Dialogic Design, into the solution space of the global problematique itself. In contrast, the *Limits to Growth* project, sponsored by the Club of Rome, treated the construction of the world model as if it was objectively separate from interventions in it. In *Limits to Growth*, Systems Dynamics served as the language to describe the world, but its use was not part of the world model itself. This is a sharp distinction from the nature of critical problems articulated by Hasan Ozbekhan – deep drivers of which implied the need for the methodology he was engaged in developing. Ozbekhan's reflectivity and critical stance was prescient.

Where are we at with a New Strategic Theory for addressing democratization? Pérez, one of the pioneers of Public Relations in Spain, engaged in debates through the Latin American Forum on Communication Strategies (Foro Iberoamericano Sobre Estrategias de Comunicación, FISEC) for seven years following his publication of *Communication Strategies*. FISEC grew from 14 participants in 2002 to more than 480 experts from 120 universities. It has 130 members of the mass media, institutions and firms from countries around the world: Latin America, the United States, Italy, France, Germany and Russia. It has produced over 150 publications. FISEC has proposed the New Strategic Theory as seven drastic changes in: the paradigm; the subject; the collective subject (organization); the object of study and its focus; the matrix of study; applicable tools; and the methodology of strategy. Those changes are viewed as transitions, respectively (16):

- from fragmentation to complexity;
- from the rational actor to the relational human being;
- from our view of the company as a production unit to that as a network of innovation and of meaning;
- from the contingent to the immanent;
- from the science of conflict and confrontation to the science of articulation and innovation;
- from a basis in economics to a basis in communication.

In 2005, the President of the United States of Mexico, Vicente Fox, (a beneficiary of Structured Dialogic Design work in Guanajuato, Mexico by our author Treviño) inaugurated the Third Iberoamerican Encounter about Communication Strategies in the Universidad Iberoamericana of Mexico D.F.. At that time, Pérez proclaimed *"The new theory received in this way its Latin-American baptism ..."* (2). Let's get ready for its communion and confirmation.

References

1) Pérez, R. y Massoni, S. (2009). "Hacia una Teoría General de la Estrategia: el cambio de paradigma en el comportamiento humano, la sociedad y las instituciones". España: Ariel.

2) Pérez, R. A., The New Strategic Theory, http://www.fisecforo.org/rap2007/rap_english/nuevateoria.htm

3) Pérez, R. A., (2001): Estrategias de Comunicación. ("Communication Strategies"), Barcelona: Ariel.

4) Pérez, R. A., (2012): "El estado del arte en la Comunicación Estratégica", (Strategic Communication: the state of the art), Mediaciones Sociales. Revista de Ciencias Sociales y de la Comunicación , nº 10, pp. 121-196. http://www.ucm.es/info/mediars/MediacioneS10/Indice/AlbertoPerezR2012/albertoperez2012.html

5) Treviño, R. y Arango, B. (2001): "La trama, articulación estratégica de acciones para enfrentar los retos ingentes del mundo de hoy", ponencia en el II Encuentro Internacional de Estrategar, julio de 2011. Inédito.

6) Pérez, R. A., (2007): "Los caminos que conducen hacia una nueva teoría de la estrategia: Aportación al homenaje a Manuel Martín Serrano", (The Roads That Lead to a New Theory of Strategy. Contribution to the Homage to Manuel Martín Serrano), Mediaciones Sociales. Revista de Ciencias Sociales y de la Comunicación, nº 1, segundo semestre de 2007, pp. 45-73. ISSN electrónico: 1989-0494. Universidad Complutense de Madrid, España. http://www.ucm.es/info/mediars/MediacioneS1/Indice/AlbertoPerez/albertoperez.html

7) Martínez Nicolás M (2006) Masa (en situación) crítica. La investigación sobre periodismo en España: comunidad científica e intereses de conocimiento. Anàlisi 33: 135–170, pg 146.

8) Samuel P. Huntington, *The Third Wave: Democratization in the Late 20th Century*, University of Oklahoma Press, 1991, pg. 138.

9) Lizy Navarro Zamora, Francisco de Lara Bashulto, Teoria General de la Comunicacion: Recorrido Hisorico, *Razon y Palabra*, November 2010. http://www.razonypalabra.org.mx/N/N74/VARIA74/24NavarroV74.pdf

10) Martin Serrano, Manuel (2007): "Prólogo para La Mediación Social en la era de la globalización", (Preface to Social Mediation in the Era of Globalization), *Mediaciones Sociales*. Revista de Ciencias Sociales y de la Comunicación, nº 1, segundo semestre de 2007, pp. 1-24. ISSN electrónico: 1989-0494. Universidad

Complutense de Madrid.
http://www.ucm.es/info/mediars/MediacioneS1/Indice/MartinSerrano/martinserrano.html

11) Civil Society Dialogue Project in Cyprus, Future Worlds Center, Nicosia, Cyprus.
http://futureworlds.eu/wiki/Civil_Society_Dialogue_Project_in_Cyprus

12) Laswell, Harold Dwight (1948). *The Structure and Function of Communication in Society*. Lyman Bryson (New York: Institute for Religious and Social Studies, Jewish Theological Seminary of America. p. 37.

13) Jesus Martin-Barbero, Communication from the Perspective of Culture - Excerpt from Media to Mediation: Communication, Culture and Hegemony, Gustavo Gili, Mexico, 1987, in Alfonso Gumucio Dagron, Thomas Tufte, *Communication for Social Change Anthology: Historical and Contemporary Readings*, CFSC Consortium, Inc., 2006, pg. 333-334.

14) Jesús Martín-Barbero, A Latin American perspective on communication/cultural mediation, *Global Media and Communication*, 2006, Vol. 2(3): 279–297, pg. 281.

15) Gerard de Zeeuw, Three Phases of Science: A Methodological Exploration, 1997 this paper appeared as a research memorandum of the Nijmegen Business School, University of Nijmegen, edited by J. Achterbergh, R. Espejo, H. Regtering, M. Schwaninger under the title of Organizational Cybernetics. It also appeared as working paper no. 7 of the Centre forSystems and Information Sciences, University of Humberside, 1996, ISBN 1 86050 025 0.
http://www.academia.edu/618520/THREE_PHASES_OF_SCIENCE_A_METHODOLOGICAL_EXPLORATION1 . See also de Zeeuw, G. (1996). Second Order Organizational Research, Working Papers in Systems and Information Sciences, University of Humberside, Hull, England.

16) ALFONSO VARGAS-SÁNCHEZ, Systemics, connectivity and innovation:
what role do we want them to play in a new perspective on strategy?, *Sinergie, Rivista di Studi e Ricerche* n. 88, Maggio-Agosto 2012, pp. 137-151.
http://rabida.uhu.es/dspace/bitstream/handle/10272/6082/Systemics_connectivity_and_innovation.pdf?sequence=2

Kevin Dye
Director of Research,Institute for 21st Century Agoras

www.ingramcontent.com/pod-product-compliance
Lightning Source LLC
Chambersburg PA
CBHW080249290526
45790CB00005B/1751